Addiction Recovery and Resilience

SUNY series in African American Studies

John R. Howard and Robert C. Smith, editors

Addiction Recovery and Resilience

FAITH-BASED HEALTH SERVICES IN AN AFRICAN AMERICAN COMMUNITY

TOWNSAND PRICE-SPRATLEN

Published by State University of New York Press, Albany

Printed in the United States of America

For information, contact State University of New York Press, Albany, NY
www.sunypress.edu

Library of Congress Cataloging-in-Publication Data

Name: Price-Spratlen, Townsand, author.
Title: Addiction recovery and resilience : faith-based health services in an African American community / Townsand Price-Spratlen.
Description: Albany : State University of New York Press, [2022] | Series: SUNY series in African American studies | Includes bibliographical references and index.
Identifiers: LCCN 2021021931 | ISBN 9781438487373 (hardcover : alk. paper) | ISBN 9781438487397 (ebook)
Subjects: LCSH: Church and substance abuse—United States—Case studies. | Faith-based human services—United States—Case studies. | Substance abuse—Treatment—Religious aspects—Christianity—Case studies. | Medical care—Religious aspects—Christianity—Case studies. | African Americans—Substance use—Case studies. | African Americans—Medical care—Case studies. | Community-based social services—United States—Case studies.
Classification: LCC BV4460.3 .P75 2022 | DDC 261.8/3229—dc23
LC record available at https://lccn.loc.gov/2021021931

10 9 8 7 6 5 4 3 2 1

To my father,
Professor Emeritus Thaddeus H. Spratlen (1930–2021)

Your humanity, discipline, and humble brilliance are among your many characteristics that I adore. Each day, you shared all of them with such unyielding empathy and a life mission for justice. Thank you, Dad, for your love and respect, your thoughtful craft of care, and willingness to listen and inspire over the years. I am so grateful that you are my father.

Contents

Acknowledgments ix

Prologue xiii

Introduction: A Place for Health and Resilience 1

PART 1
HOPE: RESILIENT PEOPLE, PLACES, AND THINGS

Chapter 1 "We, Who Would Otherwise Not Meet": The People of the Ministries 27

Chapter 2 Much More than Watermelon Roadkill: The Place of the Ministries 51

Chapter 3 Healthy Things: Resilience Resources of the Ministries 69

PART 2
HURT: DISSONANT DIALOGUES OF RESILIENCE

Chapter 4 Uncertain Sanctuary: The Ministries' Collaboration with Cocaine Anonymous 97

Chapter 5 Silence in Our Midst: (In)Visibility and Voice at the Ministries 131

Chapter 6 Change Gon' Come: The Flourishing and Decline of the Ministries 157

PART 3
HALLELUJAH! HOW HEALING HAPPENS

Chapter 7 Faith-Based Best Practices: How a Fractured Ministries Can Heal 189

Epilogue 223

References 231

Index 255

Acknowledgments

Though sole-authored, this book is a product of the contributions of many. Thank you first to the Criminal Justice Research Center (CJRC) at Ohio State University, under the leadership of Professor Dana Haynie. The 2014 CJRC seed grant allowed me to hire a graduate research assistant to help with the interviews and early data analyses, to compensate research participants, and to participate in other actions related to the organization under study. Thank you to Yolanda Gelo for your conscientious efforts as the project research assistant.

I can only begin to express my appreciation for Professor Emeritus Ruth D. Peterson, who was the leadership whisperer and whose advocacy was vital to the funding of this Ministries project. More vitally, you are the reason I am alive and sane. From your rescue of me after my car accident at the Ohio-Michigan border in the summer of 2003, to your CJRC seed grant for the Reconstruction, Inc., project that became my first book, to your incomparable friendship and quiet counsel on so many other occasions they could fill a book on their own, I thank you.

Professor Lauren J. Krivo, you have shared so much of your time and skills and commitment with me over the years. Hearing of your retirement this year gives rise to a melancholy feeling, since far fewer sociologists will now benefit from your many gifts. I am grateful to be one among those who have. Thanks also to Professor Bob Crutchfield, whose advocacy allowed my sociological journey to begin, to Professor Barry Lee for your guidance during my postdoc fellowship, and to Professor Avery M. "Pete" Guest. It was an honor to be your teaching assistant for sociological methods for those two essential quarters of my growth in grad school. And thank you for chairing my dissertation project and for all of your guidance in helping to make a "Husky sociologist" out of me. I share a special thanks to Dean Linda M. Burton, for your mentoring over the years, for your conscientious work toward economic equity with the many families and communities you have researched and worked with, and for your lessons of resilience and life renewal that I value so much. In this book, and in all my work, my social science approach extends from the foundation Dr. W. E. B. Du Bois established, to which I and many others strive to respectfully make contributions.

Thank you to my family. Mom, Dr. Lois Price Spratlen, from your bread-making, singing Thadd and me to sleep at night, and loving punishments from my childhood, to your professional excellence and pride in being a Black nurse and multiple organization endowment builder, these are among the ways in which your voice and life continue to resonate so strongly in my everyday these years after your passing in 2013. Dad, the book is dedicated to you, which is only the most partial reciprocity for all of the love and Spirit you continue to share with me and so many others. Pamela L. Spratlen, your ambassador achievements, sense of adventure, cultural curiosities, and diplomatic diversities here in the US and abroad, continue to amaze. Pat Spratlen Etem, your Olympic achievements, the family you have built, and your public health professionalism are incredible and a joy to see, feel, and adore. Paula Spratlen Mitchell, your faith-driven life, state-title-winning athletic coaching, and devotion to be a high-quality educator in settings where folk are leading hardscrabble lives is so much more than inspiration alone. Khalfani Mwamba, your name change, culturalist, Pan-African worldview and consistencies, and family and nation building since you were a teenager have been powerful to experience and share in along the way.

Thank you to Eric H. for your consistency and unyielding dedication to your mobile ministry for those years and for believing so deeply in the possibilities of what the Ministries could have been. To Pastor Orinda Hawkins-Brinkley, I am so glad your principled pastoral leadership guided a church neighbor of the Ministries for those critical years. William Goldsby, thank you for your friendship. You caringly facilitated many meetings that thankfully were much more consistent with the protocol of Reconstruction, Inc., than 12 Step meetings or the Ministries. When things were most complicated, you helped Eric H. and me process what good servant-leadership is and how to manage situations when its demands are not met.

Thank you to Pastor Ellwyn Marshall (pseudonym) for making the Ministries available to explore and explain. Your cofounding of the organization that would become the Ministries contributed to the health of so many, in a neighborhood in desperate need of those willing to address their own healing as they assisted with the healing of many others. Thanks to the hundreds of people who affiliated with the Ministries over the fourteen years of the project, for one event of a single day or for many events and years of Ministries progress. I especially thank those who responded to their active addiction, grew their own sober lives, and, by doing so, enriched the lives of their loved ones, other affiliates of the Ministries, and the health of North Lawson (pseudonym) and the larger community. Those who came to Sunday evening worship and who volunteered their time and energy to allow the Tuesday and Thursday community lunches to flourish were central to helping the Ministries be a social ecology of worth and mission. I am particularly grateful to the members of the local chapter of Cocaine Anonymous (CA) who frequented the Either-Or meetings on Thursday nights and Saturday mornings. Anonymity demands prevent me from being able to name members of the critical mass of each meeting. Your actions and principled decisions are presented in the book, and, where most relevant, your experiences are presented by pseudonym. Thank you for the many ways you gave Either-Or meetings so much life by sharing so much of your own.

I also thank Michael Rinella, senior acquisitions editor at SUNY Press, for your patience, clarity, and choice to see the value of this book's contributions. For that choice, your cautious enthusiasm during our first phone call, and for your managerial support through the publishing process, I am grateful.

I hope that I have been true to these and the many contributions of others to this work. I hope and pray I have done them justice. While all work output, including and especially this book, is collaborative, all errors, omissions, or other flaws within it are my responsibility.

Prologue

Terra's Welcome to the FACTS Ministries

When I got introduced to Pastor Marshall [two years ago] I was living at the Assurance Circle [women's homeless facility], and I wasn't clean. He spoke, and he gave me his card. I got an apartment from there, and I came to one lunch [at the FACTS Ministries] to volunteer. Then I never came back. I was bouncing from place to place, and I had went to jail, and all that. Then I didn't really start coming back until I moved over here to the North Lawson neighborhood. I live over here now, so it's easier for me to just walk around there. I've been in my apartment for, like, two years now. This is a good thing. Yes. 'Cause using, and being around the wrong people, that bring the wrong things to you, and stuff like that. I never really kept an apartment [before now]. I was on drugs a lot. I smoked a lot of dope. I drank a lot. I did everything. I did what I wanted to do. And I learned. And I feel better since I've been gettin' more active at the Ministries. And I let Pastor see my face [shared laughter]. Because I want to do my ministry. He knows that, and he supports me. I want to do something for the women, as far as the [sober] homes and, you know, and other stuff like that. You know, for us women, and he supports it.

My best thing is to get level, and get in there, and let him see my face, and we'll go from there. [Another person: He can see that you're serious]. Ya! [shared laughter] I be like, "You see me?" [gesturing two fingers back and forth quickly from her eyes toward the eyes of another woman who made the comment]. [more shared laughter] But that is my dream though. For us. For women. To have recovery houses for women. And other resources like that. Because in my addiction, I stayed homeless. I had an apartment a majority of the time, but I never stayed in an apartment no longer than a year. Or it would get turned out [become a dope spot rental, for active addiction and/or sexual encounters]. Or some other real stuff. Where I was just sleepin' and smokin' crack. Now we're all part of this thang. And we're gonna keep it movin', for real.

Kevin's Welcome

I started my search for sobriety in the summer of 2002. I was seeking an answer I was not able to ask for. How did my life get so out of control? This was the question I only came up to the edge of asking, but never did. Though it felt to me it had arrived many years too late, if my sober resilience was to begin, now was as good a time as any. Consistent with the cliché I had already been introduced to in my first hours of sobriety, you reach your "bottom" [i.e., an end point of active addiction with a necessary chaos and hardship where a possible recovery can begin] only when you stop digging a deeper hole. As the "Big Book" of Alcoholics Anonymous (Alcoholics Anonymous 2001, 30, 279) states, "All of us [were] led in time to pitiful and incomprehensible demoralization. . . . The bottom came up and hit us." I had managed to put together fifty sober hours. Not because I had run out of money. Not because I was hiding from my latest dope dealer debt. Not because I was behind deadline, trying to do another rush job at work. For the first time in my life, I wanted to be sober because my bottom had hit me hard enough. I tried to recall a time when I had been voluntarily free of all mind-altering substances for more than two days in a row since I was twelve years old. None came to mind.

I was guided by the single motive to make it through my fifty-first consecutive sober hour, and a 12-Step recovery meeting would help. It was 9:45 a.m. on a Saturday morning. I had awakened on a weekend sober for the first time in years. So often, in the days of addiction's hamster's wheel of motion without progress, I typically "came to" after I had slept off the stupor of the night before. I had begun my intensive outpatient (IOP) treatment just two days earlier. "Attend as many meetings over the weekend as you've had days with us here." That is what Bixby, the treatment group counselor, had advised. "So, here's the paperwork I need back from each of you, signed and sealed," Bixby said as he handed each of the nine people in my IOP treatment circle a piece of paper. These were the 12-Step meeting confirmation sheets for the weekend the treatment center required to bridge time with sober affiliation between the Friday-to-Sunday period that had no IOP sessions. Having attended my first 12-Step meeting that Friday night, just thirteen hours before my weekend awakening, I now needed three more meetings over the weekend. I decided to go to the closest Cocaine Anonymous (CA) meeting that was as early in the day as possible. Crack cocaine was my "drug of choice" that had brought me to my knees, nearly ending my life on four occasions. Given the violent chaos of crack, I was in range of life-threatening danger many, many more times than that. Now, in the Christian Recovery brochure presented to me in treatment, I had noticed that there was a 10:00 a.m. Saturday morning meeting at something called the FACTS Ministries (**F**aith **ACT**ions of **S**obriety). I chuckled. "Just the facts, ma'am," was the famous tagline of a cop TV show from the 1950s. "FACTS Ministries? You gotta be kidding me," I said, rolling my eyes.

A few days earlier, Wednesday night had moved me ahead far faster on my life's spiral of rapid decline. From the simmering suicide of "functional" alcoholism, my addiction had become a daily crack cocaine habit, eating up huge chunks of money at a time, with marijuana and other substances added to further fuel my madness. I was about to lose my house, and I had begun actions that could soon lead to me losing my job also. My relations with my family were little more than brief, distant phone calls made over many miles, and as rarely as possible, on a phone line that would soon be cut off, because I had not paid that bill in multiple months, along with all the other unpaid bills. Who had money for a home phone or a mortgage when the next buy of "good" dope was to be searched for, found, and somehow paid for? My relations with my neighbors were nearly beyond repair. Even the city code enforcement had come by to leave a health hazard warning sign glued on my screen door. The notice had been glued with that thick, sloppy, paintbrush glue used in guerrilla marketing on subway walls, freeway off-ramps, and abandoned buildings. At the time, it did not matter. Nothing mattered, except the next hit. Now, with these precious hours of sustained sobriety after decades of near-daily active addiction, a sober sanity was beginning to take hold.

I had brought too much of the culture of inner-city addiction into the "border" neighborhood I lived in. My neighborhood rested between an area that was a working-class college student mixture on one side, an upscale area on another side heading north, toward the first inner suburb, and the inner city 'hood bordered by the freeway divide on the other. To manage property values and perception, the local neighborhood council was formally organizing to become part of the more upscale neighborhood to the north. Any "ghetto downgrades"—like my eyesore yard, prowlers, and the late-night door knocks active addiction brings—were just what the other neighborhood's council could use to say "No." Area property values were at stake. Be it a nation state or a neighborhood, in the mechanics of place and privilege, border areas typically bear the weight of the heaviest monitoring. With sleep in my eyes from a restless Friday night, and desperation for change I had never felt before, I put a dollar's worth of pennies, nickels, and dimes in my pocket to donate for the Seventh Tradition, hopped on a friend's bike, and headed out to find the FACTS Ministries on Akron Avenue a few miles away.

Just minutes later, tired from the hurried bike ride that should have taken about twenty minutes but I had made in ten, on the broke-down bike with only part of a left pedal and a chain about to break, I stopped at a stoplight and could see a building that appeared to be the place two blocks ahead. The warm summer morning made the hot ride hotter still. Not yet 10:00 a.m. and on this sunny July morning, it was nearly seventy degrees already. This was a strip of Akron Avenue I knew all too well. I had bought some dope a few houses east of the Ministries only days earlier. It was the second-to-last crack purchase toward my bottom. Now I was in the same neighborhood to stay sober for one more hour in a meeting of Cocaine Anonymous. The light changed and I rode the last two blocks, got off the bike, and slowly walked toward the dark-green steel front door of the small brick building. I was finally ready to change my "long-term substance abuse [that] gradually disempowers and induces learned helplessness that makes those who struggle . . . decide that they cannot be successful in their efforts to eliminate substances from their lives" (Washington and Moxley 2003, 147). I had made a first step toward sustaining affiliation with a healing place, a social ecology of faith, health, and resilience at the FACTS Ministries. My bounce back had begun now that I was beginning to do the actions of sober fellowship and to value the first word of the first of 12 Steps: We.

Introduction

A Place for Health and Resilience

There are many large racial and ethnic disparities in health care access, quality of care, and other health status domains. These disparities continue to shape individual, family, and community lives of Americans in the twenty-first century, since they determine health outcomes literally from prior to conception forward. The COVID-19 pandemic has magnified many of these long-standing health disparities by race and ethnicity, by income and wealth, and by immigration status, from initial infection to hospitalization and later outcomes, including possible morbidity. The pandemic has also exposed disparities in preexisting disease vulnerability, in the effectiveness of public health efforts, and in access to health-care services, including the availability and intensity of medical care (Health Affairs Blog 2020; Michener et al. 2020). The COVID pandemic's disproportionate toxicity has placed those with substance use problems "at even higher vulnerability [since] Blacks and Latinos have lower access to needed [drug] treatment, experience less culturally responsive care[, and] have similar rates of opioid misuse as the general population [yet] in recent years Blacks have experienced the greatest increase in rate for overdose deaths from nonmethadone synthetic opioids" (Substance Abuse and Mental Health Services Administration [SAMHSA] 2020, 2–3). Very few of these disparities are new, and efforts to address them from within the communities most affected by them continue.

Among African Americans, grassroots community organizing to improve access to health care has a long history (e.g., Du Bois 1906; Sager 2012). In 1905, "the Men's Sunday Club in Savannah, Georgia, with its focus on improving community health, was one of numerous lay efforts to address the Black community's health needs" (Quinn and Thomas 2001, 44). A year later, the 1906 edited volume of W. E. B. Du Bois, *The Health and Physique of the Negro American*, was likely the first example to both document and analyze the health and well-being of African Americans. It demonstrated the importance of collaboration, at both the intervention and direct service levels, as well as in the systematic analysis of individual and public health. In more recent history, "the 1985 Secretary's Task Force Report on Black and Minority Health . . . identified the six leading causes of preventable excess death for minority populations" (Quinn and Thomas 2001, 44). Chemical dependency was one of the six listed. Then and now, responses to the Task Force Report have been, at best, uneven. The US welfare state has continued its problematic retreat, and the landscape of health-care access is shapeshifting with the implementation of 1115 Substance Use Disorder (SUD) Waiver and related resource revisions (Hinton et al. 2019).

As a result, since before the end of the twentieth century, nontraditional health service providers—both faith-based and secular nonprofit community health organizations—have been stepping in to address numerous health challenges, including substance use disorder. This health challenge has been an issue in *all* segments of American society, the wealthy as well as the impoverished, among Whites as well as African Americans and other people of color. However, as Boeri (2018, 174) has observed, "The drug problems in contemporary [US] society have been socially constructed by the War on Drugs, [whereby] entire swaths of American landscapes became ghettos of despair." This process has led many already impoverished communities to become only more so. Consistent with racial criminalization throughout the history of the United States (e.g., Foreman 2017; Muhammad 2010), the War on Drugs as a war on the Black body and African American communities in which they reside has led to addressing substance misuse in the US primarily by criminal justice enforcement. That renders drug users criminals, fails to account for relevant health disparities, and often further silences the voices of those most vulnerable (Mizelle 2014). Only secondarily is substance use disorder addressed as a medical, mental health, or spiritual ailment, as if such considerations were an afterthought. Research has suggested that "problematic drug use is often the result of trauma, poverty, alienation, and loss of hope for a better life" (Boeri 2018, 173; see also Bourgois and Schonberg 2009; Brown 2006; D'Angelo and Her 2019; White, Kelly, and Roth 2014). This calls for much more *compassionate* strategies in the epidemic of despair, addressing it with an infrastructure of equity. This is done when a responsive social ecology (i.e., beneficial people, places, and things) is prioritized.

This book, *Addiction Recovery and Resilience*, is inspired by the commitment and hard work of resilient women and men who have come together to help improve local health in an urban neighborhood. They do so as they recover from addiction through their affiliation with and support from a faith-based health organization, the Faith ACTions of Sobriety (FACTS) Ministries (a pseudonym). The FACTS Ministries was collaboratively founded in the urban core of a Midwestern city by returning citizens in long-term recovery. Prior research has shown that "faith leaders and places of worship play a key role in providing support, information, and spiritual leadership among Black and Latino communities. [Along with] community-based organizations they have established track-records [as] multi-service providers that integrate health, behavioral health, and social services [through] diverse partnerships and collaborations" (SAMHSA 2020, 4). This analysis responds to Boeri's call to explore individual, organizational, communal, and societal efforts toward making a necessary "paradigm shift of the 'drug problem' [toward] social reconstruction and social recovery" (Boeri 2018, 172–73); see also Denhardt and Denhardt 2010; Roth, White, and Kelly 2014). This necessary paradigm shift—away from individualized stigmatizing and criminalizing of those addicted to substances and toward creating a space for their health and resilience—is apparent in the work of the FACTS Ministries.

Social reconstruction and social recovery have a long history in the United States. In *The Philadelphia Negro*, W. E. B. Du Bois ([1899] 1967, 309) focused on a "mighty influence to mold and make the [African American] citizen: the social atmosphere which surrounds him." He emphasized the decisions and actions of African Americans that shaped "their culture and practices . . . and the institutions they establish and inhabit" (Hunter 2013, 9) that enrich their health and well-being. Following from Du Bois's focus on the social atmosphere—the family, organization, and community—of African American well-being, research is increasingly recognizing resilience as vital to health and as much more than an intra-individual and inherent trait. Instead, the literature suggests that we must explore how "resilience operates across multiple levels, which interact with each other [and] reflect the human ecology framework (Bronfenbrenner, 1994) . . . [and] understand people in the environments in which they live and interact with, and are influenced by" (Windle and Bennett 2012, 219; see also Shaw et al. 2016; Walsh 2003). Like Du Bois's social atmosphere and the social recovery of Boeri, a social ecology of health and resilience recognizes the role environment plays in how well people cope during and after the repeated trauma and alienations of active addiction. For its enrichment, "individual factors interact with family and community factors to bolster well-being [and] secure the cultural and community resources necessary for health while addressing the problems of stigma and alienation" (Ungar 2012, 7; see also Teo, Lee, and Lim 2017; Windle and Bennett 2012). With their tensions and uncertainties, these characteristics enrich the health and well-being of FACTS Ministries affiliates.

Like Shaw et al. (2016, 39) and others, this research demonstrates how "resilience researchers must become more ecological in their approach . . . to tell the rest of the story on resilience and better equip individuals and whole communities for success." Resilience is a social process "of community life [that] requires a different kind of thinking and planning, one that relies on raising awareness and participation of the whole, not just investment in the skills of a few" (Zautra, Hall, and Murray 2010, 9; see also Ungar, Ghazinour, and Richter 2013; White, Kelly, and Roth 2014). It is a framework of beliefs, communication, and organizational programs and "processes that foster healing and growth out of crisis [that] can reduce stress and vulnerability in high-risk situations, and empower to overcome prolonged adversity" (Walsh 2003, 67). As shown in figure 1, resilience is about engendering and sustaining a beneficial *collective* environment of support that works together toward individual, organizational, and social change.

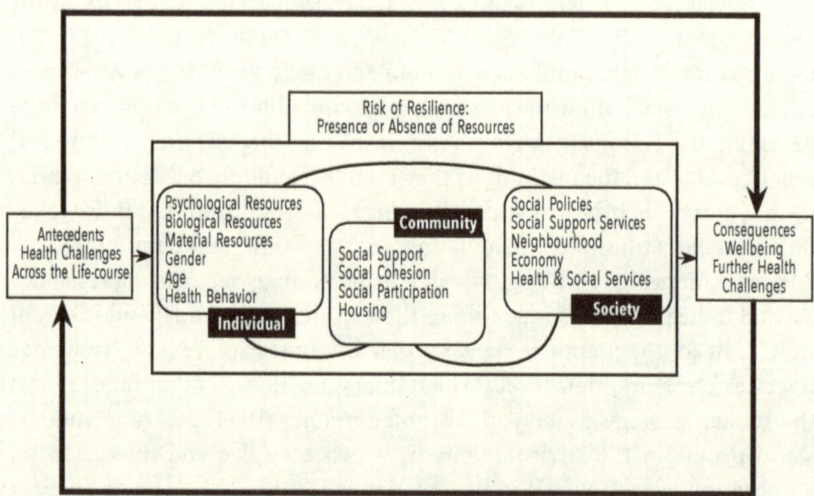

Figure 1. A social ecology of resilience framework. Source: Kate Mary Bennett and Gillian Windle, "The Importance of Not Only Individual, but Also Community and Society Factors in Resilience in Later Life," *Behavioral and Brain Sciences* 38, nos. 22–23 (2015): E94, doi:10.1017/S0140525X14001459.

The figure shows the relationships between antecedents of resilience and the availability of resources (or lack thereof) at the individual, community, and societal levels and their consequences for resilience. By focusing on the organizational level, this book details the meso-level mechanisms central to a health organization's growth and successes and the many challenges that remain. A new model of social reconstruction and social recovery has emerged that is and will be helpful in navigating the collision of interdependent epidemics that mark our present and future.

Addiction Recovery and Resilience is the result of a long-term participant-observation of an organization and its collaborations. What began as a faith-health visit in support of a loved one's recovery from addiction became something much more. Many affiliates of the organization discussed in this book have a personal history of addiction or incarceration and are engaged in long-term recovery, or they have a loved one doing so. To understand their processes of social reconstruction and social recovery, tensions that emerged at individual and organizational levels and how they are being resolved in health- and resilience-affirming ways are analyzed. Through this organizational ethnography, the book addresses how resources are being developed and mobilized at the FACTS Ministries to nurture sustained sobriety and improve health in a neighborhood of concentrated disadvantage. This includes resources that are ignored or resisted to the detriment of the organization's mission. It asks and explores answers to the following questions: What roles can community organizations play in bringing together faith, health, and collective leadership to enrich a social ecology of resilience? What are individuals in long-term recovery doing for themselves to sustain their health and well-being? And what is the role of faith-based resources in that answer (Part 1: Hope)? What tensions are being resolved beneficially as others are being silenced to the detriment of the organization's mission (Part 2: Hurt)? What are the resilience and ecological outcomes of both part 1 and part 2 (Part 3: Hallelujah!)? To answer these questions, data were collected from in-depth interviews with nearly half of the most regular affiliates; a series of focus groups, affiliate surveys, and field notes from hundreds of hours of participant observations; and historical documents, all from more than fourteen years of organizational ethnography (Berg 2007; Fox-Wolfgramm 1997; Lindberg and Eule 2020). The book extends prior health and resilience research that can enrich challenging neighborhood settings in urban America's present and future (e.g., Grim and Grim 2019; Neff, Shorkey, and Windsor 2006). Through these analyses, it specifies emergent best practices and related public policy reflected in the nontraditional health-care delivery the Ministries provides.

Cycles of individual resilience and relapse have been central to the moral economy and ecological analyses of long-term active addiction (e.g., Bourgois and Schonberg 2009; Briggs 2012; D'Angelo and Her 2019; Draus and Carlson 2009; Esbensen and Huizinga 1990; Knight 2015; Sharpe 2005). Though public perception and policy surrounding the current opioid crisis are changing (James and Jordan 2018), with the exception of recovery from natural disasters, resilience has not been thoroughly explored at a health organization or community level. Addiction to drugs and alcohol continues to rage with debilitating health consequences for individuals and their communities. These consequences are exacerbated when they are dealt with primarily by mass incarceration, while treatment (medical, mental health, and spiritual), aftercare, and long-term sobriety are relegated to a secondary line of defense. Outcomes of incarceration due to addiction, without equally rigorous health supports for recovery, wreak disproportionate havoc in communities that are the least equipped to respond to them well (Boeri 2018; Clear 2007). These community health organizations can make a valuable difference in sustaining health and resilience beyond that disproportionate havoc.

Addiction Recovery and Resilience is an interdisciplinary analysis of resilience and the ethnogenic thread. Building on prior historical research on African American ethnogenesis (Price-Spratlen 1999, 2008), the ethnogenic thread responds to a society grounded in the condemnation of Blackness (i.e., devaluing African American agency and possibilities, viewing them as frequently, if not necessarily, destructive) and in "the ideological currency of Black criminality" (Muhammad 2010, 3; see also Mizelle 2014). Ethnogenesis is "the process by which ethnic and racial groups come into being by developing and refining a communal social structure and a collective ethos from the interplay between sociocultural characteristics and American social structure" (Price-Spratlen 2003, 307; see also Myrdal [1944] 1964; Price-Spratlen 2015; Price-Spratlen and Goldsby 2012; Taylor 1979). This book builds on the ethnogenic thread by exploring a faith-based organization as a space where resilience and health flourish in a process driven by efforts "to develop and sustain group cohesiveness and identity [and] establish social networks and communication patterns as the basis of their institutional and communal life" (Taylor 1979, 1405). As White (1996, 160–61) stated, "If we conceptualize addiction as a career with predictable initiation rites and career milestones, then we should also be able to identify various pathways through which one can exit" and the collective ethos that sustains that exit.

Entering the front door of the FACTS Ministries is one such milestone and one such exit. Through its affiliations with other health organizations nearby (e.g., a 12-Step fellowship, a mental health services facility, a children's clinic), the Ministries enriches health and well-being. By hosting events and holding its regular activities, the FACTS Ministries is a "specialized institution and service . . . [for] well-being and mobilizing potential [through a] strong religious and secular organizational presence" (Price-Spratlen 2003, 310). Through affiliation, a person using substances moves from active addiction to behavioral and collaborative recovery and healing. What follows is a brief history of substance misuse in the United States. Special attention is given to cocaine and recovery from it among African Americans as a historical foundation of the FACTS Ministries. This background is followed by an account of Pastor Ellwyn Marshall's life story. His recovery from cocaine addiction is much more than a personal journey; it leads into the founding and development of the FACTS Ministries. This introduction ends with an overview of the book.

History of Substance Misuse in the US

Racialized stigma and its relationships to public policy mark substance use in the US. As W. E. B. Du Bois ([1899] 1967, 163) noted more than a century ago, "The most difficult social problem in the matter of Negro health is the peculiar attitude of the nation toward the well-being of the race. There have . . . been few other cases in the history of civilized peoples where human suffering has been viewed with such peculiar indifference." Indifference or a condemnation toward criminalization are among the most frequent societal reactions to these disparities, even when they are largely a product of societal apathy or natural disaster (Mizelle 2014; Muhammad 2010). It is at best uncertain how the indifference Du Bois wrote about has changed during the generations since he made his observation. Issues of African American health broadly defined reinforce the truism that the opposite of love is not hate but apathy, akin to the indifference Du Bois identifies. Prior research recognizes that "at the institutional level, sociological research has underscored the role of *residential racial segregation* as a primary institutional mechanism of racism and a fundamental cause of racial disparities in health" (Williams and Sternthal 2010, S20, emphasis mine; see also Drucker 2011; Johnson 2010, 2018; Woods et al. 2013). The institutional mechanism of residential racial segregation also informs substance misuse regarding the overrepresentation of African Americans incarcerated for low-level drug-related offenses, as well as the disproportionate untreated substance misuse, food deserts, and related asset limitations in many predominantly African American residential areas in contrast to White communities.

A few years after the publication of Du Bois's book in which he made the indifference remark quoted above, the *New York Times* (*NYT*, November 3, 1902, A5) published an article headlined "Cocaine Evil among Negroes" (see figure 2). Instead of indifference, it presented a health concern among African Americans as a racial demonization and criminalization. The article discussed the sale of the drug and how a Mississippi judge urged a grand jury to "punish Druggists" harshly due to "the evils attendant upon the use of the drug [which] cover the whole catalogue of crimes. . . . The negroes call it 'coke.' The coke fiend who has just taken a sniff leans back or lies down in a dreamy state [and] from this state he passes to one of wild frenzy [where] the 'coke fiend' is dangerous." This rationale suggests that severe punishment was warranted because of the agency of a racial evil unleashed by the "druggists." The zeitgeist thus moved miles away from the "peculiar indifference" toward Blacks' well-being that Du Bois observed and lamented, to an extreme fear and a necessary retribution in response to the release of evil projected onto Blacks. A similar framing was used again in the *NYT* in a March 20, 1905, column titled, "Negro Cocaine Evil." On September 29, 1913, a *NYT* column announced, "10 DEAD, 20 HURT IN A RACE RIOT. . . . Drug-crazed Negroes start a reign of terror and defy whole Mississippi town" (A1). In the column, Whites were victims, and the "drug-crazed" Black men were lynched "after they [had] killed or wounded a score of persons." This allegation was used to justify a non-trial, death-penalty punishment of White mob violence. Reading further, the unrest is said to have been brought about by a prior lynching of a Black man. A racialized association was reinforced between Blacks, cocaine addiction, crime, a legitimated suspension of due process, and ultimately, justifiable White retribution and Black death.

This pattern was repeated a few months later when a February 8, 1914, *NYT* headline read, "Negro Cocaine 'Fiends' Are a New Southern Menace." The long, detailed article suggested that cocaine made one impervious to bullets and a "better marksman," and that severe actions against its African American users were necessary: "It is literally a matter of life and death." The article ended with the recognition of public policy in relation to race: "The great stumbling block in the way of suppressing

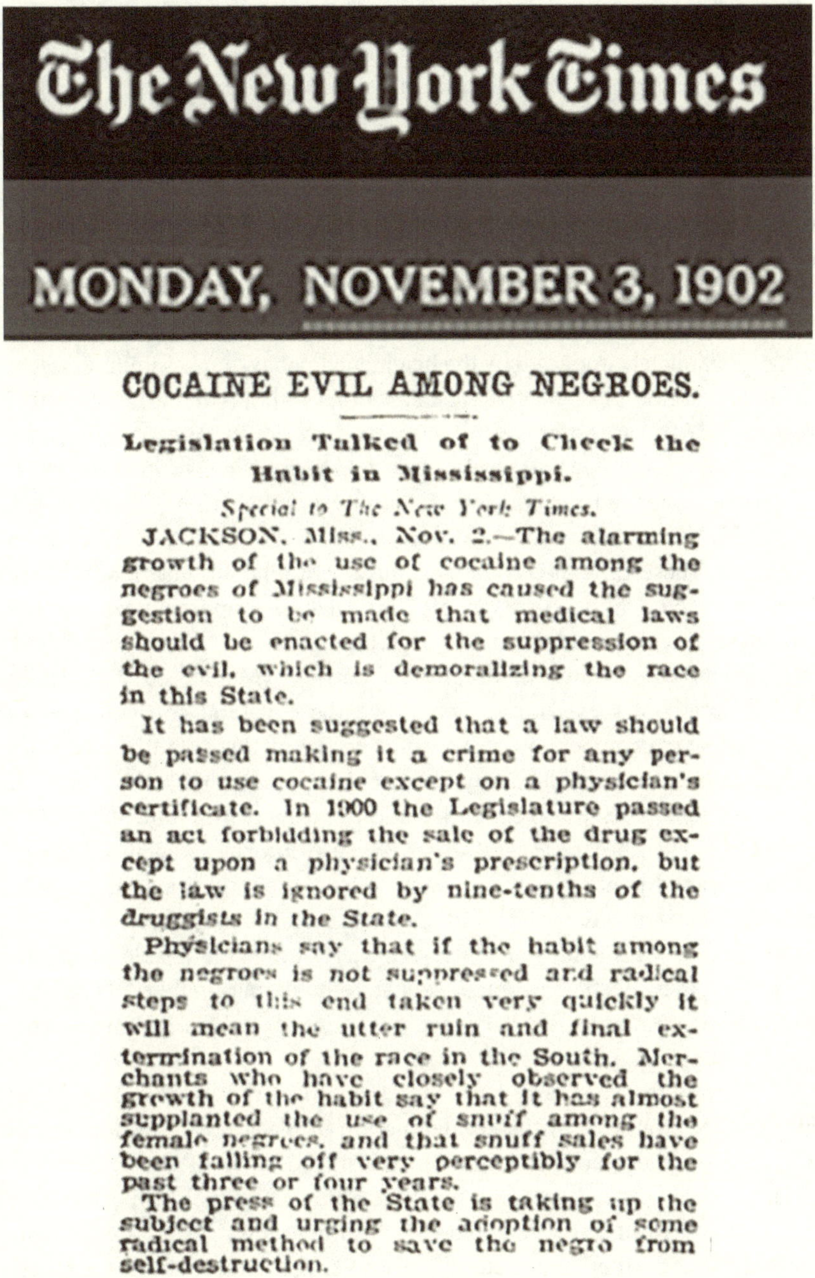

The New York Times

MONDAY, NOVEMBER 3, 1902

COCAINE EVIL AMONG NEGROES.

Legislation Talked of to Check the Habit in Mississippi.

Special to The New York Times.

JACKSON, Miss., Nov. 2.—The alarming growth of the use of cocaine among the negroes of Mississippi has caused the suggestion to be made that medical laws should be enacted for the suppression of the evil, which is demoralizing the race in this State.

It has been suggested that a law should be passed making it a crime for any person to use cocaine except on a physician's certificate. In 1900 the Legislature passed an act forbidding the sale of the drug except upon a physician's prescription, but the law is ignored by nine-tenths of the druggists in the State.

Physicians say that if the habit among the negroes is not suppressed and radical steps to this end taken very quickly it will mean the utter ruin and final extermination of the race in the South. Merchants who have closely observed the growth of the habit say that it has almost supplanted the use of snuff among the female negroes, and that snuff sales have been falling off very perceptibly for the past three or four years.

The press of the State is taking up the subject and urging the adoption of some radical method to save the negro from self-destruction.

Figure 2. Media racialization of African Americans, cocaine, and substance abuse. *Source*: "Cocaine Evil among Negroes," *New York Times*, November 3, 1902, A5.

the [drug] traffic is the fact that the causes that produce it have become entangled with a political issue [regarding] what is best for the politician." Through inaction, politicians and other policy makers of the day had "forced a new and terrible form of slavery upon thousands of colored men—a hideous bondage from which they [could] not escape by mere proclamation or civil war" (A19).

Nearly a century later, the opioid crisis has been largely presented as a "White" problem that deserves a health-challenge response over a criminalizing one (Boeri 2018; James and Jordan 2018). However, many racialized inconsistencies remain. African American youth continue to be disproportionately impacted by the heightened policy of mass imprisonment often for minor drug-related misdemeanors. Studies in 2012 and 2017 reported, "African American adolescents have lower rates of substance use than White adolescents; [yet] African Americans constituted over 85% of people sentenced for cocaine violations, although they constitute less than 15% of all crack users" (Mukku et al. 2012, 3; see also Mooney et al. 2018). These differences are systemically similar to, and magnify the effects of, the school-to-prison pipeline that disproportionately applies "punitive environmental norms of schools on . . . the impoverished, students of color [and] maltreatment victims" (Mallett 2017, 563). In the aftermath of these punishments, like the collateral consequences of being released from prison as an adult, many of these youths and their adult counterparts are ill equipped to navigate reentry with the stigma of a record, joblessness, and social isolation in which they find themselves embroiled. Health-care access disparities also inform a racialized access to the means by which someone can address their substance misuse. In treating opioid use disorders and associated health challenges, "only one in ten people with a substance use disorder nationwide is able to get the treatment they need. . . . Black people remain marginalized [and] the shortage of treatment is even more pronounced in Black communities" (James and Jordan 2018, 413).

These interdependent disparities are both a product of and a partner in a society grounded in the condemnation of Blackness. Working within and beyond these condemnations, capacity building of the ethnogenic thread has long recognized the potential value of mutual support groups for recovery from addiction. During the mid-1800s, health movements among African Americans included various temperance societies for recovery, such as the Colored Temperance Society (Herd 1991; White, Kelly, and Roth 2014). For these organizations, "liquor was used to 'narcoticize' the slave population into helpless docility and dissipation [because] liquor was the foe of liberty" (Herd 1991, 356). As part of his abolitionist organizing, Frederick Douglass (1855, 256) noted, "When a slave was drunk, the slave holder had no fear that he would plan an insurrection; no fear that he would escape to the north. It was the sober, thinking slave who was dangerous." With sober organizational initiatives in the bridge of time between them, a century later, various "addiction ministries" rose in the 1950s and 1960s. They did so in response to African American heroin addiction, placing value on religious and cultural revitalization movements. Within them, "drugs were framed as tools of genocide [and these] religious and cultural revitalization movements [provided] pathways of addiction-recovery initiation and maintenance" (Evans et al. 2014, 103). In addition to inspiring advocation for criminal justice responses (e.g., Foreman 2017), the CIA-influenced crack epidemic of the 1990s reinvigorated similar addiction ministries until the present time (Cockburn and St. Clair 1999). Yet, as one part of the condemnation of interdependent disparities that remain, crack cocaine and other drugs (prescription and otherwise) continue to plague the most vulnerable neighborhoods. Many of them have limited resources in their efforts to navigate the often devastating impact of substance misuse and its consequences.

In 2016, President Obama expressed concern regarding the growing challenges of addiction and recovery. At the 2016 National Prescription Drug Abuse and Heroin Summit, the Centers for Disease Control and Prevention (CDC) released data on the continuing prevalence of substance use in the US, now nearly two generations into the "War on Drugs." They showed that "despite decades of expense and effort focused on a criminal justice-based model for addressing substance use-related problems, substance misuse remains a national public health crisis" (US Surgeon General 2016, 1–2; see also Foreman 2017). In his 2016 report, *Facing Addiction in America*, the US Surgeon General (2016, 1-1) asserted that "the United States has a serious substance misuse problem . . . [with] devastating consequences, [including] more overdose deaths last year than in any previous year on record." The COVID pandemic has intensified these and related public health challenges (Michener et al. 2020). Many people, especially those in long-term recovery, are addressing various challenges associated with substance use disorder, as are community health organizations, often in collaboration. As the Surgeon General's report recognizes, "People in recovery, their family members, and other supporters are banding together to spread the message that people do recover through the growing network of recovery community organizations" (2016, 5-1). To improve the health and well-being of the US population, the "underlying social, environmental, and economic determinants of substance misuse and its consequences" (US Surgeon General 2016, 1–2) must be addressed.

Both faith-based and secular organizations help sustain long-term recovery from addiction, economic and health disparities, and incarceration. Among secular activist health organizations that contribute to combating addiction to drugs and its consequences is From Punishment to Public Health, an organization formed by a group of professionals in New York. Contrary to the criminal justice response associated with the crack cocaine era (Clear 2007; Foreman 2017), the group consists of clinical practitioners, public health researchers, and criminal justice officials. Together, they have collaborated to "lobby against incarceration for illicit drug possession and [to] advocate for diversion of arrestees into mental health and substance use treatment services" (Netherland and Hansen 2016, 664). From clinicians and related others, this group's "community-based interventions have helped to redress the effects of [racially] unequal drug law enforcement" (James and Jordan 2018, 415). These and other recovery organizations like them (e.g., Connecticut Community for Addiction Recovery, Faces & Voices of Recovery, People Advocating Recovery in Kentucky) enrich secular, community-based interventions helping to sustain the health and long-term recovery of many (Humphreys 2004; Laudet 2008; Morell 1996; White, Kelly, and Roth 2014).

Religion- or spirituality-informed responses to substance-related and other health-compromising behaviors have been well documented (e.g., Cheney et al. 2014; Chitwood, Weiss, and Leukefeld 2008; Evans et al. 2014). Because faith-based organizations are "particularly well-suited to provide nonclinical addiction-recovery support services . . . clergy now constitute a major recovery support resource within African American communities" (Evans et al. 2014, 103; see also Chu and Sung 2009; Walton-Moss, Ray, and Woodruff 2013). Among the questions associated with African American churches' efforts to respond to these contemporary challenges is, What contributions can such a community health organization make? Interdisciplinary research has shown such an organization's "protective role in drug addiction" (Cheney et al. 2014, 95). Cheney and colleagues add, "Religiosity is an especially strong deterrent in crack cocaine use [and is] associated with less substance use. . . . [It] minimizes doubts and uncertainties in the recovery process and helps to maintain prosocial attitudes and behaviors." Faith-based organizations have been committed to a long-standing project of improving the lives of those living in neighborhoods of concentrated disadvantage (Boeri 2018; Freeman 2001), and they sometimes collaborate with secular health organizations. African American churches are among prominent organizations that have mobilized to help in the rehabilitation of Black youths and adults in active addiction or in the aftermath of having been released from prison.

One of these Black churches is the FACTS Ministries, the subject of this book. Cofounded by Ellwyn Marshall, Raymond Daughtry, and supportive affiliates of Millwood Fellowship Church, the Ministries responded to crack addiction that had devastated the North Lawson neighborhood and the surrounding city for years. This preceded the state being declared as having an especially serious opioid crisis. Things had deteriorated so severely that in the early 1990s, a drug bust in the neighborhood was featured in a *New York Times* story, "Crack Invades the Heartland." Pastor Marshall and his wife, Cheryl, were intimately aware of this situation. Crack was, in effect, the substance of blunt force trauma, followed by its shattering consequences. It magnified long-standing inequities and health disparities—of residential segregation, high crime rates, and other concentrated disadvantages (see chapter 2). For Pastor Marshall and a board that was being developed, the Ministries could be a means to help heal these fractures. Healing could be nurtured through the Ministries' health-wellness mission by providing access to mutual support services for long-term addiction recovery, health screenings, free and reduced-rate health services, day care, free lunches, and nutritional counseling, among other resources and supports. Financial stability and commitment from Millwood Fellowship and its partners allowed Pastor Marshall to build from his own journey of recovery while strengthening the Ministries' social resilience mission.

The social ecology of active addiction both within and between various subgroups of society is well understood and has been richly detailed ethnographically. This addictive behaviors literature includes Bourgois and Schonberg's (2009) grounded theory of a moral economy regarding intravenous drug users in Northern California. In Briggs's (2012, 157) political economy of crack users, "what seems to make crack users different from heroin users is the level to which they engage in derogatory acts and high-risk behaviours." Among those in active addiction, Sharpe (2005, 142) found a gendered predatory reciprocity, where "predatory behavior among the women increased as they became victims of men more often" (see also D'Angelo and Her 2019; Draus and Carlson 2009; Knight 2015). While prior research has described and explained active addiction in great detail, far less well understood are individual and organizational components that make up a social ecology of resilience for long-term recovery. *Addiction Recovery and Resilience* contributes to this literature by analyzing the ways in which the FACTS Ministries, through its five health services domains (see chapter 3), supports the healing of spiritual/societal fractures in the lives of its affiliates, many of whom are in recovery from addiction. By doing so, the Ministries enriches the life of the community in which it is located, in a twenty-first-century Midwestern urban inner city in the US. A brief history of the FACTS Ministries, from its founding to today, is told below in more detail, in the life story of its primary founder, Pastor Ellwyn Marshall.

More Than a Personal Journey

Ellwyn Marshall was raised in the North Lawson neighborhood in which he has been pastoring since 2000. He is old enough to remember when "North meets South" was a sports battle cry for the neighborhood high school he once attended, which is now a STEM (science, technology, engineering, and mathematics) "magnet school" within the city's highly segregated public school system. Then and now, his high school alma mater has constituted part of the western border of this neighborhood. Ellwyn returned to his old neighborhood to lead a ministry where the life renewal of sobriety was central to its faith-health mission. Personally and professionally, he was well aware of the chaos of active addiction, a focus on the "good dope," pursuing the "bellringer" that the next good hit would be, which never quite delivered the anticipated high or began to gradually lead to overdose (US Surgeon General 2016; Vivolo-Kantor et al. 2019). These were the North Lawson streets for him to "hit a lick," to hustle up some money to get enough dope so that he and his then girlfriend Cheryl could get high. Cheryl, now his wife, got sober before him. Ellwyn clearly recalls her final *final* goodbye as he spiraled toward his "bottom" (the merciful end of his active addiction). Cheryl changed the locks for the final *final* time on their family home to help control the chaos in her life and the lives of their five children. Banishment from his home and family, a dinner tray on the outside steps every night, waving to his then two-year-old son through the front window as he ate his meal—these were his daily greeting and routine near active addiction's endpoint. In those days, he walked the neighborhood alleys with a very different tempo and intent. Now he navigates those same alleys with a perspective of distance-at-close-range. He had been sober for barely a year when he found the strength of faith to launch in 2000 what would become the FACTS Ministries in his father's garage. As his sobriety found its footing, motives of organization building began to define him.

In 1999, having served eight months in the county jail again for dealing drugs, Ellwyn came out with a renewed promise of sobriety. Similar to Bill W., who contributed to the founding of Alcoholics Anonymous while in search of fellowship at a moment of need in his sobriety (Alcoholics Anonymous 2001), Ellwyn realized that to sustain his own sobriety, he would need to engage with others to help realize a mission for a health-focused ministry. As he said, making "the connection between recovery and faith comes differently to different people." "The 12-Step fellowships seem to appreciate how this kind of thing can be lived. So, to grow a church, we needed to grow [interpersonal and organizational] relationships" (personal communication, August 2007). Training himself in "the Word" of Christian faith, Ellwyn set out to be a jackleg preacher (an amateur, self-educated minister). He began holding religious services in his father's alley garage, a short distance from where the storefront FACTS Ministries building now stands. This was the same garage where he had once bought, sold, and smoked dope with others. With lawnmower equipment and power tools on the metal shelves around them, gatherings became a place of shared humility and worship in the name of a sober faith. As Pastor Marshall described it years later during a Sunday sermon he gave, the garage had become a place to "put down the stem [for smoking crack] or whatever else holds you hostage, and pick up the Word of God."

Upon his release from jail, Ellwyn returned to his father's house. After a chance encounter with his longtime friend Raymond, he began to act on his dream of creating a faith-based place of long-term recovery after the use of one of the most shameful drugs. At the time Raymond was in a moment of struggle. He was lamenting having recently been "vamped" (again) in a dope deal. Raymond had given money to someone who supposedly had drugs to sell, but he had received hardened chunks of a baby formula/sugar mix. Or drywall. Or something similar that mimicked the texture and appearance of crack cocaine in a small plastic wrapper. Being vamped was a frequent cause of drug deals gone bad. The immediate aftermath of such an experience, "little moments of clarity, are times [when one] knew for sure" their substance use was a problem to them and others (Alcoholics Anonymous 2001, 284). In those moments of clarity, the person may be more open to the possibility of sustained recovery to avoid ever being cheated again. Raymond was then in the "revolving door" of getting sober for short-term motives (e.g., passing a drug test for a possible job) and briefly sustaining that sobriety, only to return to using. With little support to sustain change, Raymond continued to surround himself with the people, places, and things of addiction. At the moment of their chance encounter in 1999, Raymond was again searching for a way to maintain sobriety. Though newly sober himself, Ellwyn was already actively moving from a personal resilience to a social resilience and reconstruction. He began to realize that "unlike other forms of personal resilience, social resilience is intrinsically multilevel and includes an individual's characteristic ways of relating and interpersonal capacities (e.g., empathy, perspective taking, trust) and collective resources" (Cacioppo et al. 2015, 91). Among the collective resources Ellwyn valued were those Raymond had to offer. He shared his vision with Raymond about a place where they would not have to hide in shame their crack-addiction-informed sober walk. They talked about their hope for one another's sobriety and for launching a ministry to help others in their resilience and sobriety.

In the months that followed, Ellwyn maintained his sobriety and briefly worked with a sponsor in a 12-Step fellowship. Raymond did neither. He continued to struggle, as recovery again did not take root in his life. His return to active addiction was familiar. On more than one occasion, he came to the new meeting the two men had begun high or drunk or both. During a brief period of sobriety, it was Raymond who suggested the name for what became a newly established Cocaine Anonymous (CA) meeting: Either-Or. And it stuck. Either one was ready to end active addiction's "Step Zero," as one longtime Ministries affiliate called it, to begin the demanding work of Step One; or the person was not ready, and the repetitions of active addiction would quickly return. Raymond also named the FACTS Ministries. Sober or not, he was always welcomed back, given his contributions to the larger mission of both the Either-Or CA meeting and the Ministries. Allowing him back expressed a forgiveness of self and others and a faith in the possibility of recovery. While the CA meeting was growing, so too were the Ministries' Sunday services and its larger health mission.

Following his final release from jail, Ellwyn continued to move his life and family forward in constructive ways, and his work prospects gradually improved. First he was a short-order cook at a fast-food chain

("I remember flippin' those burgers all too well," he often remarked). Then an assistant manager at a small restaurant outlet store ("Not smellin' like french fries all day was a step up. *Way* up."). Now with a work history and a boxing background from his time in the military, he was able to apply for a security staff position for the city schools. This was because "they were looking for someone who could [go to] battle if they needed to and knew the dope game for real." Laughing, he added, "It was probably the first and only time that my background with crack and all was what a possible employer actually wanted. That was big" (personal communication, August 2007). His small garage gatherings continued as a move to a new space became possible.

In a series of letters to two prominent Millwood Fellowship board members, Ellwyn expressed his interest in growing his faith leadership, to preach the Word to "save" himself and others from a lifetime of active addiction. Throughout his jail time, his wife and their children had continued to attend Millwood Fellowship as their home church. The depth of appreciation among the church leadership for Cheryl's faith seemed to strengthen the leadership's appreciation of Ellwyn's growth and change also. While walking around the North Lawson neighborhood a few blocks from his father's garage, Ellwyn and Raymond began to look for a building that could enhance the Ministries' mission. In 2001, they noticed that a storefront building they had walked by for many years had a "For Sale" sign in its front window. It was a sturdy, one-story, 2,800-square-foot brick building on the corner of Twenty-Eighth Street and Akron Avenue.

Built in 1931, the building had undergone a number of transformations. It had housed a neighborhood cleaners for its then largely working-class Italian and Irish immigrant residents. The Depression-era cleaners gave way to a 1940s laundromat, later a 1950s corner store for candy and a small selection of grocery items, and then a day-care center through some of the 1960s. Fitting the neighborhood's general character, it had also been a bar, a tavern, and a "mini-brothel"—as attested to by some of the longtime neighbors. Since the 1970s, it had been intermittently dormant and abandoned for years at a time. A used car lot was at the end of the block, a gas station directly across the street, and rundown houses and duplexes were all around the building. Owing to its multi-use history, for many years the building's two front doors were heavy, layered metal, as if part of a security system, rather than welcoming church doors; one front door led into what became the chapel, the other into what became the community room. On each side of the southern, community room door were thick, glass-block basement safety windows, two by three feet. They allowed some light in, though no visibility. The building had two parts, split by a wall between its northern and southern portions: the larger area for the chapel, and the smaller half of the building for the community room and a small kitchen area.

Ellwyn quickly raised the possibility of purchasing the building among supportive Millwood Fellowship members. A few months later the purchase was made through a longtime friend and business owner who had shared Pastor Marshall's vision with the pastor of his large, suburban, predominantly White church. The Marshall family had been attending Millwood for a couple of years and had endeared themselves to the pastoral leadership. Many within the congregation were surprised that such a resource commitment was being made with the only African American family in its membership. Yet the commitment was made. With Ellwyn's efforts, the Millwood Fellowship leadership found two other (predominantly White, suburban) churches, Sacred Calling Fellowship and Cedar Tree Church, to collaborate with and fund an "urban outreach" satellite. Working with others is a gamble, and "power in collaboration is fragmented. Sustaining a trust-building loop long enough to achieve collaborative advantage usually requires finding ways of ensuring that shared power is maximized" (Vangen and Huxham 2003, 22). Though fragile, a trust-building loop among these collaborating congregations was established and nurtured. Pastor Marshall and his newly appointed board kept the doors open and the lights on as the building of a health ministry began.

The collaborative "demand" for the FACTS Ministries came from several White youth struggling with addiction in the three churches during the initial onset of what would become the "opioid crisis." The collaboration's goal was to establish an off-site faith-based response to substance use disorder, partially motivated by what appeared to many to be an "out of sight, out of mind" desire to keep active addiction among the White suburban youth away from the congregations and away from addiction treatment facilities. Soon Ellwyn was walking through the new building with a contractor, who was also a member of Millwood Fellowship. Generous donations from the three anchor churches were matched by those from a foundation with which an anchor church member was affiliated. Together, the funds were enough for a down payment and monthly mortgage. Ellwyn was then able to pastor full-time as an assistant pastor at Millwood and as lead pastor for what would formally be known as the FACTS Ministries: a faith-based, urban recovery and health organization.

Today, the chapel seats eighty-five comfortably. The oversized pulpit in the chapel's northernmost floorspace has a two-step staircase, and its half-octagon layout takes up one-quarter of the chapel floor plan. The pastor's office is in the far northeastern corner walled off from the step-up pulpit, and a bathroom is in the southeastern corner of this front portion of the church. A large vinyl banner on the far northern wall upon entering the chapel greets people with the message "This Thing Is All About JESUS!" The banner sits behind three throne-like, rustic chairs bestowing pastoral status to the small pulpit and chapel.

After the first year of the FACTS Ministries functioning as the urban outreach faith initiative, the Millwood Fellowship–led collaboration secured the financing of a new home for the Marshall family in a nearby suburb several miles from North Lawson; at the time, all five of the children were still living at home. The small, three-bedroom North Lawson home where the family had been living for six years was just a few blocks from the Ministries. It remained in the collaboration's "property portfolio." It served a new purpose when Millwood and Ministries leaders decided to expand their health mission with a residential recovery facility. Given the level of unmet need for sober housing within the city and the neighborhood, they recognized that "group homes help people maintain long-term abstinence from alcohol and drugs—typically referred to as 'sober living homes'—[they] can act as a buffer against the relapse risks that are endemic to many urban environments" (Heslin et al. 2012, 379; see also Boeri 2018). Thus, the first FACTS Ministries sober home opened its doors to new residents. Within a year, another small house across the street from the first was acquired. Then, in late 2009, the collaborative purchased the duplex next door, which had been empty for over a year. They recognized the vital importance of simultaneously addressing returning citizens' interdependent concerns after their release from prison: reentry and health (Drucker 2011; White, Kelly, and Roth 2014). With the acquisition and management of three sober homes, the Ministries was now able to provide sober places for a total of fourteen former felons and other marginally housed and homeless men at low rent. There, occupants could revise old relationships and build new ones, and with the new resources the Ministries offered, they could redefine their lives.

During the first few years, more services were launched in addition to the evening Sunday service. A Wednesday night Bible study was added. A faith breakfast meeting on Tuesday mornings soon followed. As donations increased and willing volunteers came forward, a weekly lunch was served on Tuesday afternoons. Word spread, and the programming, the resources, and the Ministries grew. In the community room, other health services were offered (see chapter 3). The FACTS Ministries thus continued assisting people as they established and sustained their social recovery and transformations. Until recently, activities of various kinds were offered one or more times each day, six days a week, throughout the year. Its five health service domains and programming are interactive and are reflected in the health and resilience of its affiliates. Amid its many tensions, uncertainties, and patterns of change, from its beginnings to today, the Ministries has touched thousands of lives and succeeds in regularly helping many people respond to their active addiction and lead healthier lives.

A Note on Methods

I am an African American, middle-aged male who was drawn to this project through my support of a loved one's recovery from addiction. In addition, I have known of the contexts of drug culture since my neighborhood bike rides as a child in the 1970s in West Los Angeles and the bars and back-alley objects and activities I observed then. Years later, during my first summer of research in graduate school, I had the opportunity and honor of interviewing housing-insecure, intravenous drug users about their past and present substance use practices in relation to their sexual behaviors. I have family members and friends who lost their lives to addiction to various substances, while others are practicing harm reduction and managed substance use, and still others are living a long-term, abstinence-based, 12-Step recovery. My social justice work with returning citizens (i.e., former felons) and research for a prior book on their civic engagement and principled transformation informed my perspectives on the "drug war," mass incarceration, the drug treatment industry, the opioid crisis, and the often complicated interdependencies between them. Bringing together those childhood experiences, my training as a social scientist, research and writing in the organizational intersection of faith and health disparities, and intimate, personal familiarity with all of these elements provides me with valuable perspectives. Each informs my analysis of social resilience and recovery facilitated by the FACTS Ministries.

The people, places, and (more and less healthy) things analyzed in this book were drawn from a project examining how a community health organization enriches the well-being and resilience of its affiliates. *Affiliation* is an elastic term that recognizes a wide range of types of participation in an organization. Experiences of over four hundred individuals were examined during my nearly fifteen years in the field. For analytic clarity and thematic coherence, the organization is my primary focus. Emphasis is placed on resources, patterns, and processes and the means by which each are, and are not, exchanged among different types of affiliates. Central figures and critical moments that best exemplify the ways in which the FACTS Ministries was itself a supportive environment of resilience, and contributed to the neighborhood in which it is located, are at the book's core.

The FACTS Ministries is a predominantly African American organization in a predominantly African American neighborhood. However, affiliates and their experiences at and with the Ministries represent a rich diversity of race/ethnicity, gender, socioeconomic status, sexual identity, religious background, and other subgroup differences. Affiliate social class ranged from those whose family businesses earned millions of dollars each year to those with no reported income who had been housing insecure for multiple years. Educational attainment reflected a similar broad range, including those with graduate degrees and professional careers and those who had dropped out of junior high school. Affiliate work histories were also quite diverse. Religiously, those across the Christian spectrum, along with atheist, Buddhist, Jewish, and people with no faith affiliation history of any kind, were among those who valued being short- and long-term affiliates of the Ministries and are reflected in these pages.

Perhaps most critically, the affiliates represented here include those who came to the Ministries seeking addiction recovery, those who established and sustained sober habits and maintained their long-term sobriety for many years, those on the "marijuana maintenance plan" or other form of harm reduction, and those who relapsed (i.e., returned to severe active addiction) and were in and out of the Ministries five, six, seven times or more. It includes those who attended church services or community lunches for a brief time and left on "good terms," and those who played important roles across multiple domains of the Ministries for many years whose departure was less pleasant. Throughout, emphasis is placed on the individual, organizational, and communal fractures and how FACTS Ministries resources generally contributed to healing these fractures or fell short of doing so. Resources, patterns, and policy implications examined in this book can help us understand and strengthen the ways community organizations can improve physical, mental, and spiritual well-being and help individuals, communities, and the society at large become more resilient.

Data collections for this organizational ethnography included in-depth interviews with thirty affiliates and a series of focus groups with forty affiliates. These data also include affiliate surveys, notes from the experiences of short-term volunteers, and experiences attending various off-site celebrations and other organizational events. The primary data source is field notes from many hundreds of hours of participant observation from the Ministries' five primary health service domains. All names are pseudonyms. As a qualitative researcher, my goal was to understand the tensions and triumphs of the Ministries and its affiliates. This included those who were weekly attendees of various events who kept coming back for ten years or more. Those who came just a few times to one event type (e.g., community lunches only) and did not return are also in these pages, as were those who moved in and through their own lifeworlds in the days, weeks, and sometimes years separating their direct affiliation with the Ministries. Affiliation frequency and duration did increase the likelihood of those willing to participate in the interviews and focus groups of the project, yet the inclusion of affiliate diversities was important and is reflected in these data.

Data moments ranged from urgent care waiting rooms on a Thursday night to easygoing neighborhood front porches on a slow Saturday morning. They included tense church services with surprising communication and unexpected police visits to a recovery meeting or community lunch when something got out of hand. There were late-night phone calls with raised voices of rage and the quiet, everyday tensions of a young dope dealer letting others know that "new product" of whatever type is always available, right across the street, or in the five-car parking lot behind the Ministries' building. There were burnt sweet rolls for the Men's Prayer Breakfasts on first Saturday mornings, along with other foods difficult to consume. There were the commonplace solicitations of sex industry workers during community lunches and the infrequent, though far too common, tarp-covered aftermath of shootings in the neighborhood. All of these and much more were among the aspects of local ecology for an organization located in the thick of concentrated disadvantage. Experiences of resilience, both personal and social, were central always. How the Ministries nurtured them is the analytic focus throughout.

Organization of the Book

Addiction Recovery and Resilience is organized in three parts: Hope, Hurt, and Hallelujah! In the Hope of part 1, I analyze "Resilient People, Places, and Things." Chapter 1, "We, Who Would Otherwise Not Meet: The People of the Ministries," introduces women and men of the FACTS Ministries, their identities and background diversities. Profiles of this purposive sample accurately reflect overall affiliation across the Ministries' multiple domains. In chapter 2, "Much More than Watermelon Roadkill: The Place of the Ministries," places of recovery are examined in a brief ethnography of North Lawson, the underdeveloped, high-poverty neighborhood in an economically stable and growing city where the Ministries is located. The Ministries' resilience and health-promoting resources are the focus of chapter 3, "Healthy Things: Resilience Resources of the Ministries." They include hosting twice-weekly Cocaine Anonymous meetings, relapse prevention workshops, pastoral and nutritional counseling, a women's faith-health group, a youth boxing team, community lunches, Men's Prayer Breakfasts, referrals to a women's clinic, dental and medical care, psychiatric services, and special events.

In part 2 of the book, "Hurt: Dissonant Dialogues of Resilience" are considered. The chapters of part 2 clarify how, despite challenges of strained collaboration and uncertain inclusions, hundreds benefited from their affiliation with the Ministries and many more continue to heal. Chapter 4, "Uncertain Sanctuary: The Ministries' Collaboration with Cocaine Anonymous," explores the uneven collaboration between the Ministries and the CA meetings that it hosts. It assesses Ministries-CA tensions over time and resulting disruptions to both organizations. Chapter 5, "Silence in Our Midst: (In)Visibility and Voice at the Ministries," focuses on largely unspoken and less visible persons and patterns of the Ministries. Though often unacknowledged, they are central to the Ministries' contributions to the health and resilience of affiliates. Chapter 6, "Change Gon' Come: The Flourishing and Decline of the Ministries," examines the arc of a community health organization—how it began, grew, flourished, and changed over nearly fifteen years. It details the choices and outcomes that compromised its mission.

Part 3, "Part 3: Hallelujah! How Healing Happens," links Ministries domains, resources, and trajectories with best practices in the final chapter of the book. Chapter 7, "Faith-Based Best Practices: How a Fractured Ministries Can Heal," describes an emergent model of community health and related public policy. As Tangenberg (2005b, 38) suggested, though "spiritual and scientific views of recovery will likely never be completely reconciled, attention to the person-environment context . . . can [help] provide meaningful synthesis" (see also Boeri 2018; Sager 2011, 2012). Recommendations for organizational effectiveness are specified, whose short- and long-term implications help enrich an ecology of health and resilience in and well beyond the FACTS Ministries and the North Lawson neighborhood it calls home. The epilogue considers implications of recent events in North Lawson that affected the present and future of the Ministries and can inform other health organizations in the US.

I am grateful to Pastor Ellwyn Marshall and the many FACTS Ministries affiliates who were willing to share their experiences with me. While I have used pseudonyms to respect their privacy, their spirit, personal struggles, and triumphs are captured in their words wherever possible. The people of the Ministries, within their various capacities and roles, are introduced and analyzed in chapter 1 and explored throughout the book. Their personal ecologies of resilience are at the core of the Ministries organization and of this book.

PART 1

HOPE: RESILIENT PEOPLE, PLACES, AND THINGS

Chapter 1

"We, Who Would Otherwise Not Meet"

The People of the Ministries

> Candy told me she has been off drugs for four years. She said, "I've been clean for four years going on 40." Her first husband died in the first week of their marriage from a stroke. She said she went to college and got a degree, and then got to the streets and drugs overtook her life. She used to smoke crack on the street and in the alley, 15 feet from the FACTS Ministries' back door. . . . She is an EMT, and her second husband works to get drug dealers off the street. Four years ago she was coming around to get these meals. Now she appreciates volunteering. She said, "I didn't think anything would be able to get me away from drugs. . . . I am so grateful that I got away and can now give back here."
>
> —Field notes, September 2015

The phrase "people, places, and things" is among the most frequently used expressions in substance use recovery. In the cautionary phrase, people, places, and things must be carefully weighed when supporting, rather than undermining, a person's recovery and health. Together, they are factors that can make or break one's recovery, depending on *which* people, *which* places, and *which* things one is exposed to and chooses to associate with. In a document intended for those newly sober, the Substance Abuse and Mental Health Services Administration (SAMHSA 2014, 4) warns about each with caution: "Before you walk out of detox, plan how to stay away from anyone, any place, and anything that will cause you to relapse. . . . Find good company and ask your friends or family [*people*] to help you stay sober. . . . Map out different routes to avoid dealers and bars [*places*]. . . . Put away your cash, ATM, or credit cards if having money is one of your triggers [*things*]." While this document and others mention supportive people as "good company," the phrase "people, places, and things" typically emphasizes what is to be avoided to sustain an environment of support, cultivate a social ecology of resilience (Ungar, Ghazinour, and Richter 2013; Walsh 2003), and undertake healthy decisions and actions. Whether among women returning citizens (i.e., former felons) negotiating their neighborhoods (Leverentz 2010) or among the newly sober assessing spiritual growth after substance use treatment (e.g., Brown and Peterson 1991; Dackis and O'Brien 2001), the phrase is a mantra. As Brown and Peterson (1991, 39) stated, "Perhaps the first finding we took note of was the remarkable consistency in our subjects' reported use of a broad range and large number of the 'spiritual practices' [to] avoid 'people, places, and things' not conducive to their ongoing recovery."

Recovery, that is, sustained abstinence from any addictive substance, is associated with better health and a potentially longer life (Galanter et al. 2013; McKay 2017). People led to affiliate with the FACTS Ministries valued recovery enough to see the Ministries as a safe haven where they could strengthen their resolve to heal and improve their own health or that of a loved one. Who are the people who share this motive? As Dunlap, Golub, and Johnson (2006, 115) suggested, improving the life chances of a group of people "means [seeking out] insight into the prevailing circumstances, the complex array of associated problems, and the resources and capacities available to them [in] creating (or helping them to create) a positive next chapter in their experience." Sober or resilience-affirming people, places, and things are vital in a new self-understanding that supports sustained recovery. Helgeson and Lopez (2010, 325–26) noted, "Both theory and empirical data suggest that the social environment may play a significant role in growth following adversity. . . . To examine growth, researchers should examine characteristics of the support providers [and] aspects of the social environment" (see also Freeman 2001).

The pro-social, health-affirming people of the FACTS Ministries came to it for various reasons. This chapter explores the people at the FACTS Ministries, most of whom live their own recovery as they provide support to others who seek recovery from addiction. Who are they? How do they sustain their affiliation? How do their motives for affiliating differ? Data are drawn from thirty in-depth interviews with approximately one-fifth of the FACTS Ministries' most consistent affiliates and forty additional affiliates from the focus groups of the project, as well as hundreds of field observation hours during the more than fourteen years of the research project. Taken together, over half of the Ministries' most consistent affiliates participated in this research, along with many other less frequent affiliates. This chapter profiles a purposive, yet largely representative sample consistent with overall Ministries affiliation across its six domains: Sunday services and Wednesday Bible study, 12-Step recovery meetings, sober homes residents, free community lunch patrons and volunteers, Men's Prayer Breakfast attendees, and Friday Youth Nights participants during the summer months. It also includes data from fellowship in the many rich, informal moments that occur before and after these more formal activities, all of which occur in and through a sometimes uncertain yet resilient living dialogue between their faith and their health.

People of the FACTS Ministries

A social ecology of resilience has resilient people in it. FACTS Ministries affiliates interact in many ways to achieve this resilience. In doing so, they embody beneficial resources of mutual healing and wellness. Many of them are living in a neighborhood of concentrated poverty (see chapter 2), in the "liminal urban spaces [that] are essentialized in negative terms. The assumption is that these neighbourhoods [and people in them] are *only* unhealthy" (Moore, Freeman, and Krawczyk 2011, 167; italics in original), with nothing redeeming about them. It is in such a neighborhood, North Lawson, that the FACTS Ministries functions as a space of health and hope for those struggling between bottomed-out substance use and the desire for sobriety. It sustains itself as a health resource balancing many elements—both constructive and destructive—to be useful to the health and recovery of affiliates who seek its support.

During the time the current research was conducted, people affiliated with each Ministries domain have tended to participate only in that domain with others who did the same. Church and Bible study participants interacted with similar others each Sunday and Wednesday evenings. Those who came to the Ministries to attend the twice-weekly Either-Or Cocaine Anonymous meetings rarely came to weekly Sunday services or to the monthly Men's Prayer Breakfasts. Those attending the community lunches tended not to come to Sunday services or to anything other than the next Tuesday or Thursday lunch. A few persons who had been coming to the Ministries for a few years viewed themselves as "longtime affiliates" and participated in multiple domains at the same time. Generally, this domain-specific participation or "affiliation with an identity such as 'recovery' or similar may offer group members the chance to be with a positively valenced group [i.e., having intrinsic goodness] and also the opportunity to create psychological distance from previous social connections and associated behaviors" (Buckingham, Frings, and Albery 2013, 1133; see also Haslam et al. 2009). Affiliates' domain-specific identification succeeded yet seemed to lead to a service-specific utilitarianism that might not have occurred otherwise.

Among the FACTS Ministries domains, Sunday evening services had the most equitable attendance of gender, race and ethnicity, and generation. Though varying from week to week, approximately 60 percent of those attending Sunday service were African American, with a comparable percentage of males, about one-fourth of whom were in their early thirties or younger. Community lunches on Tuesdays and Thursdays were typically three-quarters African American males. In the latter half of each month, this changed and became gender balanced, with more women and families, as end-of-month food budgets slimmed. Like Terra (church and Bible study affiliate), and Kevin (Either-Or CA meetings affiliate), whose Ministries introductions are presented in the prologue, most Ministries people were affiliated with one of three domains: (1) church and Bible study, (2) the sober homes program, or (3) the Either-Or CA meetings hosted at the Ministries. Below are profiles of a contrasting pair of affiliates from each of these domains.

People of the Church and Bible Study Domain

Perhaps the most vital at the FACTS Ministries are the people of its church and Bible study domain. These affiliates directly engage how the paradox of substances and sanctuary come together to benefit those who value living the bridge between them. They are often the most frequent attendees. With marked fluctuations, at the peak of the Ministries' mission (2008–12; see chapter 6), between fifty and sixty persons consistently attended the Sunday evening services in the eighty-five-seat-capacity storefront chapel, where nearly one hundred would sometimes squeeze in uncomfortably.

Faith affiliations have become increasingly about a sense of shared mission being prioritized over a diocese, community church, or other aspect of denominational geography. Most who attended the FACTS Ministries came from outside of the immediate North Lawson neighborhood. No records were kept of the names and phone numbers of affiliates attending the Sunday service or the amount of the most recent offering. The Ministries' success followed the more contemporary commu*ter* rather than a commu*nity* church model (see Taylor, Chatters, and Levin 2004; Warner 1993).

Two among the most regular attendees at Sunday service were Brother Darryl Hasten and Brother Warren Pomely. Unlike most affiliates, Darryl was born and raised in the North Lawson neighborhood. African American and in his fifties, he could recall how the neighborhood transformed from a stable, mixed-class African American neighborhood into one of the most socioeconomically marginalized areas in the city. His many experiences of addiction as a "family disease" (e.g., Roth 2010, 1) resonate in his comments here:

> I grew up in the Lawson area. So I've been around a lot of things for a lot of years. I'm not in recovery myself. But I've been affected [by addiction]. Siblings. Baby momma. And things through the years. I was a single parent for years [due to the addiction of his then spouse], and I feel I have learned a lot about addiction, recovery, Al-Anon.

For Darryl, sustained investment in the FACTS Ministries is anchored in an abiding appreciation for the well-being of his childhood neighborhood. Walsh (2003, 53) has noted that one finding stands out in the resilience literature: "the importance of strong relationships [as] resilient individuals turned to and recruited helpful others." Even amid complicated emotions, to establish and maintain healing, resilience must be relationally grounded. Darryl added:

> I had a lot of anger, at first, for not understanding. And for thinking, you know, I did so much. Thinking that I could make a change in loved ones. And they gon' be a'ight now. For some years I was angry at siblings. Lost many cars [from their addiction mishaps]. Went through that. My home church is [Beriah] Presbyterian Church. And I've known [Pastor] Marshall, and Doran, and others here [at the Ministries] for a lot of years.

Prior research shows how an "organization's mission uses rage as a resource for growth beyond resilience" (Price-Spratlen and Goldsby 2012, xvii,

3; see also Holmes 2017; Ungar, Ghazinour, and Richter 2013). Darryl's emotional honesty is a vital resource, even though none of his family members are affiliated with the Ministries. Like many, though his home church is elsewhere, he and his wife Andrea regularly attend the Sunday service at the Ministries as their second Sunday service. As he shared during his interview,

> The last few years I came, I've joined the Ministries to reach out and help people. I appreciate what [Pastor] Marshall is doing. What God has allowed him to do: To be a living testimony. I just wanted to be connected with a group of people helping others. When it's your family, [addiction] hits close to home. How has it affected me? It changes everything. You go through the same things they go through. And I'm just glad that I didn't give up. My siblings are no longer using. [They are] making progress forward. I'm still trying to find out what I need to do. . . . I'd like to help young people to learn to use their hands to make a way of life, and to bring an understanding of what addiction is. I'm glad to be a part of the FACTS Ministries.

Darryl values the Ministries as a means of intergenerational mentoring through a faith craft of pro-social fellowship. There is a strong "association between family processes and resilience . . . [and] it is the engagement and motivation of the family that makes it more likely [that] the individual with the addiction participates in treatment" (Ungar, Ghazinour, and Richter 2013, 353). Through proactive affiliations, Darryl engages in actions that allowed him to handle his rage regarding loved ones constructively. His Ministries affiliation allows him to contribute to the "living testimony" of Pastor Marshall and others with his many actions of empathy and craft.

Another affiliate, Warren Pomely, is a seventy-four-year-old, White, deeply religious man who has been married for nearly fifty years. His affiliation with the Ministries began in late 2007 when a close Alcoholics Anonymous friend of his mentioned to him "a minister who seems to be on the right track, in terms of valuing recovery as a Christian mission." This friend went to one of the "anchor" churches that assisted in the purchase of the Ministries building at Twenty-Eighth Street and Akron Avenue. The person his friend spoke of was Pastor Ellwyn Marshall of the FACTS Ministries. Warren attended Sunday service at the Ministries two weeks later and has been a regular attendee since. He also regularly attends the Men's Prayer Breakfast on the third Saturday of each month. When asked to introduce himself, he said,

> I'm an old drunken sinner, saved by the grace of our Lord and Savior, Jesus Christ. Five years ago, I was given the opportunity to become a member of the Willing Faith Recovery Group, and it's been a real blessing. We're celebrating five years since we began. Two years ago we expanded our ministry over to the Parker United Methodist Church. We have a breakfast group there every Saturday morning.

Warren's identity is grounded in multiple organizational affiliations, each of which strengthens both his faith and his recovery. He was among a devoted core group of men who came to the Ministries' Sunday services and Men's Prayer Breakfasts. Warren continued:

> Two weeks after celebrating our recovery group anniversary last year [2013], I got news that my youngest son was killed. He'd been fighting a lot of emotional things. And I thought I was ready for anything, but I wasn't ready for that. [Long pause.] I didn't really know what to do. And I did something that I think a lot of Christians do. . . . I kept being tormented. . . . I'd been in recovery, and God was using me to help a few others. Though others were willing, I got out of a very, very important habit of asking for help. . . . I was getting back to my old ways, saying I was fine. But I wasn't fine.

Despite having valued affiliations, Warren was not willing to reach out to others during the uncertainties of his grief. His son's death tested his resolve.

> My son was killed by a drunk driver. What's really heavy on my heart is that *he* was the drunk driver. . . . How does that affect someone in recovery? Is that discouraging? Well, ya. I'm not mad at my son, *at all.* I believe my son was saved, and just made a bad choice. [Then just] weeks after my son was killed, I did something no one expected. I went out and I got drunk. It didn't last very long. Immediately God jumped in. . . . I didn't go back to that because I missed drinking. It's a little bit embarrassing to share this. But, I wanted to die. . . . When I

> went back to Jesus and poured out my heart to him, He didn't say, "Well, you did a pretty good job [staying sober] for 17 years. We'll just let go of that." He didn't excuse me. He *forgave* me! And I'm very grateful for that.

Warren took pride in the fact that, for seventeen years, from his son's mid-twenties until the car accident at forty-two, his son "never saw his Dad take another drink. He seen me walkin' with the Lord, and *trying* to do better."

Relapse can be understood as compromised resilience. Warren's testimony acknowledges that, like many other settings, an environment of support for faith-health reciprocity has its limits. His environments of support were not enough when the drunk driver was no stranger. As he said, he was reaching for death when "God jumped in" in the form of his daughter, who confronted him about his relapse. His daughter was saddened and annoyed to realize that Warren appeared to love his son more than he loved her. Her words shocked him out of his relapse and solidified his resilient return to his sobriety.

> My question was, "Why did any of this happen?" I don't understand it. Jesus said, "I have many things yet to say unto you. But you can't bear them now. A little while and ye shall not see me. Ye shall see me, because I go to the Father" (John 16:12, 17 KJV). That's all he needs to say to me. I'm not ready to know why. I don't need to worry about why. And He's telling me that there is going to be a transformation of my sorrow [which is] still there. I'm able to have some gratitude. And I'm able to thank Jesus.

Warren contributes to the resilience of the Ministries by continuing to participate in FACTS Ministries Sunday services and Men's Prayer Breakfasts. Still, he remains "burdened about people in recovery, and people that's lost." As he said, "I'm really wanting to spend every day, if I have an opportunity to be a living invitation to come to Christ. We'll work together and be victorious." His long prior sobriety, brief relapse, and return to a religiously grounded recovery are his living testimony that, even beyond a child's substance-informed, accidental death, his own sober healing and health are sustainable.

People Living in the Sober Homes

During the years of research for this book, approximately fifty men have lived in one or more of the Ministries' three sober homes for at least one month. Ten men have lived in one or more of the sober homes for five or more years. Diversity among the residents is reflected in the profiles of Albert, who is African American and a sober homes resident of more than ten years, and Douglas, who is White and had recently moved in, living at the Ministries for just over one month at the time of his 2014 interview. Albert came to the Ministries in 2002:

> I was released [from prison] in January 2002. Within two weeks, I had visited the Ministries once or twice and I met the pastor. I felt kinship with him right away. I don't know whether it was him [also] being short. Or his humility or makeup. Something about him made me aware. I was going to other [12-Step] meetings. I had another gentleman as my sponsor. . . . But as I came to the Ministries, something attracted me to the pastor. His delivery of his [own] recovery. He had a wife and children, and had [gotten] through the pitfalls of the disease. Here they were, on the other side [of active addiction], starting a church. Amazing. From that point on, this is where I wanted to be.

As Albert quickly went from newcomer to an essential volunteer, he recognized how his success and the success of the Ministries were intertwined. Looking back on his thirteen years of affiliation at the time of his interview, he regarded the Ministries as a manifestation of practical Grace.

> Almost like a moment of clarity, God was practical in his application in my life. Once I visited here, the church invited me in. It's been amazing here. In less than four or five months of playing the guitar [for the Ministries' Praise and Worship Team], I got a key to the building door. I started chairing a [CA] meeting here. From vacuuming, to cleaning up after others. Then God blessed me with a job [as a county service provider]. I started buying [music] equipment. The Ministries *helped me go back to college!*

Each of the examples Albert gave about his increasing involvement at the Ministries reflected how the practical presence of God's Grace bolstered his resilience. Being trusted with a key to the building strengthened his ties to all other domains of the Ministries, including hosting first one then two meetings of Cocaine Anonymous each week. He shared how, once he realized he could not drink and drug successfully, he started to find himself by

> becoming involved in the meetings. They call it being a trusted servant. You can chair the meeting, or become the secretary. They call it "being in the middle of the boat"[;] the chances of you going back out and using are much less. Constantly interacting with newcomers [and] hearing the dialogue of recovery. Hearing the horror stories of "PMS": pain, misery, and suffering. All that keeps you in touch with your pain. That's what steered me. I asked God to take my will. It's the Third Step. Turn my will and my life over to the care of God, as I understand God. And the steps became those building blocks to how to live again.

The Second Tradition of 12-Step recovery fellowships states, "Our leaders are but trusted servants; they do not govern" (Cocaine Anonymous 2018, 7; see also Greenleaf 2002; Alcoholics Anonymous 1952). Albert valued the variety of leadership and service roles he assumed. The symbolism of a rescue boat reinforced the meaning of those vital, everyday decisions and actions. The Ministries and CA served as reciprocal protocols of resilience, together enriching Albert's biblically grounded program of action. The valued reminders and reciprocity of service are essential to Albert's and many other affiliates' recovery. With no significant demographic differences along gender, ethnicity, intake severity, and so forth, research shows that "helping others is related to positive outcomes in substance use patterns, improved psychosocial functioning, and psychological well-being" (Pagano et al. 2004, 770; see also White, Kelly, and Roth 2014). Albert's sober homes experiences moved him from merely attending to participating to assuming leadership at the Ministries, in CA meetings, at his workplace, and in the North Lawson neighborhood.

Unlike Albert, Douglas had been a sober homes resident for just a few weeks at the time of his interview. Coming from a rural, White, working-class background in another state, he made an investment in the Ministries as a necessary part of his fragile program of recovery. He was battling with frequent relapses and illegal actions, and he approached women with what some affiliates and Ministries leadership viewed as "unprincipled ethics." The sober homes were strengthened by differences among the residents in character, background, and behavior, even as Ministries leaders themselves struggled in earnest to understand and make the most of these differences. This struggle was consistent with Audre Lorde's (1984, 111) invitation that "difference must be not merely tolerated, but seen as a fund of necessary polarities between which creativity can spark like a dialectic." Douglas said he aimed to reduce and hopefully quit his illegal and other compromising behaviors that were inconsistent with his avowed commitment to recovery from addiction. He knew that being part of a place like the FACTS Ministries, which held out a possibility and support, was key.

> I like the involvement with everything. I like going to church. That's something I always struggled with doing. I like how the pastor, and nobody, acts like they're better than anybody. 'Cause I have met people in recovery that act like they're better than anybody. Here everybody seems to be real and open. [They] welcomed me with open arms.

For Douglas's early sober homes inclusion, resources presented with equity were essential. Making the most of opportunities in a new understanding of himself, this recovery setting demanded a self-discipline of new choices, both large and small, like going to church in an environment where status differences are not expressed in ways that alienated Douglas. An equity of drug culture familiarity and its related cross-class, cross-context similarities allowed Douglas to experience a sense of home and shared humility.

> Just being around here, and inside the house, a sober environment. Even though you sit on the porch and look *right* across the street [an active dope spot], and the things going on there. It just feels like I'm actually in a super clean environment. Same way with the 12 Steps. They don't necessarily push the so-called God on you, [but] finding that Higher Power helps me a lot. . . . I just find it real. It's building my strength by doing that.

The irony of carrying out his 12-Step "program of action" in a clean recovery environment of support, while having the immediate temptation of the drug marketplace less than a hundred feet away at all times was not lost on Douglas. His valuing a Higher Power resulted from " 'developing faith' [which] initially operates on an institutional level (developing faith in AA and the program), and [then] the inter-personal level (developing faith and trust in others)" (Morjaria and Orford 2002, 238). When asked if he had spoken with anyone about the dope spot across the street being a concern for him, Douglas said, laughing, that he had talked with "a few of the roommates in the Sober House who just told [him] to stay away from there after dark." Humor is a vital resource for health and resilience (e.g., Sumners 1988), as are simple directives, like how time of day might inform relapse risk. So too is acknowledging one's vulnerability to someone else who likely has felt the same way. Douglas was investing in his growing sobriety while valuing Akron Avenue as a "demilitarized zone." The sober home as an environment of support included listening to, internalizing, and acting on simple rules for the supportive space of the Ministries that separated sobriety from addiction. That space provided the necessary structure for Douglas and his roommates to become stable and remain sober.

Cocaine Anonymous (CA) Meeting Affiliates

Cocaine Anonymous meetings began soon after the initial gatherings that became the FACTS Ministries itself (see chapter 4). For Pastor Marshall and many others, humility is central to the behavioral and spiritual resilience vital to the process of recovery. Therapeutically, "surrender to the humility of a group process actually seems to give energy for [one's] own development" (Naifeh 1995, 157; see also Wilson 1984). Named Either-Or as a reminder of the sober choice people in recovery make one day at a time, these Ministries CA meetings offered the opportunity to achieve and share the resilience of sustained abstinence with others. The first Either-Or affiliate, now more than twenty-five years sober in CA, Carla recalled the early days:

> I was involved in CA service work, and I went to the district meetings. I was at the district meeting when Pastor Marshall came and asked that his meeting at the FACTS Ministries be

> put on our schedule. People would come to the CA office [in the Central Office Building, largely financed by Alcoholics Anonymous and shared by AA, CA, and NA, Narcotics Anonymous] when cocaine, especially crack cocaine, was a part of their drug use history.

Carla got sober in 1990 and has the longest sustained sobriety of any Ministries affiliate. Her affiliation, while anchored in her membership in CA, also includes Ministries church services. She and her boyfriend, Jonathan, a former Ministries sober homes resident with a more uneven sober history, participate in both religious and recovery aspects of the Ministries. They are among the six most visible couples who come to the Ministries. Like (sober homes resident) Albert, Carla continues to deeply value her service work in CA. She said,

> I do a lot of service work for Cocaine Anonymous, and I've been doing it ever since I got sober in 1990. I wanted to because I wanted to be a part of something. CA is the youngest fellowship there is [among AA, NA, and CA]. AA had like maybe 100 meetings a week in [the city]. We might've had three meetings a week when [I got sober]. And the most sobriety in CA back then was maybe two to four years. So, everybody got an AA sponsor because there wasn't enough sobriety in CA.
>
> My most significant [tool in recovery] was service work. In the fellowship we say, "You gotta give it away to keep it." I was going to this AA meeting and they said, "If you want to get involved, you need to chair or do something." So, you go up to the chair and you ask them what can you do to help out. [At that point,] I probably had only about 45 days sober. I went up and I asked the chair and they said, "Well, you can bring the donuts." Well, I couldn't drink that week because *they had to have sober donuts. Them donuts couldn't be drunk* [laughs]. So that kept me sober. Then we were having a convention. I was chair of entertainment, so I couldn't get high until after that convention. Then after that convention, I would have ten months sober. That was the first CA convention in [the city]. People came from all over the state to show us how to do it right.

For Carla, resilience was having—and using—a most important recovery tool: service to others in need. By serving in CA and at the FACTS Ministries, she moved from presence, to visibility, to involvement, to expectation, to leadership. She valued the risk and vulnerability of asking questions and then acted on the healthy suggestions provided. Her resilience was informed by her appreciation for having been at the CA district meeting when Pastor Marshall asked to list the first meeting hosted at the Ministries in the local CA meetings brochure, valuing that history for having contributed to it. Her humor and symbolism ("sober donuts") enriched her gratitude for being sober while sharing her sobriety with others. In addition, Carla participated in planning the first CA convention hosted in the city, which also contributed to her reciprocity of resilience with the FACTS Ministries.

As Ostrom and Janssen (2004, 251) noted, "Development may be enhanced by multi-level governance involving the capacity to initiate or veto action at multiple scales." In CA, the multiple scales ranged from chairing a single meeting to representing that meeting at the city level to representing the city at the state level for support in planning a regional convention in the Midwest. At the simplest level of holding a meeting, members benefited from the value one gains from simply knowing one is not alone. Carla shared during her interview that the Ministries played a role at each level, beginning with guiding her in choosing a sponsor and in changing her degree of trust toward women. She confided,

> When I first came here, I didn't trust women. I thought they would stab you in the back any moment they could. They's always after your boyfriend. You couldn't trust 'em. Whatever you told 'em in confidence would be spread all over town the next day. And what you didn't tell 'em, they'd make up. So, I hated women.
>
> When I was told I had to get a sponsor, I was looking at the men. I said, "Well, he's pretty cute. He's gonna be my sponsor." And my treatment counselor group leader said, "No, Carla. It's [gotta be] someone other than your sexual preference." And I said, "Well, you expect people to get sober, but why would you make it so hard for a person? A woman?!" So, I eventually picked somebody in the same zip code as me, from a sheet with women's names and numbers. And that happened to work out.

For Carla, levels of service began with her initial self-sabotage of the expected sponsor-sponsee structure. To remove the risk of the profoundly dangerous "13th Step," the sexual or romantic pursuit of newcomers or vulnerable others, a person in recovery (the sponsee) is required to be guided in her sobriety by a sponsor of the same gender, assuming heteronormativity to be "the standard." This requirement, intended to reduce the likelihood of fractured trust, dates back to the origin of AA in the 1930s. In one of the few systematic analyses of this phenomenon, researchers found that "at least 50% of the participants experienced 7 of the 13 13th-stepping behaviors [and] 77% [of the female participants] reported that men had flirted with them at least occasionally" (Bogart and Pearce 2003, 45). Carla's willingness to raise her concern in her treatment aftercare group allowed her to address it professionally. She criticized the same-sex sponsor protocol yet adhered to it anyway. She acted against her preference to choose a male sponsor, which she felt would have been "easier." Being asked to allow women in as allies led her to gradually revise her uncertain trust. As Carla continued to return to the CA meetings, she found out that, in fact, women in the fellowship were not violating her trust regarding information she shared in confidence. As she noted, perhaps she had overgeneralized from her prior experiences. Carla's choices can be understood as means through which a program tension could inform the resilience of recovery.

Like Carla, Conrad was another Either-Or CA member. He had more than six years of sobriety at the time of his interview. His affiliation was also informed by the reciprocity between the spiritual foundation of the CA program and the faith foundation of the Ministries.

> I'm the vice-chair of the [CA] district, and also Chair of the unity [committee]. Where I'm at right now in my sobriety, I am in dire need of enlarging my spiritual condition. I have a real strong faith in God and Jesus Christ as my savior. [But] I have trouble with churches. So, I'm looking for the guidance of the FACTS Ministries, because they're different. Their particular meetings [are] a more spiritual atmosphere, a stronger God sense atmosphere. . . . My primary [recovery] group is Cocaine Anonymous. I like CA because it [specifically] mentions in Step 1, "cocaine and all other mind-altering substances." I've been in and out of the rooms of recovery for over thirty years. But in CA we focus more on the spiritual program of recovery

> than the other fellowships do. And I'm a firm believer that it's all about God. All about His power that relieves me of my addiction. I believe that the people I come in contact with at CA have the same understanding. That it's spiritual.

Conrad recognized the importance of identifying a primary recovery group through comparative experiences. These comparisons took decades for him to refine the right "fit" to reinforce his recovery through the spiritual content of CA at the FACTS Ministries. For him, affiliating with the Ministries was consistent with the Big Book's foreboding caution that "if an [addict] failed to perfect and enlarge his spiritual life through work and self-sacrifice for others, he could not survive the certain trials and low spots ahead" (Alcoholics Anonymous 2001, 14–15). As Conrad acknowledged, many who have "trouble with churches" experience a spiritual dissonance with structured worship.

In Conrad's case, he was led to the Ministries "because they're different," and he valued resources from the affiliation between CA and the Ministries. For him, CA's local history being two decades longer than that of the Ministries was one of those beneficial differences. He fully realized that the longevity of an organization would not necessarily be positively associated with resource increases. At the FACTS Ministries as in the social sciences, organizational "commitment may be defined as the process through which individual interests become attached to the carrying out of socially organized patterns of behavior which fulfill those interests" (Kanter 1968, 500; see also De Leon 2000; Krentzman 2013). Conrad's affiliation with and commitment to both CA and the Ministries extended from the value he placed on these beneficial differences between them.

> Cocaine Anonymous is 30 years old in the city this year, and I'm Unity chairperson. [The Unity committee helps to] unify our group and our fellowship. I started this last month. I'm going to all meetings, and I'm going to stress unity. Diversity, with our personalities. It's not a weakness with us. It's a bigger issue than anybody knows. God uses each one of us for our specific personalities. Just like pieces of a puzzle they always told us about. We fit. God knows where He wants everybody to fit . . . 'cause we need to be united together in this. Go forth. That's what our 12-Step [program] talks about.

For Conrad and many other affiliates, diversity is among the most valued resources that sustains bonds in both CA and the Ministries. For him, longevity nurtures unity and his expectations regarding what thirty years of unity "should" be associated with. The Ministries in affiliation with CA and the 12-Step program as a whole were parts of his stated recognition of the "need to be united in this." As Conrad stated, "This is my passion, my mission. First, get you sober. Then we can give you some concepts and basic instructions about living [your] life. Spiritual principles. Then, live them. That's CA's mission. That's [also] the FACTS Ministries' mission."

Other Affiliates of the Ministries

In addition to the church/Bible study, sober homes, and Either-Or CA meetings, Ministries affiliates in other domains also contribute to the resilience of the organization, including those from the free community lunches hosted each Tuesday and Thursday, those who come to the monthly Men's Prayer Breakfasts each third Saturday morning, and young people who attend Friday Youth Nights during the summers.

Larry, an African American in his late sixties, has been volunteering at the Ministries for over six years at the Tuesday community lunches. He is a retired civil servant and longtime resident of North Lawson. He drove a cab for many years and was part of the "alert squad," as he described it: a group of cabbies willing to get folks to health-care services more promptly than might otherwise be possible, given the neighborhood's reputation and allegedly slow emergency responsiveness during those years. Larry discovered the Ministries through his church and through a relative he was supporting, who struggled with an addiction to crack cocaine.

> I've been in this neighborhood for a really long time. I now come to the Ministries for lots of things. I came to this building years ago. Way back in the day, it was the Wind Star Tavern. The bar was set up in this area [motions to specify the floor layout]. Now, in that same building, in that same room, through my church, I'm serving meals to the community, and helpin' others to lay down the drugs, and come to the Lord as they will.

Larry has a strong and diverse sense of fellowship and faith, and he is unique in the longevity of his affiliation with the location. Chance, another lunch volunteer, is a small-framed, freckle-faced, Jewish man in his twenties. He shared his first impression of Larry: "In just my second volunteer visit, the individual who was treating me like family was Larry." Sober for many years at the time of his interview, Larry had never spent much time in the rooms of recovery; his sobriety was about spiritual deliverance. The depth of his religious devotion dating back to his childhood, coupled with the active addiction of many adults during his childhood, led him to his scripture-driven affiliation with the Ministries. During his Sunday sermons, when Pastor Marshall would begin a phrase from a given scripture and pause, the vast majority of the time either Larry or (sober homes resident) Albert would recite its remaining words. Larry's resilience is reflected in his serving as a good Samaritan through his cab-driving vocation and in warmly welcoming other volunteers to share in and enrich the Ministries' resilience mission.

While most lunch volunteers and patrons appreciated the community lunches made available on Tuesdays and Thursdays, experiences and feedback of a few lunch patrons were more negative. In his late forties, Copter had been coming regularly for several years to lunches offered on both days. With an inconsistent work history, magnified further by a lengthy prison sentence in his thirties, he was among the growing pool of marginalized African American men without a consistent income (Western 2018; Western and Pettit 2010). Given the many collateral consequences extending from his prior incarceration (Leverentz 2010; Western 2018), like many other returning citizens, Copter's difficulties finding and sustaining employment continued, now six years after his release from prison. He heard about the Ministries during his most recent time in prison when Pastor Marshall came to speak there. He said,

> The Ministries is a bunch of freaks up in there, for real. On the regular, those lunch women—and some of the volunteer men, too, now—they up in there tryin' to get with Black men in the lunch lines. All the time. Two of those folks [mentions specific names]; they be white-on-rice on a mothafucka. I tried to keep away. For real. Told pastor about 'em. All five times it happened. Got to where he accusin' me of bein' a womanizer. Demanded that I stay away. They was up in *my* grill! And I gotta go?!

A proud man of limited means, Copter felt that he was blamed for the burden of exploitation that was not of his own making. The decision to silence him by asking him to leave was one of several organizational tensions at the Ministries (see chapter 5) that made the process of recovery even more challenging for Copter and others. Copter was one of the many patrons who moved among the group of churches throughout the city that serve free meals to ensure the stability of their weekly meals. He felt that the lack of transparency in the decision-making that informed his being barred indefinitely from the Ministries' lunches was galling. Multiple residents of the sober homes who also volunteered during the community lunches mentioned that they found Copter's banishment from the church problematic. While complete, secondary corroboration was not possible, other African American male lunch patrons mentioned to multiple longtime sober homes residents that they too had experienced or witnessed this occurring due to the inappropriate behavior of more than one lunch volunteer. In each apparent instance, the Black male lunch patron in question was asked not to return for some period of time.

Among female lunch patrons, Carol is an African American grandmother in her forties who frequently comes to one or both lunches. She extends her food budget with the twice-weekly meals at the Ministries in the latter two weeks of each month, as many North Lawson women do. At the time of her interview, she had been coming to the Ministries for just over three years and shared this reflection during a Saturday morning Either-Or CA meeting:

> This is a place where Grace can grow, you know? I've never been able to stick with this thing [being sober] for all that long. It's just too rough sometimes, what with the streets bein' like they are, with the drugs and all. A "bottom." Whatnot . . . I 'on't know. I'm glad Fridays [Youth Nights] happen here. Good to have family videos, and coloring books, and popcorn to bring up my grandkids with the Lord.

Carol began bringing a couple of her grandchildren and her youngest child to the Friday Youth Nights during the summer of 2011. She soon began coming to the Saturday morning CA meetings and took great pride in the increments of her sober time, celebrated with colorful key tags in the first year of one's sobriety. For her, the Friday nights were an opportunity to be without her children and without day-care responsibilities for a few hours during a summer evening. When Friday Youth Nights were abruptly ended in 2013 without explanation, many neighborhood women like Carol and their families suffered the consequences. After that, any affiliations that the neighbors had with the Ministries became unpredictable (see chapter 5).

Among the regulars at the Men's Prayer Breakfasts, unlike any of the persons profiled above, Andrew was a member of Millwood Fellowship, the predominantly White, suburban, "parent" church that led the church collaboration that funded the FACTS Ministries. White and stocky, he came to the breakfasts wearing clean, old, blue overalls over his thick build. He had by far the longest beard of any Ministries affiliate. Another patron who frequented the monthly breakfasts was Lawrence, a slight-built, African American man in his early seventies with thinning gray hair, a face full of freckles, and a calm manner. Andrew and Lawrence came to the Men's Prayer Breakfasts almost every month. Andrew was a close friend of Warren Pomely's and would warmly greet him and share hellos with everyone else. Lawrence kept to himself and never shared a greeting or spoke to anyone. Yet he was there on time, every third Saturday morning, always with multiple coats on, regardless of the weather or season of the year.

The Men's Prayer Breakfasts were small gatherings because of their 8:00 a.m. start time Saturday mornings. For those who came, who were mostly neighborhood men across a wide range of ages, the breakfasts were a place to get a good meal for the day, share in the Word of God, and be less lonely for a couple of hours on a weekend morning. In each domain, diverse groups of resilient people came together. The FACTS Ministries, in personal characteristics, motives for affiliation, and experiences of the organization over time, reflects the rich diversity of those who valued one or more domains of its mission.

Conclusions

This chapter has explored the four main groups of people in the Ministries' ecology of health and resilience: affiliates of the church and Bible study, residents of the sober homes, those who came to Either-Or CA meetings, and others including volunteers and community lunch attendees. Affiliates from each group were central to the ethnogenic thread of the Ministries (see introduction)—i.e., ways that each group contributed to a process of refining a communal social structure and collective ethos that helped turn reasons for stigma and alienation (e.g., prior addiction, family food insecurity) into assets for resilience and enriching health for themselves and similarly situated others. Health and education are essential to the viability of any organization or setting. These two vital "enabling resources . . . support health and human development and the manifold ways these resources are generated and utilized" (Duff 2011, 150; see also Ungar, Ghazinour, and Richter 2013). The people of the FACTS Ministries are African American, White, Latino, and Native American. They are women, men, and transgender. They are young and old, employed, unemployed, or retired, single and married, some with children, some without any dependents. They are Christian, Jewish, and nondenominationally spiritual. Their sexual orientations are as diverse as can be encountered in the human family. These are the people striving for health and resilience, while affiliating in a neighborhood of profound health-care disparities. They are most often committed to a single domain anchoring their affiliation there. Many are informed by diverse motives and resilience resources that contribute to the distinct characteristics and challenges that define the Ministries.

Among church service and Bible study affiliates, many reject the 12-Step "spiritual program" of recovery. They believe they are "sinners [who have been] saved by Grace," rather than persons with a "disease" seeking support with managed abstinence. Like Shirley Timmons's (2012, 1158) theory, these "church-side" affiliates have an "understanding of God as sponsor [which] happens as addicts assess their addiction and recovery in the context of God's plan for their lives." This perspective is reflected perhaps most clearly in Warren's belief that things that have occurred in his life are part of the plan and, furthermore, that events he cannot reconcile, like his son's death, are not meant for him to understand. His faith and the faith of other affiliates is reflected in the large vinyl poster at the front wall of the Ministries' chapel: "This Thing Is All About JESUS!" As stated frequently at Ministries' church services and Bible studies, to many Ministries people, the presence or absence of this deliverance in one's life was the only recovery question worth asking. At the same time, potential limitations of this perspective emerge in Warren's and Darryl's distinct personal testimonies.

For almost half of the church domain affiliates, personal recovery is of secondary importance. Many of them do not have a difficult history of substance use and are not in recovery. Many had made individual attempts to be a loved one's evangelical means to sustained sobriety and were not successful. They recognize addiction as warranting a deeply relational response, celebrated through service to and with others (see Humphreys 2004; Walsh 2003). For example, Darryl was in search of a mentoring role through his Ministries affiliation, and he sought to share his love of carpentry, contracting, and woodcrafts with the next generation of North Lawson youth.

The primary motive of the vast majority of community lunch volunteers was rituals of evangelical charity. Whatever their relationships to substances were, generally they were not in recovery but simply valued the Ministries' mission grounded in giving meaning to Matthew 25:35: "I was hungry, and you gave me something to eat. I was thirsty, and you gave me something to drink" (KJV). Motivated by Christian service, they had a near-missionary zeal. Some, like Larry, gave special meaning to the Ministries building and areas nearby as a space of "counterpoint" memory (i.e., having been a tavern). He could reclaim it with value now as a sacred space of breaking bread in faithful service as the best way to live his retirement years. A few, like sober homes resident Albert and Candy (reflected in the opening field note to this chapter), gave back with a "both/and sensibility," as people of recovery and people of faith.

Among Either-Or CA affiliates, the Ministries is a place for a reciprocity of mission to flourish between the "spiritual program" of the 12 Steps (Cocaine Anonymous 2018) and the cultural competence of a nondenominational church pastored in the Black Baptist tradition. In the Big Book of Alcoholics Anonymous, the primary text for CA and the Ministries' Either-Or CA meetings, "You have to act the Good Samaritan every day if need be, [because] helping others is the foundation stone of your recovery" (Alcoholics Anonymous 2001, 97). They value the good Samaritan embodied in the legacy of Sister Ignatia, a nun who worked with thousands of alcoholics in the early years of AA (Darrah 2001).

More than the affiliates of any other Ministries domain, Either-Or CA affiliates tended to also give attention to criminal justice issues. They made efforts to ensure that Either-Or meetings were available to those currently institutionalized in community corrections facilities, halfway houses, and drug treatment facilities. Their sense of empathy was strong, since they too had experienced, and had been able to remove themselves from, the chaotic circumstances of active addiction and its carceral consequences. They were especially aware of the Ministries' potential for partnering with secular and health organizations in an equity of resource sharing.

Perhaps the clearest motives among all Ministries affiliates are those of sober homes residents, who came to the Ministries informed by the desire to have a roof over their heads and a place to call "home." Their affiliations began with a material desperation grounded in the Ministries' mission to be a safe space for those at the worst of their bottoms as they build a life free of substance use. They valued freedom in the comforts of a sober environment where, as Douglas stated, "nobody . . . acts like they're better than anybody." That residential freedom is highlighted in the repetitions of active addiction's "bondage" they see repeated directly across the street, seventy feet from the front porch of the Ministries' third sober house. Through Pastor Ellwyn Marshall's leadership, they see their own life possibilities and strengthen their investments in the importance of sober service.

Most organizations value keeping track of their membership numbers in some way. From its beginning, the Ministries and its leadership kept no list of membership in the organization. There was no member listing, no compiled phone tree, not even a wooden placard in the chapel to share how many people attended the prior Sunday evening service or the total number who affiliated across the six domains in any given month. When asked in 2007, during the Ministries' eighth year, why no records of affiliation were kept, Pastor Marshall said, "Because we are *not* a church. We are a health Ministries. For us, membership is inconsistent with the mission we are trying to build here." That is, given the private and the public, the permanent and the transitory, the formal and the informal, and other related dimensions, in the eyes of Ministries leadership, any permanent record of affiliation would have somehow taken away from the Ministries' mission.

As in many organizations, the Ministries' domain affiliates are "siloed," with few overlaps. Only sober homes residents are required to participate in all Ministries activities, unless an activity conflicts with their work schedule. So Tuesday and Thursday lunch volunteers have very little to do with CA 12-Step meeting attendees, just as most Sunday service attendees would never participate with others beyond Wednesday night Bible study. In short, these separations matter—as do distinctions between the people of the Ministries across domains and leadership. Alongside these affiliation silos, there was never even a more traditional means for an emergent, affiliate leadership to have a voice in Ministries decision-making. Deacons were never selected. No usher board or youth leadership of any kind was developed. This lack of a traditional church leadership along with little interaction among affiliates in different domains afforded the Ministries little opportunity or encouragement to develop multi-domain allegiances. For example, community lunch volunteers and Friday Youth Night attendees could have strengthened the mission of both domains if Ministries activities and traditional leadership had brought them together. This marked, domain-specific affiliation seemed to weaken internal between-domain interactions and the Ministries as a whole. Yet within each domain, strong attractions to the domain's mission included highly engaged affiliates.

An environment of support for health and resilience extends from interactions in a given place. Domain-specific affiliation is what anchors the people of the FACTS Ministries, with each domain making valuable and unique contributions to the effectiveness of the Ministries. Yet a social ecology amounts to much more than having quality people to work with. It requires sustaining compassionate, empathetic, respectful interactions among them and sharing resources of value toward a collective end. Such a social ecology rests on the idea that, in its construction and expression, resilience (a) is multilevel and multidimensional, (b) has a set of protective factors at each level operating interdependently, and (c) has "a multitude of considerations [which] interact to either activate or suppress resilience processes" (Stajduhar et al. 2009, 314). Together, these characteristics can assist the health and well-being of the people and the organization. Still, domain-specific affiliations make valuable and unique contributions to the "pieces of the puzzle" to which Conrad refers, which come together due to the resilient people of the Ministries. Consistent with Boeri (2018), Duff (2011), and Ungar, Ghazinour, and Richter (2013), the fellowship and resource exchanges among affiliates of the Ministries enable healing in an environment of profound challenge. A health ministry can be an enabling place that addresses many disparities and adverse consequences of addiction and other health challenges. These challenges are often most severe in communities least equipped to address them. Building on this affiliate-centered view of resilience and the ethnogenic thread, chapter 2 explores contextual detail. It moves from the people of the Ministries to the place of the North Lawson neighborhood where the FACTS Ministries is located.

Chapter 2

Much More than Watermelon Roadkill

The Place of the Ministries

> Our tiny community garden in [North Lawson] started with the biggest of ironies: an acre of weeds growing on top of a nearly unmovable weed tarp. It would not be the last. We called our project [Who Knows]—as in, we know it has value to grow. With nothing more than a love of tomatoes and concern for an impoverished neighborhood, members of my church and I soon encountered Ohio's notorious clay, broken equipment, a late frost, mislabeled plants, fertilizer shock and the fattest, laziest groundhog in [the city].
>
> —North Lawson volunteer, August 2009

A social ecology for health and resilience is an environment of support located somewhere. As the volunteer notes in the quote above suggest, with proper care and devotion, even the least-promising clay earth taken over by weeds can become nourishing and life-affirming. Be it a community garden or the FACTS Ministries located in the impoverished North Lawson neighborhood, quality care matters for social reconstruction and social recovery (Boeri 2018). Here, open-air drug markets, nearly around-the-clock sex industry workers, and bootleggers selling knockoff watches, downloaded DVDs, or perhaps even stolen items or weapons conduct their business across several blocks, while every night sirens for emergencies blast at all hours. The chaos is not constant—simply more frequent and visible than in other settings. Strewn along the curbside gutters of Akron Avenue and Hayworth Street, which demarcate this neighborhood, are food wrappers, empty soda cans, beer bottles, half-eaten sandwiches, moldy lunch meat, and more, discarded by patrons of the nearby fast-food outlet just off the freeway. In the gutters, one finds the carcasses of squirrels, possums, and rodents that dare-deviled their way into traffic and met their demise. They have been jokingly called "roadkill stew" in a movie. Rotting banana peels, watermelon rinds, and slices of watermelon left behind after a food fight are aptly called "watermelon roadkill" by a couple of passersby. What's more troubling are the remnants from substance use: small paper bags for packaging the dope-smoking "works" sold in corner stores, parts of a lighter, an occasional needle for intravenous drug use, burnt-out aluminum foil for smoking crystal meth, heroin, or crack cocaine, and "corner store chore"—threads of copper used and discarded after smoking crack, now in a smashed ball after having been run over by cars and bikes. Yet, in spite of these environmental challenges, several local conditions also inform a social ecology of resilience in the North Lawson neighborhood in general, and at the Ministries in particular. From gutter details, to building and local area history, to community gardens and libraries and more, this chapter considers the place of the FACTS Ministries, to analyze its social ecology, the neighborhood, and the greater community.

The traditional social disorganization model suggested generations ago that a local, chaotic ecology is an incubator for illegal activities and for antisocial development and outcomes (e.g., Landers 1954; Shaw and McKay 1942). Others have critiqued this ecological model for a variety of reasons, including its "erroneous" premise that "social areas are homogenous [and that . . .] all people residing in the same neighborhood have similar life experiences" (Esbensen and Huizinga 1990, 693; see also Hennessy 2017; Kubrin and Weitzer 2003). Addiction recovery centers and other community health venues can be more effective when they "apply an ecological framework to understanding drug addiction and recovery" (Matto 2004, 5). The National Institutes of Health (NIH) and other health science institutions have long valued incorporating social and cultural factors into health research. The social disorganization model and ecological health research take it as a given that local area context—i.e., place—is an important factor influencing (lack of) individual, organizational, and communal health and resilience. As noted in chapter 1, people, places, and things must each be carefully weighed when supporting, rather than undermining, a person's recovery. Having analyzed the significance of the people of the Ministries in chapter 1, we turn to the Ministries and its surrounding neighborhood as places of healing in chapter 2.

Like most American social and health sciences, this book's recognition of and research on place extends from the legacy of W. E. B. Du

Bois. On the generational heels of Dr. John Snow's discovery of the field of social epidemiology in mid-nineteenth-century London, "Du Bois was a social epidemiology frontrunner [exploring] whether or not the host is socially or biologically exposed to the infection of systemic inequality [as] a determinant of death" (Jones-Eversley and Dean 2018, 230, 231). In *The Philadelphia Negro*, Du Bois ([1899] 1967, 156, 160) linked inter- and intra-racial disparities in tuberculosis outbreaks to distinct local settings, stating that "Negroes live in unsanitary dwellings . . . partly on account of the difficulty of securing decent houses by reason of race prejudice. . . . [There is] considerable proof that the Negro death rate is largely a matter of conditions of living." Then and now, conditions of living inform how a place may function as one of resilience or may function as one of apathy. A social ecology of resilience is premised on the ideas that (a) resilience is multilevel and multidimensional; (b) protective factors at each level operate in an interdependent fashion assist in the return to form and function of affiliates at each of those levels; and (c) "a multitude of considerations interact to either activate or suppress resilience processes" (Stajduhar et al. 2009, 314; see also Shaw et al. 2016; Ungar, Ghazinour, and Richter 2013).

The places one returns to on a regular basis inform the interrelationships between addiction, faith, health, and resilience, and a "relational perspective incorporates information about settings that are drawn from reported views of residents, as well as from independently measured local conditions" (Cummins et al. 2007, 1830; see also McRoberts 2003; Walsh 2003), both historical and contemporary. This relational perspective was reflected in the profiles in chapter 1 and in the people's relationships to the tension between the health- and resilience-affirming front porch of the Ministries' sober home and the active addiction going on directly across the street. In their consideration of residential support for addiction recovery, Mericle et al. (2017, 358) note that "some homes were in a two-block radius of other types of resources such as churches, an AA club house, a community garden, gyms/fitness centers . . . and a barber shop." Consistent with the access assessment of Mericle et al., the FACTS Ministries provides—within close proximity—access to church services, Either-Or CA meetings, gym equipment in the garage behind one of its sober houses, a barbershop across the street, and a community garden a few blocks north. The garden described in the epigraph to this chapter is often tended on Saturdays prior to the 10:00 a.m. start of the CA meetings. The care and attention to new growth reflected in volunteers' actions in the community garden metaphorically and temporally parallel new growth in the relationships among faith, health, addiction recovery, and resilience taking place at the Ministries.

In their consideration of residential support for addiction recovery, Mericle et al. (2017, 354) note, "Given [the] growing evidence of the role that neighborhood factors play in increasing risk for substance use, another important gap in the literature [is that we . . .] know little about the neighborhoods in which residences that blend peer support and professional recovery support services are located." This chapter addresses this important gap in the literature by exploring the historical and contemporary ecology, and the characteristics and patterns of change over time, in the North Lawson neighborhood.

How North Lawson Came to Be

As the recent Confederate statue controversy in US cities and violence associated with it have again demonstrated, history shapes all places. North Lawson is no different. It was a residentially settled space in which a block-to-block racial and ethnic patchwork characterized the World War I–era and pre–Great Migration patterns. The North Lawson community is a product of land expansion westward and the formative process of urban development during the nineteenth century in the US. In the state as elsewhere, early residential settlement and urban formation began soon after the nation was formed. As Manuel Castells (1970, 9) stated, "We are concerned here with the cultural system characteristic of capitalist industrial society . . . [which] presupposes the correspondence between a certain technical type of [industrial] production, a system of values ('modernism'), and a specific form of spatial organization, the city." This logic was central to the settlement of many areas, including the greater Lawson neighborhood.

The neighborhood began in the early nineteenth century when a presidential gift was made to a local war hero of the American Revolution. Toward the end of the 1800s, the first post–Civil War African American families moved into a nearby neighborhood of "Bug's Borough," which eventually became a predominantly southern European immigrant and African American area. According to one area historian, Bug's Borough was a community where residents experienced a common economic distress, yet it was a place with a strong sense of community despite the stress of racial differences.

In its history, Bug's Borough experienced a pattern that was repeated in other neighborhoods of the city and throughout the US. Deed restrictions were used to keep "undesirables"—be they Italians, African Americans, or others—from being able to buy homes along particular streets. This process of American apartheid (Massey and Denton 1993), its currency and very deep roots, was especially apparent at the time when post–World War I settlements were expanding residential opportunity for various immigrant and other groups. In 1920, an observer of the city's housing color line said, "There seems to be an unwritten law which says exactly where Negroes shall reside. And . . . in the majority of cases it is very effective" (Giffin 2005, 124–25). As noted recently, "the 1920s was the height of segregation [with] an increase in restrictions on where African Americans could buy property in newly opened subdivisions. . . . Lots were for white people only, [where] all of the lots were sold on the first day" (Landmarks Foundation 2014, 54). Similar circumstances occurred in North Lawson. A collaboration among private citizens, realtors, lending institutions, and government officials was the foundation through which the North Lawson to come was established. Most of the neighborhood housing was constructed immediately following World War II. By war's end, it was largely made up of returning GIs making their first home purchases, along with the Appalachian immigrants doing the same. Italian and Irish settlements becoming largely GI and Appalachian strongholds was the first of many twentieth-century neighborhood turnovers in this area.

Like all places, North Lawson's streets establish its appearance. Two bridges over Hayworth Street set its northwest edge: one for trains and the other for a six-lane highway and its on- and off-ramp intersection. This is a common urban placeholder, both old and new, often created and used to set intentional boundaries of community. Writing about Birmingham, Alabama, Connerly (2002, 101, 106, 112) aptly describes practices that informed most urban areas of the US, similar to the city in which the North Lawson neighborhood is situated.

> Interstate highways bisect[ed] historically Black neighborhoods . . . displace[d] Black households, [and] had a deleterious impact on the city's Black neighborhoods. [They] caused a disproportionate number of them to lose population, and threatened the viability of neighborhood businesses and the commercial areas that served them. [This because] local state government manipulated the interstate highway program to

> perpetuate neighborhood racial segregation and [had a] dramatic influence. (See also Bayor 1988; Hirsch 1998; McRoberts 2003)

More than a century before the interstate highway system, the railroad system created or reinforced divisions of class, race, and urban settlement, just as the train bridge on the northwest corner divided, and continues to divide, the two sides of the tracks in North Lawson and in many other American cities. As E. Franklin Frazier (1930, 718) noted, "The lower occupational groups tend to concentrate in the transition area of the city and along the railroad tracks." Traditionally, this divide was informed by a variety of factors, including the increased viability of work opportunities for laborers of that era and the desire for greater access to them. There is a residue of these socially and geographically constructed patterns today, which was reinforced through the much more recent interstate construction. Similar to the railroad system before it, in a state court case, highway construction was determined to have a disproportionate impact on predominantly minority neighborhoods. Despite this resolution, the project proceeded because "the selected corridor created fewer adverse impacts on minority populations than the alternative corridors that had been under consideration" (Cole and Foster 2001, 225; see also Ard 2016). In this city and throughout the US, when privilege-protecting social and geographic structures reinforce existing inequalities, they are valued and sanctioned to proceed. This because the approach chosen posed slightly less than the worst impact it could have had on the marginalized area. In North Lawson and elsewhere, the "shell game" of ignoring and minimizing internal/indigenous input—whether it has sanctioned, legal merit or not—and instead prioritizing the external assessment of underdeveloping alternatives is not unique and quite consistent with the larger histories of class, race, and place.

The busiest street along North Lawson's eastern edge, Akron Avenue, has long been a primary thoroughfare connecting the city's downtown with its north and east sides. Once a hideaway neighborhood, from Thirteenth Street North to Hayworth Street, this two-mile stretch of the Akron Avenue corridor eventually runs into the eastern suburbs. Howston is the city's primary north-south street. North Lawson was far enough east of Howston Street, through which the horse-drawn carriages and then eventually streetcars traveled. Now the routes of all primary bus lines travel on Howston. Further east, Akron Avenue was also one of the main north-south thoroughfares onto which streetcar technology extended at the turn of the century. Similar to another city in the state, the city's primary racial divide was east-west, with predominantly White neighborhoods to the west and predominantly African American neighborhoods to the east. This was magnified through the second suburbanization of the 1950s.

In the late 1950s, the racial makeup of the neighborhood quickly transitioned through blockbusting and other residential racisms of the time. Demonstrating how abruptly the process of American apartheid can function and reinforce race-separating changes (see Massey and Denton 1993), rapidly growing Great Migration flows of African Americans could not be restricted to previously established community borders. As in the 1920s, African Americans slowly moved into older White neighborhoods. The "white flight" of blockbusting and panic selling soon followed. These in turn led to the flight of capital and to physical decay. In North Lawson, less than one in ten residents were a racial minority in 1950. By 1970, more than 80 percent were a minority, and more than 90 percent by 1980 (Jacobs 1998; Massey and Denton 1993).

In North Lawson and elsewhere, this removal of multiple capacity-building resources at the local level led to a corresponding shift in various institutions, including health-care access and public schools. North Lawson is home to a long-standing and respected, predominantly African American, high school in the region. Lawson-Lee High changed from being nearly two-thirds White in 1967 to 90 percent African American by the early 1970s. Since that time, the neighborhood, the high school, and other schools in the area have remained predominantly African American. Due to these shifts of population and resources in the neighborhood, real buying power decreased severely and has remained largely the same since 1980. North Lawson has the highest proportion of abandoned homes among all areas of the city and one of the highest violent crime rates. It also has the second-highest rate of returning citizens (i.e., former felons) being released from state prisons and the second-highest percentage of schoolchildren eligible for the city school lunch program. This economically underdeveloped, high-poverty neighborhood in an economically stable Midwestern city exhibits many of the characteristics associated with the "school-to-prison pipeline" (Christle, Jolivette, and Nelson 2005, 69; Price-Spratlen and Goldsby 2012).

In the first decade of the FACTS Ministries (2000–09), there were a few hopeful changes in North Lawson. As reported in the 2010 US Census, the percentage of residents twenty-five and older with no high school diploma dropped from 35.6 percent to 28.4 percent, and single mothers with children under the age of eighteen declined from 23.9 percent to 19.4 percent (Kirwan Institute 2012). Still, a number of other high-risk factors saw little to no improvement during these years. Forty-three percent of North Lawson residents live below the poverty line, and its public schools at every level remain in "academic emergency." According to reported school district statistics, the academic emergency includes an elementary school math proficiency of 34 percent, which is worse (30 percent) at the high school level. Reading and language arts proficiency is even worse (City-Data.com 2010). While 50 percent of elementary school children were proficient, only 21 percent of North Lawson high schoolers were proficient in reading and language arts. Perhaps what is most shocking is a chronic absenteeism of 32 percent in elementary school–aged children, which confirms that nearly one-third of North Lawson students are missing more than two full weeks of school during the school year (City-Data.com 2010). This rate more than doubles among North Lawson high schoolers, as nearly three of every four students (74.4 percent) are chronically absent.

Clearly, like many other neighborhoods, North Lawson has been marked by long-term disinvestment and by limited access to the benefits of many mainstream social, economic, and political institutions. In the period immediately preceding the formation of the FACTS Ministries, local neighborhood disinvestment included virtually no new construction during the entire decade of the 1990s (Ard 2016; Johnson 2018). The process of marginalization is not new, and the process of profound resource disparities is only growing in the global environment of the late twentieth and early twenty-first centuries. Among the historical tensions and paradox of North Lawson are the dissonant truths of many African American communities in general: sustained marginalization in an environment of relative prosperity for some. And just as that is selectively true for groups of Americans, states, and regions of the US, it is also true far more locally, of cities and the neighborhoods within them, including North Lawson, where the FACTS Ministries was founded and continues to operate today.

A Present Place: North Lawson Today

In North Lawson and similar neighborhoods, the underdevelopment process literally begins in the womb of expectant mothers, feeding a pipeline that runs not only school-to-prison but, in fact, *cradle*-to-prison. According to recent (i.e., the last five years) analyses of change, the North Lawson infant mortality rate is among the worst in the city. It is nearly three times that of the county as a whole and is comparable to that of the lowest national infant mortality rates of any country in the Western hemisphere (CelebrateOne 2016). This extends from low-birth-weight babies being born at a rate nearly twice that of the county and among the worst in the entire US (Health Map 2016 [source details withheld for confidentiality]). The city is among the top-ten worst areas with racially disparate impacts from pollution (e.g., Kirwan Institute 2012). Investigations continue into why the state's low-income and minority communities continue to be more affected by environmental pollution and degradation than do wealthier and/or Whiter communities.

Furthering the cradle-to-prison pipeline, the out-of-school suspension rate for North Lawson elementary school students is 25 percent, meaning one of every four K-6 students experienced an out-of-school suspension in the 2012–15 period. This rate more than triples by the time students are in high school, where 76.3 percent of North Lawson high schoolers experienced an out-of-school suspension during this same period (Health Map 2016). That is nearly three times higher than the suspension rate of high school students in the city as a whole. When considering suburban schools in the comparison, it is more than six times the rate of metro area high schools. All this occurs among a student body where 90 percent of students across all levels are eligible for the school's free lunch program, and area schools overall have one of the lowest district rankings in the state. Christle, Jolivette, and Nelson (2005, 70) stated, "Academic failure, exclusionary discipline practices, and dropout [rates] have been identified as key elements in a 'school-to-prison pipeline,' especially for minority students and those with disabilities."

Like all neighborhoods, North Lawson has its borders and points of entry. From the FACTS Ministries' front door two miles northwest as the crow flies begins the northern edge of North Lawson. As noted earlier, the Hayworth Street bridge goes over the broad, six-lane highway, with on-ramps and off-ramps that comfortably manage the often-heavy traffic. Long before the economic downturn of the COVID pandemic, a common sight was people holding signs asking for money as they stood or sat by the off-ramps, positioned for high visibility. They do so primarily at two locations of a traffic light's pause: on the northwest and southeast off-ramp railings. Consistent with environmental criminology, "within a transient, poor section of a city there will be places that have some regularity and repetitive appearances of particular individuals . . . a true vagrant might be identified by the regulars" (Brantingham and Brantingham 1993, 23) as being out of place. Both the physical structure and the behavioral patterns are markers of a neighborhood's class transition and a means of generating whatever dimes, quarters, and dollars that drivers at a stoplight are willing to give someone holding a "NEED HELP" sign at a freeway off-ramp. Past the train and highway bridges of its northwest corner, heading east on Hayworth into North Lawson, class- and race-based changes of housing stock and people on the street are visible. The White flight that racially transformed Lawson-Lee High School in just six years during the late 1960s and early 1970s is long past. Yet its loud echoes remain. The railroad-track bridge over Hayworth, a mid-1950s update and revitalization project, reinforced the racial residential divide at the time of President Eisenhower's Highway Acts (Rothstein 2017; Jacobs 1998). Just east of the train bridge on either side of Hayworth used to be the eastward and westward bus stops, the latter of which was recently removed due to service cutbacks—despite the fact that buses provide the city's only public transportation. There is a "Welcome to the Lawson District" sign on the southeast corner of the broad intersection. It is always obscured by overgrown tree branches from the highway greenspace.

Heading further east on Hayworth, the next notable intersection is at McGandry Street, with the look of the "'hood" on every corner. Both sides of McGandry have corner stores, and there is a car shop just off one corner, where they also sell barbeque ribs during the summer months. A chicken and shrimp spot on another corner offers "deep fried, Southern style" dishes. The small Apostolic church on the third corner of the intersection is known for the size of its cross, which dwarfs the church itself and its small, gravel front yard. On the fourth corner stands a retail space that has been unoccupied for many years. The corner stores at McGandry Street are near two cell phone outlet stores and a small, four-pump gas station. Of all the items sold and bought in the area and of all the businesses that come and go in North Lawson, likely the most lucrative is crack sales on the streets, supported by the sale of crack pipes, or "stems," in any corner store. A tiny polyester rose is inside to decorate the small, four-inch-long glass tube, which is about the diameter of a pencil. The rose is an ode to art or a nod to the pretense that the stem can be used for a purpose other than what it is most often meant for. It markets an illusion, rooted in the everyday tensions of how a social ecology of resilience can be muted in the contexts of oppression. It is dissonant symbolism: a pleasant piece of art inside a glass utensil used almost exclusively for illicit drug consumption in a neighborhood where a great deal of money goes to drug sales of various kinds in the neighborhood's day-to-day.

North Lawson has been a "food desert" (Walker, Keane, and Burke 2010, 876) since at least the mid-1990s, when the last grocery store closed along the Akron Avenue corridor, two blocks north of where the Ministries would locate a few years later. These are among the place characteristics in the North Lawson neighborhood marked by poorer prenatal health, low birth weight, high infant mortality, elementary school underachievement, and high school levels of (non)participation that collectively lead to an academic emergency. As further evidence of structural divestment, not surprisingly, the district per pupil spending is far lower than in the city as a whole. The area's high level of dependence on federal property tax funding relative to the local area makes the prospects for sustained change unlikely.

Beyond dilemmas of food and funding is rampant crime. In early 2013, a couple blocks north of the FACTS Ministries, two teenagers shot each other, killing one of them, in the parking lot of a fast-food chain outlet. That led the fast-food company to close its doors, then raze the building. In a very short period, the plot went from a neighborhood landmark where elderly men played checkers and chess in the large front window on Saturday mornings to yet another fenced-in empty lot along Akron Avenue. From 2011 to 2017, a couple blocks south of the Ministries, a theater renovation as a cultural arts center was established. It gained momentum, then sputtered and never took flight. In the years in between, a few small business ventures were established and quickly closed in those blocks just north and south of the Ministries. Two neighborhood landmark churches closed. A different church purchased and moved into one of those buildings. The other remains vacant. A large laundromat nearby recently closed. After it lay dormant for nearly a year, a day-care center opened in that space in 2015 and has been there since. Yet amid these local uncertainties, the popular branch library completed in 2004 at the neighborhood's northern edge initiated a sustained, beneficial access to more than just the community garden across the street.

A Resilient Ecology

In "severely distressed" neighborhoods like North Lawson, "poverty and long-term joblessness have been associated with a constellation of other negative consequences [yet] there are strengths in these families and communities . . . that can facilitate resilience" (Dunlap, Golub, and Johnson

2006, 116–17, 134). North Lawson's places of today are informed heavily by the systemic defunding they have experienced across generations. Yet in those intentionally underdeveloped local spaces, resources of resilience rise. Sometimes through municipal initiatives (e.g., the library branch). Sometimes through neighborly initiatives (e.g., the community gardens). Sometimes through faith-based, organizational initiatives (e.g., the FACTS Ministries). With its location, along with adjacent health service outlets and the churches of the Akron Avenue corridor, the Ministries is part of a social ecology of resilience.

North Lawson's present yet underdeveloped resilience is intensified by many challenges. Its social ecology is a place of possibility. It has many levels and dimensions, protective factors within each that operate interdependently, and all of which operate in a location with a mixture of assets and constraints that, taken together, provide an environment of support to improve and sustain one's health and well-being (Stajduhar et al. 2009). At its core, the neighborhood has an underdeveloped infrastructure of community resilience, leading to many impositions of compromised progress. American apartheid and its related process, and the cradle-to-prison pipeline, mar the neighborhood's potential for resilience. Both have informed both the past and present of North Lawson. Both are being challenged through the interaction of municipal resource investments, acting in collaboration with grassroots capacity-building initiatives. In North Lawson, and in cities throughout the US, grassroots organizations are acting on the need to create broader opportunities as a vital means of fostering a more hopeful present and future. Just one block south of the Hayworth and Akron intersection, two places of growth demonstrate a very different neighborhood tempo: the Lawson Library and a community garden across the street from it.

The Lawson Library was dedicated and opened on February 20, 2004. The goal with this and several other neighborhood branch libraries renewed or constructed at that time was to encourage beneficial local area foot traffic and increase the amount of pro-social spaces for youth. The library has remained true to its mission. Its Homework Help Center typically draws twenty or more students on any one of the three days of the week the services are offered, enhancing the library's utility for young people and many others. The library is well used by people of all ages. It was difficult to schedule use of its community meeting rooms for events related to this research project because of how often it was booked for use by two standing organizations with long-term reservations. The rooms are frequently also being used by other organizations for single events, including sewing clubs, the local chapter of the NAACP, the YouthBuild initiative for fostering young people interested in carpentry and contracting skill development, and many others. The line from the parking lot to the front door on Saturday mornings typically began to build nearly an hour prior to its opening. Youth of all colors and cultures lined up with their elders, causing one to be hard-pressed to secure any time for the twelve library computers. Prior to the onset of the COVID pandemic, during ethnographic spot-check look-ins in the most recent years, that continued to be the case.

Security for the library is quite visible. While there has never been an incident of note at the library that made the evening news, many incidents of varying severity have occurred nearby. So in the interest of nurturing a family- and child-friendly space, security in and immediately around the Lawson Library is closely monitored. This is not without controversy. A security guard is visible at all times. An exterior security camera has been damaged and replaced near the main exterior entrance several times. Consistent with the surveillance culture in which we now live (e.g., Pecora 2002), at least five visible internal cameras extend from the ceiling at multiple locations. The seeming ever-presence of being watched in public space is an assumed part of the North Lawson neighborhood. A formal, citywide request for proposal for unarmed security guard services was publicized in early 2013, and multiple forms of security have been visible at the branch since its opening.

There is a small, cement, patio-style entry area of fifty square feet in front of the library and its small parking lot. This patio area is raised a few feet above the sidewalk, just inside the wheelchair accessibility ramp. In one corner of the entry area, for many years a statue was on a three-foot pedestal. The pedestal was accessible and allowed the statue to greet all who came to the branch's front door. The statue was of an African American male child, perhaps nine or ten years old, sitting cross-legged on a couch, with a pleasant half-smile, reading a book in his lap. It sat at a level where even a child of six or seven years old could almost meet his eyes. The image symbolically affirmed that any youth with the support and willingness to value the written word could grow from the joy and possibilities in those pages. In February 2014, the statue was knocked over for the first time, not having been secured to the pedestal. Perhaps this was poor artistic construction or an unintended oversight. The damage to the statue was repaired. Within a month, it was back on the pedestal.

Then every few months, the statue was knocked over again. Sadly, by November 2015, rather than repair the damage and reset it for a fifth or sixth time, the statue was removed. The pedestal is empty, and now Lawson Library patrons are no longer greeted by that welcoming image. That absence may be neutral to some. To many others, it is a symbolic challenge to the developmental value of the shared public good the library and the publicly available resources within it provide.

Still, shortly after the library opened, its resilience effects included a group of faith-affirming near-neighbors who initiated a community garden directly across the street. The long-abandoned plot was first marked, then fenced, and then its soil was tilled. Planting rows were set on what is perhaps a two-hundred-square-foot plot. These steps progressed slowly. With each of them, a sense of shared public good was enriched. The quote that begins this chapter was written by a cofounder of the garden, who continued:

> A bunch of first-timers who were green in everything but their thumbs learned quickly to take manageable steps, celebrate tiny victories and avoid sweating the small stuff. Slowly but surely, a vacant plot became four beds of vegetables and herbs bordered by a simple network of mulched paths: . . . neighbors have started poking their head over the fence to see what's growing on. (August 2009)

A year later, a second, larger community garden was planted two blocks north of Hayworth Street, three blocks north of the first community garden neighboring the library. The second garden had a business dimension, having been started by a transplant from Milwaukee who planted the plot next to the coffee shop he owns. Much of the produce that coffee shop garden generates is given away to North Lawson neighbors in need. This is how a largely unplanned collaboration can nurture the shared benefits of neighboring ties and more nutritious food in one among the city's many food deserts (e.g., Walker, Keane, and Burke 2010), which neither the library nor the community gardeners likely could have created independently. Benefits of community gardens have been demonstrated in prior research and include enhancing values, improving environmental equity, the economic benefit of improved property values, helping community responses to obesity, and creating other dynamics of resilience (Allen et al. 2008; Ohmer et al. 2009; Okvat and Zautra 2011). Recognizing challenges of claiming causality, and the need for better data and methods, from their meta-analysis, Okvat and Zautra (2011, 382) conclude, "[Despite] tensions regarding how private or public the garden should be in terms of access, the data reviewed suggest a relation between community gardens and individual, community, and environmental well-being."

The figurative bridge between the library and the garden across the street is among North Lawson's most vivid affirmations of neighborhood resilience. Still, site-specific revitalization of even a single block in North Lawson is always uneven. On either side of the community garden are two retail spaces that have been vacant since before the library opened in 2004. Retail or other uses of those spaces may "catch up" as the municipal investment and sweat equity vitalities of both the library and the garden continue and grow.

The resilient ecology of North Lawson and the presence of the FACTS Ministries in it are also reflected in the building of the Ministries itself. Like several buildings in North Lawson, across its history, it has been a laundromat and a cleaners. A bar and a tavern. A carryout and a corner store. After it stood abandoned for many years, a prior owner converted it into a church. Nearby, a jackleg preacher who had recently gotten sober was holding what he called "redemption meetings to stop smoking crack and help others to do the same" in the alley garage of his father's house. A faith friendship between the preacher and a man he barely knew led to a partnership and the establishment of an urban ministry. Soon thereafter, the Ministries began.

Conclusions

This chapter has explored characteristics and constraints of the North Lawson neighborhood that are marked by the long-standing, defunding outcomes of apathy and intentional underdevelopment. American apartheid creates and sustains race-separating changes that reify place-related resource differences and cultural caste. North Lawson is also the social ecology for health and resilience in which the FACTS Ministries is located, with health and education being central to the viability of the organization. These two vital "enabling resources . . . support health and human development and the manifold ways these resources are generated and utilized" (Duff 2011, 150; see also Ungar, Ghazinour, and Richter 2013). The Ministries is part of the proper care and devotion of the ethnogenic thread of social reconstruction and social recovery. It helps refine a communal social structure and collective ethos that, in turn, helps reasons for neighborhood stigma and alienation (e.g., high poverty, health disparities) to become potential assets for improved health and other life-affirming outcomes. An understandable question remains: What, besides a church, can succeed as a neighborhood business? Like the larger neighborhood, the blocks of the Akron Avenue corridor experienced an all-too-typical urban marginalization, punctuated by periodic violent crime that either took lives or simply added to gun challenges that furthered class/race alienations of the urban core. All the while, the FACTS Ministries' doors have remained open.

Reflecting on her volunteer work in North Lawson the year before, a 2015 fellow of an international scholarly organization remarked that "the absence of attention to all the good going on in the neighborhood [was] the most surprising element" of her fellowship experience. She said that, far too often, "they don't get credit for their work and people ensure that the negative is consistently amplified via various media channels." No longer surprised that low-income African Americans are working to support their neighborhood, she says that she is surprised "at how so much of the work is going unnoticed." A social ecology of resilience is much more than having quality people to work with. It requires caring interactions between them and sharing resources of value toward collective ends.

Many affiliates see the FACTS Ministries as an "oasis" of healing in an environment of profound challenge. In order for it to be appreciated as an urban ecology of health and resilience, a detailed consideration of its spiritual things provides an important and necessary next step. As Leverentz (2010, 649) noted, "While avoiding people, places, and things related to drug use may be feasible for a subset of [former] drug users, it is done at significant cost and difficulty for many." Thus, a vital invitation to those seeking recovery from addiction is to surround themselves with resilience-nurturing, pro-social, and health-affirming people, places, and spiritual things alongside the reminders of active addiction. Consistent with Castells (1970), "in a society where the powerful will not relinquish power, where the rich will not redistribute wealth, and where self-interest precludes social interests, liberation can begin only in the black community . . . somewhere between the pastoral nurture of personal faith and the prophetic demands upon religious communities" (Andrews 2002, 9; see also McRoberts 2003).

Together, the people and places introduced in the first two chapters are fundamental to the health and social resilience at the FACTS Ministries. A health ministries can be an enabling place that addresses many disparities and adverse consequences of addiction that are often most severe in communities least equipped to address them, like North Lawson. The Ministries sustains resources and services that are essential to resilience in a challenging neighborhood setting. Building on the people of chapter 1 and places of chapter 2, chapter 3 considers the "things," or the faith and health resources of the Ministries. Consistent with prior research, these resources enable healing in an environment of profound challenge. The FACTS Ministries' structure, programs, and patterns are the means through which its faith and health resources/services work for its affiliates. Exploring what they are and how they matter is what follows.

Chapter 3

Healthy Things

Resilience Resources of the Ministries

> Community-based organizations that provide social services and food assistance, serve vital community needs each day. . . . The centrality of health to both societal and individual wellness suggest that commitment to building human resilience should be at the forefront of any workable model. . . . At its core, a resilience-centered framework provides concrete actions people, organizations, and institutions can take to sustain [the] long-term well-being of communities in the face of adversity.
>
> —Wulff, Donato, and Lurie 2015, 363–64, 367

Introduction

As chapters 1 and 2 demonstrate, a social ecology of resilience is informed by the people and places that come together to further individual, organizational, and communal health and well-being. Research shows that "assertive linkage procedures rely on actively connecting [prospective affiliates] to meetings and shaping/reinforcing their attendance. Procedures may include early referral to support groups, education about potential benefits and risks of attendance [and] discussion of each person's prior . . . obstacles and participation" (Passetti, Godley, and Godley 2014, 188; see also Roth 2010; Bellamy et al. 2014). As reflected in the chapter 1 profiles, be it through treatment center referral, social ties, organizational outreach, collaborative invitation, mainstream media, or other means, some form of initial affiliation is a necessary first step. Chapter 2 showed how place-informed history and the resilience-centered motives among municipal service providers and community gardeners alike can help enrich an environment of support for the services and success of a community-based organization. The triangulation of municipal information sharing (i.e., the library), volunteers addressing food insecurities and abandoned plots of the urban core (i.e., the community garden), and a faith-based health organization (i.e., the FACTS Ministries) affirmed a symmetry of whole health even in the midst of a neighborhood of severe concentrated disadvantage. Having explored the people of the FACTS Ministries in chapter 1 and the places of challenge and resilience in the North Lawson neighborhood in chapter 2, extending from the Wulff, Donato, and Lurie (2015) quote above, the things—or resilience-centered, health-affirming resources and practices of the Ministries—are analyzed here in chapter 3.

Consistent with Passetti, Godley, and Godley's and other researchers' focus on assertive linkages, prior research has also established how "churches are a trusted resource in African American communities; however, little is known about their presentation of health care information" (Harmon et al. 2014, 242). To learn more, this chapter explores the health resources of the FACTS Ministries and how they nurture pro-social responses that enrich individual, organizational, and communal health and well-being. Centered at the intersection where the Ministries sits, there were fourteen churches within a two-mile congregational corridor of Akron Avenue, including two blocks east and west of Akron. Two health-care centers were within this same set of blocks. Among them, the Ministries made a faith-health interdependence its mission, adding visibility to the importance of the relationships between them. The FACTS Ministries was the one resource along the corridor that served as both a health and a faith resource. It did so by challenging a silence-as-shame cycle of stigma in the substance use recovery process. When addressing health inequalities in general, and recovery in particular, to nurture resilience, "stigma is met head on as participants [develop] the ability to effectively manage and rebound from disappointments and setbacks. [They] learn to explore themselves, their relationships with others (such as family members), their relationships in the community, and how it all fits in within the larger society" (Bellamy et al. 2014, 159). The "radical" act is prioritizing visibility with substance use recovery, one of the most stigmatized health challenges, at the core of its organizational identity and resources.

The Ministries is a health resource of assertive linkages. It is surrounded by several trap houses, frequent drug sales, sex industry workers, and other neighborhood characteristics associated with all three. The location of the Ministries allowed it to be understood in terms of a spatial tension or dissonance that prioritized pro-social, health-affirming actions of sustained change in the midst of this challenging yet hopeful setting. As reflected in chapter 2, in "severely distressed" neighborhoods like North Lawson, "poverty and long-term joblessness have been associated with a constellation of other negative consequences [yet] there are strengths in these families and communities . . . that can facilitate resilience" (Dunlap, Golub, and Johnson 2006, 117, 116–17, 134). Adjacent health service outlets in the Akron Avenue corridor help. With its location and its five health service domains, the Ministries can be understood as being, and being a part of, a social ecology of resilience.

Health Service Domains

The FACTS Ministries offers various health resources (see table 1). While founded to focus on substance use recovery, almost from its origin other health dimensions were recognized as being central to the effectiveness of the Ministries achieving and sustaining its primary mission. As Peterson, Atwood, and Yates (2002, 409) noted, "To promote health and wellness in light of our diverse society and health needs, health promotion professionals and churches can be dynamic partners." Consistent with its health mission, the Ministries provided "equity-oriented health care services" (Andermann 2016, E477). Its contributions were sustained primarily through the financial sponsorship of two anchor churches, grants and donations, and willing on-site volunteers. Its services included sober homes and other substance use recovery resources, pastoral counseling, nutritional/meal-based support, youth/developmental/preventive initiatives, and other health and resilience resources.

Substance Abuse Recovery Domain

The Ministries was founded as a faith-based, substance use recovery resource to be "a safe haven" for those with substance use concerns "to live in freedom again" (promotional materials). While the Traditions of the 12-Step fellowships emphasize autonomy from all other organizations, the Ministries collaborated with the city's Cocaine Anonymous (CA) chapter to offer addiction recovery resources. As previously noted,

Table 1. The five health service domains of the FACTS Ministries and nurturing resilience. Source: Developed by the author for this book.

Health-Service Domains	Collaborations ——— Resources/Strategies of Action	Contributions to Resilience	Areas of Limitation/Challenges	Possible Change
Substance use recovery	Sober Homes program, CA meetings' spiritual program of abstinence; ride-share service (Thursday nights); dialogue between 12 Steps and religious affiliation	Millwood Fellowship, Sacred Calling Fellowship, Cocaine Anonymous ——— Residential stability (Sober Homes program), long-term sobriety; 4 essentials of recovery (Kaskutas et al. 2014)	–Protocol inconsistencies (Sober Homes program) –Perceived as drug specific, –Not open to "radical recovery" (i.e., the personal as political in recovery)	Multiple recovery affiliations, harm reduc./MAT, 12 Step critique (i.e., challenging ideological hegemony, both secular and religious)
Pastoral counseling	One-on-one and family counseling; health/recovery, premarital, couples, and grief counseling	Referrals made to nearby county behavioral health clinic ——— Religiously grounded mental health; cultural competence, empathy	–Single pastoral resource (Pastor Marshall only) –Traditional religious views only	Improve therapeutic diversities, continuing education(?)

Nutritional/meal-based support	Free community lunches, men's prayer breakfasts, food pantry, dietician-support visits, Thanksgiving meal	Local restaurants, food pantries ———— Beneficial calories, countering neighborhood as a food desert; the fellowship of food (i.e., challenging isolation, improving psychosocial exchanges)	–Donation dependence –Limited menu, limited days –No forthright consideration of the faith politics of food (e.g., Parson 2014, Food Not Bombs approach)	More available days, potential collaborations with nearby community gardens
Youth/developmental/ preventive	Boxing club, Friday youth nights (summer), Bible study summer school	Branch library, recreation center Prosocial peer support, challenging youth obesity; training, discipline, the "religion of sports"; lessons of victory/defeat, faith socialization	–Boxing only, –Off-site/ministries disconnect –No visible consideration of the politics of youth prevention	On-site youth leadership/ voice, greater visibility
Other health and resilience resources	Health screenings, women's leadership event, referrals for free health services; clothing donations; lending library (tapes of prior sermons, Bible study); special events	Children's hospital, women's clinic ———— The importance of prioritizing health maintenance (e.g., regular screenings), life course promotion; women-centered fellowship	–Inconsistent –Expert outsiders only –Not enough value on women's health –No visible consideration of the politics of health disparities	Valuing collective leadership (e.g., health-wellness cmte.), respecting women's leadership

the Ministries hosted two CA meetings each week. With no more than twelve total CA meetings taking place at any given time, the Either-Or CA meetings hosted by the Ministries constituted no less than one-sixth of all CA meetings in the city. Through much of its history, outside of treatment centers, it was the only venue hosting more than one CA meeting. Despite its name, CA is not a single-substance fellowship, taking pride in its intentionally worded Step 1: "We admitted we were powerless over cocaine and all other mind-alternating substances, and that our lives had become unmanageable" (Cocaine Anonymous 2019, 6). Cocaine was the substance of priority given the unique and most severe stigma associated with its consumption and amplification in the "War on Drugs" during the late 1980s and 1990s (Hood 2012; Sharpe 2005). Their collaboration was beneficial to both the Ministries and the local chapter of CA, enriching the health and resilience missions of both organizations. First two, then three of the most vocal and visible CA affiliates in service leadership positions at the city (i.e., district) and state (i.e., area) levels of CA were among the most consistent affiliates of the Ministries.

In addition to the Either-Or CA meetings, three other resources were central to the Ministries' substance use recovery domain: a men's sober homes program, relapse prevention workshops for sober homes residents, and other events and activities related to recovery hosted at the Ministries. The sober homes provide a residential alternative that creates a total mutual help culture (Kelly and Yeterian 2008), extending from the long-standing value placed on a therapeutic community approach for recovery and healing (De Leon 2000; Hennessy 2017). Therapeutic community builds on the notion that "the experiences of ordered living provide an essential therapeutic element [to] strengthen capacity for orderly living [by] establishing values and norms that contrast with the street, drug culture, and prisons" (De Leon 2000, 74). Its benefits demonstrate how "a community where residents live without professional treatment staff and length-of-stay restrictions [provides] a greater opportunity to develop a sense of competence toward maintaining abstinence" (Jason et al. 2006, 1727; see also Hood 2012).

The sober homes program is based on the social ecology model, where residential environments of support are at the core of one's "protective factors that enhance the individuals' coping abilities, which in turn decrease vulnerability to negative outcomes" (Jarrett 1997, 219; see also Werner and Smith 1982). The model includes peer influences, bonding, self-efficacy, family climate, and a sense of collective efficacy (Kumpfer and Turner 1990). Its success is reflected in the chapter 1 profiles of Albert, a long-term resident, and Douglas, a recent sober homes arrival. As Douglas noted in his interview, "it feels like I'm actually in a super clean environment. . . . I like how nobody acts like they're better than anybody [and] here everybody seems to be real and open." Their success included what appeared to be a greater appreciation for each other's assets of recovery (i.e., warmer interactions, or at least less apparent friction among the newest residents) and other characteristics of an environment of shared respect (e.g., sharing prospective job referrals, collective food and meals, and working out together). This warmth and appreciation were often expressed in an exaggerated, mocking tone and always received with good humor.

Across the three sober homes, their twelve to fourteen residents participated in relapse prevention workshops designed to "help individuals learn to employ effective coping skills while dealing with external challenges that impede management of complex addiction and health-related conditions" (Collard, Lewinson, and Watkins 2014, 469). Two Either-Or CA home group members (i.e., frequent affiliates who defined this group as the main meeting of their recovery affiliation and primary commitment for service) were living what Ministries leadership viewed as two of the strongest programs of recovery among all Ministries affiliates. In 2011, Pastor Marshall asked them to facilitate a series of relapse prevention workshops for the Ministries' sober homes residents. In their curriculum, they included role-plays of risk settings they were likely to encounter and "trigger" exploration for street and neighborhood, family, and sober housing settings. They were guided through exercises in how empathy can enhance one's active listening and relationship to other "tools of recovery." The workshops revisited past prison/criminogenic contexts of risk and helped the participants respond to them in health-affirming ways. They also discussed sober masculinity and its relationship to faith-based masculine self-perceptions (e.g., Flores 2013; Travis 2009). The leadership of Millwood Fellowship (the primary funder "anchor" church) and Ministries leadership began raising questions about the efficacy and contributions of this component of sober homes programming. Worksheets, writing, and the process of having to do "homework" elicited responses from several participants like, "What *is* this? You think we gotta go back to school for this s—? I'm tryin' to stay sober. Didn't know I'd have to go back to doin' homework and s—." One of the workshop facilitators became ill soon after the workshops began, which limited their availability and consistency.

Still, amid the internal leadership uncertainties, resident reticence, and facilitator challenges, these workshops contributed to behavior changes and improved health outcomes. As one sober homes resident noted,

> Real talk, those relapse prevention things were a hassle, for real. After the Saturday morning CA meetings, I needed to go get my hustle on, or try to find some work or catch an extra wink of sleep. But they was useful. Yep. Knowin' that bein' sober ain't about bein' no punk, just 'cause you ain't all out there, like that. Role playin,' and acting' out and shit. Goal plannin.' What would bein' sober for 3, 4 years mean to me and my family? Shit like that. All that faith walk stuff, too. Ya, I kinda got into it, a little bit.

If sober homes residents were not working, they were required to participate in all Ministries activities that did not conflict with their work or family responsibilities. Attendance at the workshops remained steady, with nine or more of the sober homes residents attending, as well as other invited affiliates. Several longtime Either-Or meeting affiliates noted that newer residents were more willing to speak at the CA meetings while the relapse prevention workshops were taking place, as if they gained greater confidence in their ability to participate in group activities. Research has shown that "multiple forms of mentorship and support, such as sponsorship and 12-Step programs, significantly increase the potential for continued abstinence or decreased substance use" (Heyer et al. 2020, 1; see also Witbrodt et al. 2012). It was somewhat unclear what aspects of a program of recovery were required as a sober homes resident. Still, while the relapse prevention workshops were taking place, there were more apparent meetings between sponsors and their sober home resident sponsees as well. While the workshops were taking place, there were fewer relapse-informed evictions from the sober homes, as only one resident was asked to leave due to relapse during the months of the workshops. The equivalent of no call–no show absences in other Ministries' activities occurred more often after the relapse prevention workshops ended. Though crediting the workshops or any single health resource for improvements in resident behavior is not possible, some improvement appeared to be associated with the number, and level of participation, in them. Sober homes resident Albert, one of the people of the Ministries introduced in chapter 1, served as the long-standing secretary of the Thursday night

Either-Or CA meetings. Because of his willingness, ride share services were available for getting all those in attendance safely home from Thursday night meetings. His choice to do so was part of his "mobile ministry" and personal devotion to the Ministries' mission. It was yet another resource that improved health-care access among affiliates.

Pastoral Care/Counseling Domain

Like all good counseling or psychotherapy, pastoral caregiving at the FACTS Ministries involves listening to a person's words with empathy and care. Clebsch and Jaekle (1975, 8–9) state that the functions of pastoral care are a "ministry of the cure of souls . . . directed toward the healing, sustaining, guiding, and reconciling [among] persons whose troubles arise in the context of ultimate meaning." Among all Ministries health resources, this resource had the widest range of experiences and perceived outcomes. Pastor Marshall had personally experienced a harrowing active addiction and had subjected himself and his family to a severe "bottom" at the end of his drinking and drugging. His wife Cheryl had gotten sober over a year before he did. As a result, being empathetic to affiliates who sought him out for counseling was made somewhat easier given his own personal history.

The Ministries' contributions to resilience included providing affiliates with access to religiously grounded counseling so they could sustain a level of mental wellness they likely would not have otherwise had. Pastor Marshall approached sessions with the goal of sharing a cultural competence (Stansbury et al. 2012), or as he described it, "I'm tryin' to be, what to say, Biblically authentic in the ol' school church tradition. On my better days, my more sober days, so to speak, I think I help folks to a breakthrough. Bein' faith-filled, them knowin' His Word in their lives in ways that can make wa's happenin' that much more manageable. That's what we're doin' here" (personal communication, July 2010). After having had individual and family sessions with Pastor Marshall, one affiliate remarked,

> After all that was over, sittin' down ev'ry couple weeks or whatnot, jus' to see wa's up. I'm glad pastor was there when I needed him. It was a rough patch, 'cause my teenager was startin' to get into some real scary trouble, even though he just hit middle school. You know, more than just a little thing, here or there. So I was worried. Still am. And for me, stayin' sober

> is kind of a struggle, still. And my momma's been doin' better. Sittin' down with the pastor, kinda helps, you know, smooth out some of that stuff.

Crisis and prior trauma are frequent among persons in recovery and were in the personal history of many Ministries affiliates. As William White (2007, 231) noted, "Recovery is a medical term that connotes a return to health following trauma or illness." Being in recovery is embraced as a process among affiliates, be they persons in recovery, volunteers, anchor church supporters, or caring family and friends. A very short list of prior traumas among affiliates included the shooting deaths of loved ones, ongoing spousal abuse, weathering the elements of substandard housing, and surviving police brutality or penal system assaults, among many others. Unwilling to stay in an overcrowded and unpleasant shelter, a homeless affiliate got frostbite and nearly froze to death in an "abando" (abandoned home) behind the gas station across the street from the Ministries. A survivor of at least one documented difficulty while in police custody and involved in numerous other life-threatening situations of active addiction, he had an apparent though slight developmental disability and uncertain mental well-being, which were reflected in some incivilities toward others while at the Ministries. A niece of his looked after him and was distraught about his near-fatal outcome. Both the homeless affiliate and his niece came to a better understanding of addiction as a "family disease" (Roth 2010, 1). While his housing insecurity and substance-related choices remained precarious, and he remained estranged from most of his family, his niece continued meeting with Pastor Marshall for several months after the frostbite incident. She never attended religious services at the Ministries, having a home church elsewhere and not being in recovery herself. Still, she was seen bringing either another family member or a friend into session with Pastor Marshall at least a few times. While what happened to her uncle was rare, on at least four other occasions during the more than fourteen-year period of this research project, a similar situation was either shared from the chapel floor during testimony in church services or referenced during 12-Step meetings.

Things did marginally improve with this affiliate and his family. Gradually, he began attending more Saturday morning Either-Or CA meetings. "The shakes" of his hands from his long-term alcoholism seemed to occur less often during his participation at Ministries events. He repaired things enough with family to be able to stay in the basement of a relative's house.

Though he never said anything at the Either-Or meetings he attended, over time he was willing to respond when greeted with a hello and a handshake as meetings began. At one meeting, an affiliate who was a history buff and a fan of W. E. B. DuBois quoted him. A promise of Step 9 says, "We will not regret the past nor wish to shut the door on it. We will comprehend the word serenity, and we will know peace" (Alcoholics Anonymous 2001, 83–84). The affiliate linked those promises to a line from *The Souls of Black Folk*: "It is a hard thing to live haunted by the ghosts of an untrue dream" (DuBois [1903] 1969, 110). For this affiliate, the untrue dream is active addiction. Ghosts are the residue of not making amends with those one has harmed during one's active addiction, or taking "too long" to do so. When a person in recovery does Step 9, healing grows as the untrue dream fades, though it never disappears. The haunting ghosts subside as one completes the step and moves on to Step 10 in their spiritual program of action. As the shares of that meeting continued, the affiliate who had almost frozen to death in an abando just six months earlier asked for a piece of paper and a pen. Slowly, carefully, he wrote down the DuBois quote, word for word. When he finished writing, he looked up with a self-satisfied smile. Though his struggles continued, Either-Or meetings for him, and pastoral counseling for his niece and other loved ones, were among the resources that contributed to the resilience of his family and of the Ministries.

Pastor Marshall also provided grief and premarital and marital counseling. One couple, Roman and Cindy, who were not married, began counseling with him shortly after Roman became affiliated with the Ministries. Having recently moved from the upper Midwest, Roman was originally from the Deep South. When he arrived at the Ministries in 2009, he had just lost his youngest son to gun violence down South. He was in search of a safe space to sustain his newly established recovery in this new place of opportunity. While in the rooms of recovery, what is sometimes derided as "the geographic cure" occurs, where a person seeks out and expects a new location to help them establish a new identity and sustain a sober self. This decision is regarded with caution, often seen as a choice of addictive denial: "The 'geographic cure' is well known in the addiction recovery world, where former addicts are told to avoid 'people, places, and things' associated with their old addictive behaviors to maintain their newfound sobriety" (Maruna and Roy 2007, 106). This is called denial because one takes one's addiction with them wherever they move. Still, some moves are beneficial, as Roman found his to be.

Raised in a Southern Pentecostal church, he expressed appreciation for Ministries' Sunday services soon after his move to the city, in his thick, beautiful, resonant drawl:

> 'Cause sometime, Marshall gon' give you that ol' time preachin' and teachin' and all. Give it to ya without all 'at book learnin' and whatnot. 'Cause that's what I got back home. Back home for real, ain't no time for all that showin' off and whatnot. Naw. Praisin' Him and savin' souls. Yep. [Pastor Marshall] give it to ya 'cause he a crackhead for real too, just like the rest of us.

Pastor Marshall worked with Roman and Cindy through Roman's grief at the loss of his son and on their relationship of formative trust. After a year together, eight months of which they had lived together, Roman did not trust Cindy to have a key to the apartment they shared. He kept everything in his name and did not allow her access to any house-related resources without first asking for his permission. In therapy, they explored how restrictive patriarchy becomes oppressive, in a language and with examples that were accessible to all. They explored how the absence of access can become pathological distrust and whether they could find and sustain a new balance. Some months into their pastoral counseling sessions, Roman was able to speak about his son's shooting at Either-Or meetings. During open topic meetings, when those in attendance volunteer two or three topics for discussion during the meeting, Roman volunteered "grief in sobriety" and "emotional honesty" and other similar ideas. At one point many months into their pastoral therapy, Cindy was overheard talking about going to the apartment early to begin to prepare their meal prior to Roman's return home. This suggested that she now had a key to their home. The progress of resilience in various forms grows at different paces.

While these and other similar triumphs were experienced by many, several other Ministries affiliates were highly skeptical of Pastor Marshall's counseling skills. Translating empathy to counseling communication is a skill and is certainly not guaranteed simply because of a prior addiction history. His pastoral training was entirely self-taught, and he was public and even boastful about not having studied much of anything outside of the Bible. He was particularly reticent, if not outright hostile, toward the Big Book of Alcoholics Anonymous. He would regularly remark, "I don't have a sponsor. I don't, what you people say, 'work' the Steps. I'm not much on the Big Book. But I do live recovery, saved by Grace and one day at a time." Pastor Marshall was a devoted client of a therapist and talked frequently and openly about his experiences in individual, couple's, and family counseling.

He was a "jackleg" pastor, having received a Calling during his final stint in jail. Consistent with the apostle Paul, "the Grace contained in the Gospel of Christ [recognizes that] God can use even the efforts of jack-leg preachers to enable the words of human beings to become the Word of God" (Hein 2005, 565). His decisions, behavior, and counseling style were inspiring to some, eliciting strong allegiance to, and confidence in, him. They were a caution to uncertain others. Especially in a storefront setting of faith leadership, "in pastoral care, who the minister is has much more significance than how he goes about counseling. His love for his people motivates him to . . . search out the most effective procedure for the communication" they share with affiliates (Oglesby 1973, 326; see also Andrews 2002).

At his best, Pastor Marshall valued

> the thoughtfulness inherent in inviting multiple sources of support to work together, including the family and other organizations involved with the addict, to create the kind of community of recovery that offers stability to both addict and family. [It includes] locating strengths and assets in the system rather than focusing exclusively on a deficits approach [which] seems compatible with a "searching and fearless moral inventory" (Fourth Step of AA), including an inventory of assets as well as liabilities. (Roth 2010, 2)

Consistent with Roth (2010), Pastor Marshall's commitment to and recognition of the interdependence of these healings in recovery were among the most valued aspects of the interactions between him and those in pastoral counseling. According to Doehring (1992, 25), "where the chain of being is hierarchical and oppressive," therapeutic goals are to empower and liberate the care seeker. The degree to which this or any similar therapeutic motive guided Pastor Marshall is unclear, and this may not have been the foundation of health service provision at the FACTS Ministries. Still, pastoral therapy services did provide affiliates with access to a resource toward well-being and sustained sobriety.

Nutritional/Meal-Based Support Domain

The North Lawson neighborhood has been a "food desert" (Krohn 2013, 97) since at least the mid-1990s, when the last grocery store closed along the Akron Avenue corridor, two blocks north of where the Ministries would locate a few years later. Regarding the role of food in resilience and health outcomes, culturally grounded education for food production is being valued in substance use recovery and in other health recovery in new and important ways. Among treatment center clients, research is showing that food production is among the "community health programs that will increase the likelihood that they will maintain their sobriety" (Krohn 2013, 98). Improved access to quality calories can be a beneficial boost to sobriety and other health outcomes. Prior research has noted a relationship between concentrated poverty, addiction, and food insecurity (Chilton and Booth 2007; Krohn 2013). In a sample of women using a food pantry, "the experience of hunger . . . was also related to eating poorly [and] with extreme circumstances [including] periods of homelessness and drug addiction" (Chilton and Booth 2007, 119; see also Strike et al. 2012). Among these struggles to sustain recovery, "the competing demands of addiction and subsistence represent a daily struggle, wherein eating a nutritionally adequate diet may not always be a priority" (Strike et al. 2012, 2). The Ministries' nutritional/meal-based resources are a collaboration of several organizations and people, including: the anchor churches' monetary donations; two chain restaurants that donate food; volunteers from the neighborhood, anchor churches, CA, and the Ministries' sober homes program, who staff these community meals. Health provider volunteers periodically make nutritional counseling, obesity, high blood pressure, and pre-diabetes screenings. Because "church leaders can play a significant role in making some desirable changes in food habits" (Pawlak and Colby 2009, 62), the Ministries recognized the importance of improving affiliate relationships to food. The twice-weekly community lunches, monthly Men's Prayer Breakfasts, informal/periodic food bank, and annual Thanksgiving Day meals were the on-site means to help them do so.

On Tuesdays and Thursdays, food was served at noon, and the line for the meals often began forming just after 11:00 a.m. On a typical day, forty to one hundred mostly local residents came, many of whom walked to the chapel. Numbers fluctuated dramatically, informed by end-of-month budgets and other financial strains. Most weeks, about three out of every five lunch patrons were African American men. Toward the end of each month, more women and diverse younger people arrived. Both patrons and volunteers often described the atmosphere at the lunches as "family-like" and "welcoming with lots of loving grace" and other similar expressions. As one volunteer noted:

> When I was in the kitchen, I met with a female who told me that she was once a crack addict and at one point was living on the street. Like the pastor, she too was not shy of her past. She was willing to share it freely with me, a complete stranger. This reaffirms my belief that the individuals who volunteer and come around, view [FACTS Ministries] as a safe space where they can be open and honest. She seemed to be content with where she is and how she managed to come to this point in her life where she can help other people who were like her and make their day better simply by cooking a fresh meal.

Consistent with these frequent displays of resilience, lunches are also a time when other health resources are made available. A volunteer observed on her third visit to help prepare and serve,

> When the break between the first and second helping came, I went into the dining room and *saw a doctor in the room*. He stated that he goes around to organizations like this to give a medical exam, including a check of one's blood pressure and their general physical condition to anyone who wants one. He said he is a retired surgeon and enjoys meeting individuals [and having] experiences at community-based help organizations like this.

Even though "every once in a while an individual will come in drunk or high when trying to get food, volunteers don't necessarily look down upon them, but they [aren't] happy that individual is around in that state. Many of the individuals there though [seem] to be down on their luck and [aren't] afraid to plainly show it on their faces or in their actions" (volunteer field notes, October 2012). The lunches are spaces of good food and good fellowship—quality exchanges of resources among lunch patrons, volunteers, Ministries leadership, and others in attendance. Lunches also provided access to free health-care services and referrals to further health services for those whose health screening information warranted them. Such screenings and other direct health services informed how the lunches contributed to healing Ministries affiliates and all in attendance.

The third Saturday of the month Men's Prayer Breakfasts were small, intimate gatherings of twenty to twenty-five men that began Saturday mornings at 8:00 a.m. For these mostly neighborhood men of all ages, the breakfasts served as a place to share food, fellowship, and faith-based, health-affirming moments. "Social support plays an important role in maintaining psychological wellbeing" (Pidd, Roche, and Fischer 2015, 357), and the spaces of male-centered caring the breakfasts provided were especially valuable. Residents of the Ministries' sober home next door were often the first to arrive to prepare the breakfast and greet others as they arrived. With the help of volunteers, sober homes residents also cleaned up afterward. Persons in recovery are most often understood as recipients of services in treatment settings. As Pagano, Post, and Johnson (2011, 23) noted, "the helper therapy principle (HTP) observes the helper's health benefits derived from helping another with a shared malady [and] is embodied by the program of Alcoholics Anonymous" (see also Padfield and Pagano 2018; Riessman 1965). This principle informs all mutual support groups, including other 12-Step fellowships like the Either-Or meetings of CA. The Men's Prayer Breakfasts were a way for men to be in sacred service to other men in an equity of shared health and well-being, a concept that was prevalent throughout Ministries health services.

The prayer breakfasts encourage those in attendance to shift their understanding of Saturday morning to a time of waking up to a valued responsibility and expected health fellowship, rather than "coming to" from a stupor of active addiction. The breakfasts place value on the shared leadership of a guest speaker, often vesting respect and active listening in their testimony regarding traditional leadership as men of faith. However minor, the breakfasts challenge gender roles of who cooks, does dishes, or vacuums: all tasks, from the preparing a meal to closing and locking up the building, were carried out by the male residents and volunteers as part of their nurturing a healthy, sober self.

Finally, the annual Thanksgiving Day meal also provides an opportunity to engage in food- and family-centered mutual support. What began as a shared potluck meal to precede the Thursday night Either-Or meetings on that Thursday holiday (2006–08) became a Ministries-sponsored holiday extension of the community lunches (2009 forward). The family-like atmosphere was always more visible during the Thanksgiving meals, with special attention given to child-centered activities (e.g., coloring and craft activities to adorn the placemats) and family take-home meal plates a priority for all those in attendance. While the politics of food access and related inequalities were never addressed (e.g., Parson 2014), this omission was consistent with most Ministries health programming, which most often acted as if the "good works" of faith were apolitical exercises in charity, rather than a place where the personal and the political meet.

Youth/Developmental Preventive Domain

In addition to its adult health resources, the FACTS Ministries also valued the health of youth. Developmental and preventive youth health initiatives were a collaboration of volunteers from the anchor church, two other churches, and the North Lawson neighborhood. Consistent with its mission as a social ecology of resilience, the Ministries believe resilience can be learned through developmental strategies and preventive actions (Walsh 2003). This learning is especially true and necessary among youth, including youth being reared in environments of concentrated disadvantage (Forrest-Bank et al. 2015; Williams and Bryan 2013). Youth would accompany adults at the community lunches, CA meetings, Sunday services, Men's Prayer Breakfasts, and Thanksgiving Day meals. The Ministries' developmental health focus also included a year-round boxing club, Friday Youth Nights during the late spring and summer months, and an annual summer Bible study youth camp. Though too often understood stereotypically, there is much truth to the perception that "in inner city slums fighting was a necessity not only for survival, but [also] as a psychological release and a form of expression as youths and adults fought others and a frustrating, unintelligible system" (Gems 2004, 89; see also Morton, O'Reilly, and O'Brien 2016). The boxing club was an asset for North Lawson boys.

Under the leadership of Pastor Marshall, the youth boxing club, Fists of Faith, connected religion and sports. More than seven hundred churches nationwide have incorporated boxing and mixed martial arts "into their ministry in some capacity" (Borer and Schafer 2011, 167). Fists of Faith was an off-site collaboration with the neighborhood recreation center. The center was willing to donate space and to help facilitate donations for purchasing equipment the young men used for their sparring. The club was initiated in late 2007 when one of the young single mothers who attended Ministries Sunday services asked Pastor Marshall what to do to help curb her young son's increasingly volatile behavior. The mother was in search of an activity that might help reduce the difficulties her son was having in school and address the related risks of gang activity and drug sales that were part of their family business. At the same time, Pastor Marshall was interested in returning to the sport he had had some success with as a youth at the Golden Gloves level and in his twenties while serving in the military. These factors combined with his desire to respond to his own growing weight problem and related health challenges. Upon this mother's request, Marshall began a boxing initiative he had been thinking about as an after-school outreach program for North Lawson youth. At the neighborhood recreation center a few blocks west of the Ministries, eight to ten boys, aged eight to sixteen, began coming together twice a week to develop skills in the "sweet science" of boxing.

By summer 2008, Pastor Marshall had secured consistent gym space and funding for equipment rentals. Fists of Faith became a consistent, three-days-a-week after-school program. It provided pro-social, extracurricular mentoring through sport, where boxing techniques were partnered with biblical references to battle and the preparation process to pursue victory. Boxing club participants learned to compete in a sport with deep historical roots. Not only did the local area have a strong boxing history, but Pastor Marshall had a personal connection to a famous fighter, a prize-winning boxer and family friend who taught him the sport. This led him to include boxing as a central part of his military service. As older boxers supported the growth of the younger boxers, peer mentoring developed among participants both within and outside of family ties. The resulting character building, sportsmanship, discipline, and improved self-worth helped to reduce risk behaviors, not only for the young man whose mother had made the original appeal to Pastor Marshall but also to several other boys willing to engage in the training and skill building of the sport. The young men were able to move from the training regimen to regular sparring, and then to neighborhood boxing matches with other recreation center competitors nearby. Ministries affiliates who followed the sport stated prior to an Either-Or CA meeting that three Fists of Faith boxers had begun to participate in formal amateur fights.

The main successes of the boxing initiative included: prevention as a pro-social option for youth athletics; nutritional assistance for fight preparation and other related obesity-risk-reducing activities; organizational collaborations for increased funding, space, and related resources for the gym, equipment, and training supports; and mentoring and other productive youth boxing supports from sober homes residents. For the men who assisted Pastor Marshall, there were beneficial secondary benefits. One was on disability and two others experienced long-term unemployment and had limited job prospects due to the nature of their criminal record and work history. Examples of their improved self-worth were quite clear, reflected in their increased willingness to speak at CA meetings, to be of service at the Men's Prayer Breakfasts and elsewhere at the Ministries, and to participate actively in their own programs of recovery.

The other primary youth-centered, faith-health initiative at the FACTS Ministries, the Friday Youth Nights, took place during the late spring and summer months. The Ministries' community room was made available to children and youth of all ages from the neighborhood. Twelve to twenty youth came on a regular basis. Activities included day care for toddlers to early adolescents, youth Bible camp, family-friendly movie night, and youth workshops on substance use prevention and self-worth in faith. From Play-Doh and coloring books to faith in movement exercises, from efforts to avoid neighborhood bullying to guest youth pastors discussing emotional well-being in a youth-accessible content ("What do you do when you feel this way?")—these Friday nights were a time for fruit, popcorn, and hot dogs, preceded by words of prayer. Each youth night began with a "call to caring in God's Grace" prayer for one's faith, health, and safety. One of the older adolescents was asked to lead those in attendance in saying grace prior to the food being served. Each youth night ended with a "call to caring until we meet again" for the faith and health of each youth and their family. The call to caring was especially moving for many youths who were coming to an understanding of what it meant to have a parent in active addiction and beginning to realize the importance of support they could receive for their own well-being through the family's affiliation with the Ministries.

The opportunity for safe, free evening neighborhood day care during these summer months helped to spread the Ministries' name, along with the opportunity for church volunteers to build up skills that could improve their employability. Several women affiliates of the primary anchor church of the Ministries regularly volunteered, along with Ministries-affiliated women in recovery. Men from the sober home next door were available to help with any "heavy lifting" tasks and security. Two of them often read to the youngest children and responded supportively to any boisterous behavior that arose. Special attention was given to the children with a parent or other family member in an especially severe or uncertain place in their active addiction or vulnerable sobriety. The "16 Prevention Principles" of the National Institute on Drug Abuse (NIDA) and the NIH (NIDA 2003) or any of their related curricula were not a part of Ministries youth nights. Promoting critical awareness of substance use, law enforcement inequalities, or the school-to-prison pipeline was not either. Still, they provided a pro-social environment for faith-affiliated personal and family health and youth resilience.

Other Health and Resilience Resources

Additional health resources at the FACTS Ministries included a women's faith wellness group, men's workout group, and on-site screenings from and referrals to one of the three health-care outlets in the neighborhood. In the fall of 2010, the Ministries hosted a Women of Faith and Wellness event to celebrate the faith and good works of North Lawson women and to initiate a women's health initiative at the Ministries. It was one of the few events where Cheryl, Pastor Marshall's wife, provided visible, substantive leadership. At the event, awards were given and speakers provided inspirational messages. The organizers prioritized bringing added attention to, and addressing, health inequities and the role of faith leadership collaborations—led by African American women—in doing so. As one African American woman attendee recalls,

> I remember enjoying the program, and the music was good. But the wellness piece? Not so much. . . . I do remember questioning whether it was well-spent time and effort. I don't remember any moments of great inspired unity. Rather, it was more about maintaining [Cheryl's] position. I guess she couldn't allow other women in what was totally her domain. Even when we began "Resilient Moms, Healthy Kids" [a follow-up youth initiative established at a nearby church] I never saw Cheryl again. . . . Unfortunately, women's wellness is not all that salient to me about that day.

Two other women who also attended the event and were asked about their experiences of it echoed a similar sentiment. The event apparently was not given the opportunity to have "legs" of sustained participation and leadership, so no women-centered initiatives followed. Because the North Lawson neighborhood is recognized as having one of the worst infant mortality rates of all neighborhoods in the city, the need for targeted initiatives was apparent. However, despite this recognition by Ministries leadership, the event lacked a life course approach that placed value on the importance of prenatal health as a vital starting point to the health and well-being of mothers, children, families, and the community. Many participants and event organizers went on to lead several funded initiatives, sponsored by units of the local state university and a philanthropic organization that funded intergenerational, healthy child initiatives. The FACTS Ministries played no part in any of them. The Women of Faith and Wellness event was one of a few at the Ministries that valued, yet also seemed to fear, women's visibility and leadership. Two other efforts at collaboration with the Ministries leadership were briefly initiated by a nearby woman pastor. Neither proceeded because, as Brown (1997, 73) has noted, "in order for womanist thought to survive as a viable transformative agent in the lives of African American women [and others, organizers] must develop methods of sharing womanist perspectives with . . . 'ordinary' African American women, families, churches, and community organizations." When efforts to develop and respectfully collaborate with those womanist methods are not made, possible initiatives quickly wither.

From Du Bois (1903) to Lincoln and Mamiya (1990) to Taylor, Chatters, and Levin (2004), prior research has demonstrated that "the Black Church created a dialogic relationship between black women's faith and secular social activism" (Barber 2015, 251). This dialogic relationship was present, though muted, at the FACTS Ministries. How much that both could contribute to the improved health of women affiliates and the Ministries as a whole seemed uncertain much of the time. The women's wellness event was one of several at the Ministries on the dividing line of what could be characterized as a feminist or womanist avoidance. Selective inattention by Ministries leadership (i.e., Pastor Marshall and the board) coupled with a traditionalist-driven silencing of faith-centered Black women regarding tensions of women-centered leadership were present, though largely unspoken (see chapter 5). Though the theme does not resonate in the memory of several participants, women's wellness initiatives were designed to be a part of the event and to contribute to the Ministries' larger health mission. As another example, an Akron Avenue Faith Alliance, led by two women pastors of two other neighborhood congregations, grew out of their fellowship at the Ministries-hosted women's wellness event. Through the alliance, they engaged in other, interdependent initiatives, such as writing for a community newsletter, contributing to a small-scale local development collaboration, and church-sponsored prayer walks. No FACTS Ministries affiliates were a part of these activities.

Among the other health and resilience resources of the Ministries, around the time of the women's wellness event, three sober homes residents put together a workout space in the garage next to the Ministries' parking lot. Darnell was in his fifties, African American, disabled, and small-town born and raised. He was one of the many affiliates who had a complicated family history, with generations of addiction. Donald was in his twenties, White, fully able-bodied, and suburban born and raised. He had what he described as "an uncomplicated family history" with very little active addiction across generations. Though there was never a formal mentor-mentee program arrangement among sober homes residents, several of the men participated in and valued informal mentoring situations. The friendship between Darnell and Donald was one of them, and the workout initiative extended from it.

On Saturday mornings after the Either-Or CA meetings, Darnell and Donald would lead all who cared to join them in a workout regimen. They jokingly called it "The Crackhead Workout: From getting' lit to gettin' your lift on." As one participant put it,

> It was good to join the men to, you know, deal with the aging thing, and move our health to a whole other level. For real, we were just gettin' together to be healthier. The garage is a matchbox [i.e., small and hot]. The crackheads and hoes and other folks up the alley are more of a distraction than they should be. The equipment? Nothin' fancy. But it works, and we're gettin' there. It's the fellowship and the faith that does it.

After several years of regular but unsteady workouts and fellowship, the men's workout group waned. Donald had been struggling with sustaining his sobriety across those years, cycling into, out of, and back into the Ministries' sober home next door. Darnell and the other men continued the workouts. After his return from his relapses, and through his challenges, each time Donald returned to the newcomer sober home and the workout group. After Donald's final relapse and overdose death in 2015, the group declined. As one regular participant said,

> When Donald left that last time, and went back to ol' girl and all that, it kinda put everyone out of sorts. For him to end up

> dead a couple months later, right around the corner in one of those abandos, was just . . . just . . . real tough for everyone. Still is. [Long pause] For all of us to go from the Faygo-Grippo diet [i.e., eating junk food and little else during a "dope binge" of active addiction] some of us had been on, to workouts on Saturday mornings after Either-Or was all good. Hopefully, we'll pick it up again.

Health referrals are another, visible health service available through the Ministries. Consistent with the health professional visits and screenings that periodically occurred during the community lunches, the health-care outlets were conveniently located within a mile of the Ministries, and referrals to them were made often. Holden and her colleagues (2012, 63) stated, "The social determinants unique to African-American men's health contribute to limited access and utilization of health and mental health care services and can have a deleterious effect on their overall health and well-being [and] health-seeking behaviors." Among the poorest Ministries affiliates both before and after the passage of the Affordable Care Act (ACA), though free "community commitment" health services were not officially available, uninsured affiliates had consistent health screening access. As one example, Jess had not had any dental or medical care of any kind for over six years. He was many pounds overweight and came from a family with a long history of heart maladies. His father and an older brother both had died from heart attacks at a young age. Through his affiliation with the Ministries, and prior to the ACA being signed into law, Jess gained access to a heart health assessment that demonstrated compromised heart functioning and the need to have a procedure. A medical doctor on the FACTS Ministries board arranged for Jess to undergo the necessary procedure at a globally recognized health facility nearby. Another affiliate, Carla, also gained access to a health service through the Ministries. Together with her teenage daughter, who had a two-year-old child, Carla participated in a "toddler health" initiative operated by the nearby satellite facility of the local children's hospital. She then shared this information with a neighbor who was in a similar situation with her daughter and grandchild. Carla's neighbor and her neighbor's daughter affiliated with the Ministries for a short period. While the specific details varied, situations like those of Jess and Carla occur frequently among Ministries affiliates.

A women's clinic is also nearby. It shared a curious tension of access and mission with the Ministries. It offers family planning services, valuing a woman's right to choose her relationship to a present or potential pregnancy. Ministries leadership did not articulate a position on these services. Informally, family members of Ministries leadership and others displayed open hostility toward a clinic volunteer who came to barbeque fundraising events. Others displayed tacit ambivalence and made occasional remarks indicating they were not in favor of a woman's right to choose. Still, throughout the years of the project, women's clinic brochures were frequently displayed on the information handout table in the Ministries' chapel.

Mental and behavioral health referrals were made regularly as well. A satellite office of the County Community Mental Health Program was close by, and several affiliates were clients. Through the local community college, at least three longtime Ministries affiliates were paid interns in the facility's training program. At least two were also taking classes to become a drug and alcohol specialist and licensed practical therapist. The Ministries had a behavioral health screening process for its sober homes program. While Either-Or CA meeting attendance by sober homes residents seemed largely unchanged by this access, health outcomes from these behavioral health referrals included: (1) improved mental and behavioral health professional access, as well as improved referral efficiency during the time the newcomer sober house next door had a house manager employed; (2) fewer calls to, and responses from, the police for frantic or other moments of intense breakdown at any of the three sober homes; and (3) greater participation in the Men's Prayer Breakfasts and Sunday services by newer residents. Reduced cigarette smoking, greater work regularity, improved family relationships and other outcomes also seemed to be associated with resilience from these behavioral health referrals.

Conclusions

The five health service domains of the FACTS Ministries analyzed here are valuable resources in the lives of Ministries affiliates. Each is a vital aspect of the ethnogenic thread that helps refine a communal social structure and collective ethos among domain affiliates. This ethos in turn helps individual and neighborhood stigma and alienation (e.g., prior addiction, high poverty, health disparities) become assets for improved health and other life-affirming outcomes. Studies of health care and patient relationships to it have often found clients more satisfied with religious alternatives (e.g., Levin 2014a). Yet, even in a state that has prioritized faith-based community initiatives, quoting a state-level liaison, "When faith-based substances abuse treatment providers were brought together none of them knew each other [or] talked to one another" (Sager 2012, 69). This lack of basic cohesion among them likely reduced the potential contributions any one of the organizations was able to make.

Still, in the African American church tradition, and as summarized in table 1, the FACTS Ministries functions largely as a social service and therapeutic system (e.g., Barnes 2005; Gilkes 1980). It is a community organization that provides resources to help people improve their health and resilience. As Wulff, Donato, and Lurie (2015, 363) have noted, at its core, "resilience embodies a vision of healthy individuals and thriving communities, and a resilience-centered framework provides concrete actions people, organizations, and institutions can take to promote the sustainable and long-term well-being of communities in the face of adversity" (see also Ungar, Ghazinour, and Richter 2013). In a neighborhood like North Lawson, with an underdeveloping history characterized by concentrated disadvantage, that resilience-centered framework is reflected in the resources of its faith-based and other community organizations, including the Ministries. Though recovery was its core health focus, over time a diversity of services were provided, cultivating a social ecology of resilience and health.

Holly Matto (2004, 12) stated that in spaces of recovery, "individuals may experience heightened sociological ambivalence or cultural cognitive dissonance . . . a disequilibrium [that] can foster growth, or alternatively can lead an individual toward" destructive outcomes. Responding to that disequilibrium to foster growth, the FACTS Ministries rests in the collaborations and resources that contribute to a neighborhood and community organization of healing and change, where the shared goals of an enriched faith and a sustained sobriety are. W. E. B. Du Bois (1904, 292) suggested leadership begins from "the solidarity of human interests [and] desire to do good [because] the causes and incentives to human advance when the advance of all depends increasingly on the advance of each." At their best, each health service domain valued this Du Boisian sensibility and was the most consistent means of its resilience mission. Their visibilities and community accessibility led to other events that further enriched the FACTS Ministries.

A social ecology of resilience requires multiple domains of possible healing, with each domain helping to improve the quality of care, increase affiliate numbers, engage newcomers, and sustain long-term affiliates. According to Rebecca Sager (2012, 19), who has analyzed state-level variations of faith-based initiatives, there has been "a culture shift . . . refram[ing] the debate surrounding church and state to one about cooperation, collaboration, and institutionalization rather than one about separation." As this chapter has shown, these health domains and the healing they provide operate at individual, family, organizational, and community levels. At each, collaboration matters. Multiple levels of government have important roles to play in order for long-term, equitable community well-being to be sustained (see chapter 7). Some argue that "collaborative relationships between government and faith-based groups nurture civic engagement and highlight the benefits of recruiting efforts from the faith-based sector" (Sager 2012, 13–14). Other nongovernmental, secular collaborations also inform the contributions faith-based organizations can make. These organizational relationships are among the sometimes tense, dissonant dialogues many faith-based groups participate in. Chapter 4 explores one of the FACTS Ministries' most vital collaborations with Cocaine Anonymous. Their collaboration was among its most consistent and most troubled, as it enriched a resilience mission they shared.

PART 2

HURT: DISSONANT DIALOGUES OF RESILIENCE

Chapter 4

Uncertain Sanctuary

The Ministries' Collaboration with Cocaine Anonymous

> Developing strong, transparent partnerships across the board, at the organization, community [and other] levels . . . and greater coalition functioning are all supports for sustainment. Indigenous communities [have] demonstrated that when this type of capacity building framework is used, it can enhance the chance of program sustainment success. Partnerships and study of those partnerships between intervention and service delivery . . . and their communities hold great promise for effective program sustainment.
>
> —Hodge and Turner 2016, 203

A social ecology of health and resilience must be a space of shared mission, where individuals and organizations with similar motivations come together. This chapter explores the FACTS Ministries' affiliation with the local chapter of Cocaine Anonymous (CA), the Ministries' most consistent on-site organizational interaction. In the context of Hodge and Turner's (2016) consideration of resources most consistent with sustainment, even at its peak, the affiliation between the Ministries and CA could not have been characterized with words like "partnership," "coalition," or "collaboration." When it worked, collective efforts of these two organizations sustained a social ecology of resilience—one in which abstinence from cocaine and all other mind-altering substances and a program of health and recovery were enriched by the presence of, and participation in, CA meetings at the Ministries. The ultimate decline of their affiliation resulted from Ministries leadership challenges that slowly fractured the ability of the affiliation to be sustained.

The Substance Abuse Recovery and Sober Homes Program composes one of the five core domains of health services offered at the Ministries (see chapter 3). An essential aspect of this domain was the CA meetings hosted twice a week. The Ministries' affiliation with CA began when Pastor Ellwyn Marshall requested to host a CA meeting. Ministries affiliate Carla (the first of the two Either-Or CA affiliates profiled in chapter 1) was doing CA service work in the early years of her sobriety. Sober for over twenty years at the time of her interview in 2014, Carla stated that in August 2000, she was there when Pastor Marshall attended a district meeting of each of the city-level CA meeting group service representatives (GSRs) of the local district. Described by Pastor Marshall in a very similar way, according to Carla, at that meeting Marshall "asked that his meeting at the FACTS Ministries be put on [CA's] district meeting schedule." After discussion, the CA GSRs took a vote with a quorum present, and a substance abuse recovery meeting was formally established as a CA meeting at the Ministries. Pastor Marshall was given meeting materials and received instructions on CA protocol. The new recovery meeting at the Ministries was put on the district schedule for that month. With this shared decision-making, a mutually beneficial affiliation between the two organizations began.

The Ministries' CA meeting was named "Either-Or" to remind members of the sober choice for sustained abstinence they had to make anew each day. Pastor Marshall knew the value of appealing to Cocaine Anonymous, the smaller but well-established recovery fellowship in the city, if the Ministries' mission was to succeed. Pastor Marshall's motives for reaching out to CA included the shared value of healing beyond harm and stigma and moving from a place of health-compromising active addiction, first to a place of unhealthy sober shame and at some point—in a sober future—to an empowered collective of active, long-term recovery. From its origin, surrounded by trap houses and the regular open-air drug sales of the North Lawson neighborhood (see chapter 2), Pastor Marshall hoped that the Ministries would be strengthened by working with an organization that directly addressed substance use of "cocaine and all other mind-altering substances" (Cocaine Anonymous 2018, 5). CA had proven its effectiveness for decades. As noted in this portion of CA's Step 1, CA is *not* a substance-specific fellowship. Stigmas vary in severity, and the Black-"crackhead" identity intersection of stigma is especially severe (e.g., Briggs 2012). Compared to other 12-Step fellowships, CA effectiveness includes its willingness to more openly address the lived experiences and recovery consequences of the racialized stigma of crack cocaine and other highly charged aspects of substance use with more openness and empathetic care (e.g., Boeri 2018; Cheney et al. 2014; Humphreys 2004). The Ministries was unique in its willingness to embrace that heightened stigma in its motives for CA affiliation, in particular. As reflected in Carla's experiences, "advice to the stigmatized often deals quite candidly with the part of his life that he feels is most private and shameful; his most deeply hidden sores are touched on and examined. [Yet] the most private and embarrassing is the most collective, for the stigmatized individual's deepest feelings are made of just the stuff members of his category present in a well-rounded version" (Goffman [1963] 1986, 112). For affiliates of a faith-based community health organization that visibly prioritizes overcoming a highly charged stigma to sustain sobriety, a 12-Step collaboration with CA made good sense.

A shared respect of mission and adherence to protocol are fundamental to sustained collaboration between any two organizations. The Ministries' collaboration with CA extended from long-standing resource sharing for mutual benefit. First once, then after a few years, twice each week, a healing circle of CA affiliates contributed to the Ministries by enriching the faith-health relationship at the core of its spiritual things (see chapter 3). In turn, the Ministries contributed to Cocaine Anonymous at the district level. Other benefits of the Ministries-CA resource exchange included increased opportunities for engaging in readings and rituals that would reinforce recovery, as well as more chances for affiliates to be of service in diverse ways and to be more civically engaged. Furthermore, the shared resources allowed those at the Ministries who had a longer and more diverse sober history to access a broader network of personal contacts for education and other skill building, job and housing opportunities, and other vital resources.

At the organizational level and consistent with Hodge and Turner (2016) quoted in the opening to this chapter, from the eighteenth-century origin of Native American recovery circles to today, mutual aid societies have been exchanging resources with other organizations for improved health and other shared benefits (White 1996). Among African Americans, research on the relationship between faith identity and individual and community health dates back at least to 1906, with Du Bois's *The Health and Physique of the Negro American*. In it, he called attention to "the formation of local health leagues among Colored people for the dissemination of better knowledge of sanitation and preventive medicine" (Du Bois 1906, 110). At that time African American "health professionals, hospitals, churches, and civic organizations cooperated in a variety of efforts to improve the health status of black Americans [and] spawned two events that constitute the origins of National Negro Health Week" (Quinn and Thomas 2001, 45). The living legacy of those historical collaborations includes the affiliation between the FACTS Ministries and Cocaine Anonymous. As prior research has noted, "effective church-based community health programs must take a holistic approach when dealing with health problems among African Americans. [They] must also ensure the complete involvement of clergy and church members, thereby engendering a sense of partnership in the process" (Sanders 1997, 373). Consistent with the National Negro Health Week history, the presence of CA at the Ministries was a safe space to support sobriety, resilience, and health.

The first CA meeting hosted by the Ministries occurred on a Saturday in August 2000. For the first few weeks, the meetings were at a formative stage. Attendance fluctuated. Sometimes only two or three people came; at other times up to fifteen came. Over time, as word spread, stable attendance increased, programming and resources grew, and the format of the meetings was consistent. Soon, a Thursday night meeting was added. The two CA meetings (Saturday morning and Thursday night) became reciprocally beneficial, reinforcing each other's viability and visibility. Given the CA-approved readings and protocol carried out in these newly launched meetings, as in all CA meetings, experiences of trauma that CA affiliates shared and the empathy they expressed and responded with were consistently of far greater depth and detail than those offered in the Ministries chapel during Sunday services.

Central to active addiction is the disbelief in and rejection of the resilience of recovery, since "long-term substance abuse gradually disempowers and induces learned helplessness that makes those who struggle . . . decide that they cannot be successful in their efforts to eliminate substances from their lives" (Washington and Moxley 2003, 147). It is a sentiment of dismissal and desperation, with no hope for the possibility of a life different from that of active addiction, familiar and uncomfortable. As one approaches a "bottom," the life spiral of a learned helplessness is the most familiar repetition. One lives a chaotic repetition of punishment and reward that, to many, is a necessary part of trauma and growth toward sustained affiliation with a social ecology of health and resilience. The turnaround can begin when desperation turns to actions of fellowship and when one engages with others without judging oneself or others and values the collaborative first word of the First Step in the program of recovery: "We."

CA affiliates begin by taking the First Step: "We admitted we were powerless over cocaine *and all other mind-altering substances*—that our lives had become unmanageable" (Cocaine Anonymous 2018, 6; italics added). With that acceptance each affiliate chooses to value CA. The following section describes Either-Or CA meetings at the Ministries when things worked, as they did, for several years of the Ministries' affiliation with CA in the city.

Sacred Repetitions of Resilience

Of the three most recognized 12-Step recovery organizations, CA was then and is now far smaller than Alcoholics Anonymous (AA) and Narcotics Anonymous (NA) (Laudet 2008). CA also has the greater diversity (i.e., more people of color affiliates, greater balance between women and men, and more consistent leadership with both diversities) than AA and NA. CA began in 1982 in Hollywood, California. Meetings are held in most US states and in many other countries in addition to ongoing online meetings. CA respects the larger "parent" fellowship of AA and the "cousin" fellowship of NA. The reasoning behind AA's substance-specific approach is to make sure to keep alcoholism "relentlessly in the foreground, [or else] other issues will usurp everybody's attention" (Vaillant 2002, F12). Too often, the "singleness of purpose" doctrine of AA (Alcoholics Anonymous 2001) has led some AA members to scold anyone who speaks of substances other than alcohol in AA meetings and has minimized the complexities of multiple addictions, gender differences, or other aspects of difference that are often silenced yet warrant deeper consideration (see chapter 5).

Like many organizations that value shared space, 12-Step meetings and the churches that host them establish a wide range of relationships with each other. For some churches, 12-Step meetings are little more than tenants-at-a-distance that may receive a reduced rental rate from church charity. For other churches, they are partners of "identity in [an] empathic community" (Waters 2015, 769), with a division of labor in a mission they share. The organizational relationships are fluid, uncertain, and characterized by a sense of safe space. Together, they create and sustain a valuable environment of support for spiritual progress and improved health. Sustaining a safe space is essential when linking social and ecological systems as one system for resilience in addiction recovery (Dossett 2017; Laudet 2008). Resilient "microsystems represent activities, roles, and interpersonal relations where the developing person is directly involved with particular physical and material features like the . . . neighbourhood or church" (Ungar, Ghazinour, and Richter 2013, 352; see also Flores 2013; Morell 1996).

The FACTS Ministries is a product of the Black faith socialization of its pastoral leadership and many of its long-term affiliates (see introduction). It shaped the images on the walls, including one stating, "All men fall, but great men get back up." This placard is right next to a composite image containing bust drawings of Malcolm X as a symbol of faith-driven sobriety, along with Rev. Dr. Martin Luther King Jr., South African president Nelson Mandela, and Hon. Marcus Moziah Garvey. The social ecology of resilience at the Ministries is reflected in the music heard during choir rehearsal as the Praise and Worship Team (PWT) rehearsed prior to the Thursday night Either-Or meetings, with songs conjuring Shirley Caesar, Hezekiah Walker, and others. It is in the call-and-response patterns of signifying in Black culture and fellowship that often permeate Sunday services at the Ministries and Either-Or meetings (Hall 1997; Lincoln and Mamiya 1990). These culturally anchored violations of the one-voice, "one-meeting" expectation of much of 12-Step fellowship are in the mm-hms and the yep, yeps and praise laughter central to the church testimony and recovery shares. The ecology is also reflected in the handshakes and hugs, the bodily adornment among the diverse women and men who come, the (dread)locks of several young Black men in attendance. Perhaps most importantly, the Ministries' social ecology of resilience can be felt in the demonstrated commitment of those who attend the meetings, assuring their continuing presence and possibilities.

Among the vital features in the rooms of recovery is the ritual of listening to the readings and contemplating the narratives they provide. In CA, the approved literature and primary texts that outline its program of recovery are the Big Book and *Twelve Steps and Twelve Traditions* of Alcoholics Anonymous, from which approved adaptations are selected. Through the readings and other meeting rituals, those of service engage in governance to further the "common welfare" of Tradition 1. Service is reflected in the chair, secretary, and group service representative (GSR), along with the readers and greeters, the coffee maker, and the post-meeting cleanup crew. While secretary and GSR positions typically serve for months or years at a time, meeting chairs generally rotated monthly when the

CA-Ministries affiliation was functioning well. These service roles renew investment in a personal and communal resilience and in the health and recovery for those in attendance, for the fellowship and the host site.

As in all 12-Step fellowships, Either-Or CA meetings at the Ministries begin with the chair opening the meeting saying, "Welcome to the Either-Or meeting of Cocaine Anonymous. My name is _______ and I am an addict." Following the call-and-response church tradition, all those in attendance respond in unison, "Hi, _______," sharing their greeting with the chair. The chair then reads the Preamble of the fellowship out loud:

> Cocaine Anonymous is a fellowship of men and women who share their experience, strength, and hope with each other that they may solve their common problem and help others to recovery from their addiction. The only requirement for membership is the desire to stop using cocaine and all other mind-altering substances. There are no dues or fees for membership; we are fully self-supporting through our own contributions. We are not allied with any sect, denomination, politics, organization, or institution. We do not wish to engage in any controversy and we neither endorse nor oppose any causes. Our primary purpose is to stay free from cocaine and all other mind-altering substances, and to help others achieve the same freedom. We use the Twelve Step Recovery Program, because it has already been proven that the Twelve Step Recovery Program works. (Cocaine Anonymous 2018, 5)

The Preamble expresses the norms and values of CA at the core of its social ecology. These permeate every meeting and transcend timing uncertainties, since "assessing attributions of recovery is a complex task, particularly in regard to the timing of when the improvement is measured, when recovery is determined, and when individuals are asked to identify the contributions of various factors to their recovery" (Flynn et al. 2003, 407, 408). Despite these and other attribution uncertainties, the Preamble is valued as an important repetition, assisting in the enrichment of another sober day.

At Either-Or CA meetings, the readings that follow the Preamble and their sequence are valued as a helpful part of the meeting, the fellowship, and the Ministries. "How It Works" follows first, read to the group by a willing affiliate. This is the seminal reading from the Big Book that lays out the basic details of the 12-Steps program. This reading is adapted from chapter 5 of the Big Book of Alcoholics Anonymous: "Rarely have we seen a person fail who has thoroughly followed our path" (Alcoholics Anonymous 2001, 58), it begins. It ends with three vital reminders of the role of spirituality, a necessary faith in a power greater than the person in recovery, and the need to call upon that power as essential in one's process of recovery. After "How It Works," the Twelve Traditions are read out loud by another willing affiliate. The Traditions place the individually oriented program of the 12 Steps in their collective context of Tradition One: "Our common welfare should come first; personal recovery depends upon CA unity." For CA, this unity "is the most cherished quality our Society has. Our lives, the lives of all to come, depend squarely upon it. We stay whole or [CA] dies. Without unity, the heart of [CA] would cease to beat" (Alcoholics Anonymous 1981, 129). The third reading is "The Promises of the Ninth Step." They begin, "If we are painstaking about this phase of our development, we will be amazed before we are halfway through. We are going to know a new freedom and new happiness" (Alcoholics Anonymous 2001, 83–84). The promises speak of the pathway or means of realizing what unfolds in one's life of recovery when one "thoroughly follows" the program of recovery.

Next, newcomers—those new to recovery or simply new to this particular meeting—are invited to introduce themselves. The invitation is followed by a patient pause of shared silence, to give newcomers the space and time to decide if, and how, they want to be welcomed, as they learn to express their wish for a sober self, perhaps for the first time in their lives. Also, by tradition, when an individual expresses being new in some way or makes clear in their share that they are newly sober or attending this meeting for the first time, someone passes around an approved CA brochure that has a space for phone numbers (e.g., "The Home Group"). All those who care to do so give the newcomer their first name and phone number to provide that person with an instant set of empathetic others, as a gesture of welcome to new sober affiliation. To reduce the likelihood of inappropriate intimate pursuit, newcomer women get only women's numbers and newcomer men likewise get only men's numbers. Then, typically, when the person who began circulating the brochure gets it back, that long-term affiliate presents it to the newcomer. He or she calls attention to the phone numbers and invites the newcomer to use the numbers to reinforce their newfound sobriety as they choose to.

After the new persons have been welcomed, the final reading at

Either-Or meetings is "Who Is a Cocaine Addict?" It meticulously reviews details of active addiction to any substance, giving special attention to the highly volatile chaos of cocaine. It provides many vivid examples of the substance-driven behaviors that became or "led in time to pitiful and incomprehensible demoralization" (Alcoholics Anonymous 2001, 30) of which the Big Book speaks. It is a strong testament to the shared trauma reflecting the truths, both symbolic and behavioral, valued and painfully familiar to any person in recovery. In the clean time that follows, those in attendance are invited to share their length of sobriety with the group. Colorful plastic key tags are given to those with milestones of early sobriety (e.g., thirty days, sixty days), and copper anniversary coins are given along with a key tag for those celebrating particular years (e.g., two-year or five-year coins). Clean time is followed by any announcements for the good of CA and requests for prayer or greeting cards to enrich spiritually the well-being of others not in attendance.

These "front matter" rituals that include the readings, introductions, and announcements take about fifteen or twenty minutes altogether. Requests are made for the participants to bring up two or three topics "related to recovery, the 12 Steps, the program, or about CA." Most often, silence follows while people consider what topics they might suggest or simply wait for others to do the same. This post-request pause is often a dissonant mix, both pleasant and uncomfortable. A moment that has its own healing value, it is similar to other silent engagements of faith, be they Buddhist, Quaker, Taoist, or another, that value "communal silence as generative, playing an active role in decision making through a process . . . as participants wait and listen for guidance" (Molina-Markham 2014, 155). Many affiliates view these moments, in the midst of the safest of spaces that rooms of recovery provide, as among the most valuable. From them, they learn opportunities for growth provided by uncertainties within the program. More specifically, they experience the utility of discomfort in shared silence. The First Step, relationships in early recovery, dealing with family members still in active addiction, or the value of "living amends" are a few of the many topics that have been suggested over the years. With topics volunteered, the sharing begins, and the bulk of the meeting is taken up with discussion on those topics.

A departure from the above was the dual format of Thursday night Either-Or meetings. Following the open-topics format of most Thursdays, on the last Thursday of each month someone would give a lead: i.e., one person sharing "in a general way what we used to be like, what happened, and what we are like now" (Alcoholics Anonymous 2001, 58). Leads are where this three-part journey is shared in the forty or forty-five minutes left after the readings, clean time, announcements, and other meeting rituals have been completed. Chairing the Thursday night Either-Or meeting for a month included securing a lead speaker for that last Thursday night meeting.

Finally, like meetings in all 12-Step fellowships, Either-Or meetings may occasionally be followed by a "Group Conscience," which are "the collective conscience of [the] whole fellowship" (Cocaine Anonymous 2018, 8, 11). In them, many important decisions to a particular group are made. Examples are deciding the amount to send to the district (city-level) CA from their Seventh Tradition donations, or choosing to change a reading or other ritual, or holding an election for a person to represent the meeting as its GSR, or simply deciding about a cake for a home group member approaching a sober anniversary. Any affiliate who values that meeting as their "recovery home" or primary meeting of CA affiliation can call a Group Conscience (Sandoz and Dupuis 1998). They typically occur after the regular meeting and are open to all, though only home-group members can vote on any decisions. In the case of Either-Or CA meetings at the FACTS Ministries, these engines for the fellowship as a whole had enough affiliates claiming Either-Or as a home group and coming to meetings regularly for Group Consciences to be well attended. Sometimes, such formal meetings-after-the-meetings include non-home-group affiliates who request more information about the larger fellowship and living a sober life beyond recovery meetings.

When Their Affiliation Flourished

Like all affiliations, Either-Or CA meetings at the FACTS Ministries experienced phases of change. As in Beckhard's (1969) definition of healthy organizations (e.g., delegation, information sharing, egalitarianism), many characteristics of the early years provided the foundation for what was to come (see also Beheshtifar, Borhani, and Nekoie-Moghadam 2012; Boyd and Stahley 2008). After the first meeting in 2000, and spanning their first eight or nine years of growth, the affiliate ecology of resilience and healing at the Either-Or CA meetings was characterized by three beneficial attributes of the Ministries: (1) charismatic leadership and service, (2) food, family, and community, and (3) rituals of celebration and grief. These three attributes of ecological resilience showed how those in attendance contributed to the best of an environment of support for healing in their lives and in the lives of other Ministries affiliates. The outcomes were clear: consistent attendance numbers in the range of sixteen to twenty people, and sometimes more than thirty-five, gave the Either-Or meetings a "standing-room only, hot ticket in recovery" feel. Those in attendance often arrived early and were willing persons of service, reading things, helping to set up chairs, or contributing in other ways. Good things were often being said about Either-Or meetings at other recovery meetings in the city, including at the monthly district (i.e., citywide CA) gatherings, where the well-being of all meetings of the district are considered and evaluated. These three attributes that defined Either-Or meetings and the Ministries' successful work of recovery are discussed below.

Charismatic Leadership and Service

When Either-Or CA meetings flourished at the Ministries, they were led well by affiliates willing to serve the meeting, the CA fellowship, the Ministries, and themselves in the space where their missions met. In the first eight or nine years of Either-Or meetings, starting in 2000, ample people were willing to lead and follow as they valued both roles and the interdependence between them. This principled leadership is "the equitable role relationship of servant-leader in a dialogue of transformations . . . between [more] healthy and less healthy decisions and actions" (Price-Spratlen and Goldsby 2012, 36; see also Greenleaf 2002). It included having long-term GSRs for both meetings who maintained the positions for a year or more. This allowed for monthly representation at the district meetings. GSR representation also meant that when fellowship brochures, new coins and key tags in celebration of sober progress, and other program materials were to be ordered, or announcements of budget or events going on elsewhere in the area (i.e., state), they could easily be secured from the CA World Services office in Southern California. Respecting being of service at the Either-Or meetings also included persons familiar enough with the program of recovery to value adhering to protocol at the place where the formal meets the informal in meetings. Sarah, Jonathan, Troy-Allen, and Jerry were among those most charismatic affiliates who regularly attended Either-Or CA meetings and came to be perceived by other home group members as unsung leaders.

Sarah was a White, brash, thickly built, and friendly long-haired woman who made a performance of every arrival. She arrived on a loud motorcycle that she parked in the small, five-car, off-alley parking space behind the Ministries. Her black leather chaps, vest, and other clothing added to her comfortable tensions as a self-proclaimed "sober biker chick." Like most in recovery, Sarah had a multiple substance use history, with cocaine imposing her most severe consequences. She regularly attended the Saturday Either-Or meetings and nearly every week repeated that her home group and fellowship were in "the mighty AA." Hers was a well-informed, symbolically laden participation that valued her biker-associated identity while living a program of recovery. Her dual fellowship affiliation and enthusiasm for living an "edgy" recovery in a biker culture led Sarah to be valued as a role model to many.

Like Sarah, Jonathan was another charismatic personality who regularly attended when the Either-Or meetings thrived. He was a large-framed African American man with broad shoulders and a deep love for the Big Book. Proudly active in service at several levels of the fellowship, he had attended CA World Services conventions for many years in a row and regularly brought one or both of his preadolescent sons to the meetings. Quietly displaying a youthful discipline learned from their military grandfather, they were the children of a natural scientist father who cherished them as part of his reward for a sober life, started two years before the birth of his older son. Jonathan's shares were long and, regardless of the topic, included word-for-word quotes from the Big Book each time. His strong familiarity with the Big Book, long history of service at multiple levels, and deep ties to the international headquarters of CA led many to place a great deal of value on what Jonathan shared and how he lived his recovery.

Troy-Allen was a resident of the Ministries sober homes. His demonstrative hypermasculinity and allure were reflected in his well worked-out body and visible "prison" tattoos, which he displayed by wearing tank tops at all times of the year, regardless of the weather. His shares were commented on by many. Troy-Allen presented a strong desire for sobriety. He also repeatedly expressed a challenging tension between his sober self and a very strong pull toward what struck many as a romantic view of returning to active addiction. He was as likely to celebrate the rewards of living sober as he was to longingly describe things he missed about getting high. Troy-Allen put into words what several others who attended Either-Or meetings regularly also valued, with approving head nods and other affirming body language. Like many affiliates, Troy-Allen struggled to claim his vulnerability as a necessary resource for sustained sobriety.

Meanings of sober masculinity and sexualities, and what they can and cannot be within the program, are unclear to many in recovery.

His shares and those of many other men at meetings indicated how gender constructions of crack cocaine and other drugs are often about sexual control (Bourgois 1996; Lejuez et al. 2007). For many, recovery is about redefining a healthy sexuality in sober terms, regardless of one's sexual identity, race/ethnicity, generation, or gender (see chapter 4). At Either-Or meetings, Troy-Allen's shares were among the more overt recognitions of this reframing of "the uses of the erotic" (Lorde 1984, 54) as sober motivations and behaviors. What he shared in the meetings were often laments about what his life had become while sober and what he desired it to be. He often repeated not knowing how to get to and sustain a sense of self that did not include sexual encounters as conquests, guided by the "lever" of control the next piece of dope—presented or denied—allowed one to impose on one's sexual partner. A risk of relapse rested in a drug-informed hypermasculine consumer. His sense of self extended from a substance-informed position of power and control which determined his self-worth in relationship to others, especially sexual partners. For Troy-Allen and many other men, without these rituals, what their sexuality-masculinity mix could or "should" be was a mystery. That "mix" often manifested itself as vulnerability behind their hypermasculine veil. The men expressed their uncertainty as a perceived "surrendered masculinity" (Travis 2009, 175; see also Lejuez et al. 2007) of health-compromising tension between a sober self and stereotypical "manhood" (i.e., machismo) of very particular expressions of power and control. Either-Or meetings of CA provided some of these men an outlet to express their concerns, which in turn led to a discomfort felt by many women and other men. Because this seemed to be the struggle of several men, Troy-Allen's shares were appreciated. Dap or other affirmations were often shared with him when he finished.

Jerry raised many of the same issues Troy-Allen did. White, in his sixties, and heir to a successful local family business, he was in a similar struggle, one generation later. Jerry's one relapse during his more than ten years of affiliation with the Either-Or meetings and the Ministries had been for only two days. By not managing that paradox in a sober way, his brief relapse was centered on a sexual encounter. Jerry picked up a female sex industry worker in the neighborhood and purchased crack for her. He then watched her smoke it, as he had done many times before he got sober. He soon found himself in addiction's spin cycle again for two days. On the night of the first day, the police stopped Jerry. He had been followed, and they had spotted his late-model, high-priced car parked at 3:30 a.m. outside an abandoned house on a street just one block from the Ministries' front door. He was not physically or even verbally harassed, arrested, or ticketed. He missed only one Saturday morning meeting during the hours of his relapse. In the weeks that followed, Jerry shared in the Either-Or meetings that what resonated with him was the police officer scolding him in a tone he respected. That helped to snap him out of his brief malaise and return to active addiction. His brief relapse ended quickly. Jerry restarted his recovery just one day later.

Troy-Allen's and Jerry's contributions constituted a symmetrical discourse across race, class, and life-stage differences, as their "surrendered masculinity remained entwined with heterosexist, patriarchal, and capitalist institutions and ways of being. [Their sobriety demanded an objective] critique of some of the most extreme elements of masculine identity" that were most familiar to them (Travis 2009, 185). Troy-Allen typically came to the Thursday night meetings. An African American from the South, he had spent extended time in prison and had a limited education and an uneven work record. He relied heavily on his girlfriend for various forms of emotional and material support, including the ego salve of driving her high-priced car to meetings. Jerry was a regular on Saturday mornings. He was White, owned his home and other rental properties, and was college educated. Both men's openness and parallel uncertainties about their substance use and masculinities were beneficial contributions to informal leadership.

During these years of the CA-Ministries affiliation, a steady division of labor and mission was developed and sustained between the Thursday night and Saturday morning Either-Or meetings. Albert, a sober homes resident, was always ready with pizza and a ride for the Thursday night meetings. Jerry was always open to bringing the donuts on Saturday mornings and his CA district fundraising 50-50 raffle enthusiasm. "You don't sell the steak; you sell the sizzle" was among his most frequently repeated lines and became a Saturday morning mantra. On the chapel side of the wall, the Ministries sustained a small, consistently successful Praise and Worship Team (PWT), when both its membership and musicianship were strong. Their Thursday night practices ended just as the Either-Or meetings began. Further solidifying the stability of both meetings, the Community Correctional Facility (CCF) established a relationship the Either-Or meetings. At that time, nonviolent offenders serving their sentences in community were allowed to attend 12-Step meetings outside of the facility. Women serving CCF sentences came to Thursday night meetings, and CCF men attended Saturday morning meetings. Each meeting had a different group of consistent affiliates who attended. Though the readings and CA recovery program were largely the same, these and a few other differences lead each meeting to have its own distinct "feel."

The PWT and the division of labor between the two CA meetings lost a great deal of their momentum when, in late 2004, Arnold, the lead guitarist, relapsed and was killed during what appeared to be a drug-buy gone wrong. A couple of blocks south of the Ministries, Arnold was attempting to buy some crack cocaine. Something had apparently gone wrong enough to lead him to run from an encounter. When he was shot at, a bullet hit the pavement, bounced up, and struck him in the back of his head. Arnold was one of the few who regularly attended both Either-Or CA meetings on Saturday morning and Sunday worship. Given his military service and kind manner, his sudden relapse and immediate death was especially unsettling to many. Arnold's passing was a severe, shared leadership loss.

Still, from Sarah to Arnold, from Jonathan to Jerry, the sustained presence and leadership of charismatic CA members such as those described above have been frequent characteristics of organizational growth and the sense of an allied mission. They thoughtfully articulated the fellowship's program of recovery and displayed a reverence for the Big Book and its applications to their lives. Whether in 12-Step recovery or other settings, "Max Weber believed that the basis for charismatic leadership was a perception by followers that their leader was extraordinary" (Conger 1999, 152). When it thrived, the largely informal charismatic leadership enriched their own affiliation and that of others and strengthened the resilience of Either-Or CA meetings and the FACTS Ministries.

Food, Family, and Community

Food was a simple resource for good fellowship. Similar to the origins of the 12-Step model, it was a vital indicator of the health of, and resilience in, Either-Or meetings at the FACTS Ministries. From the earliest national coverage of Alcoholics Anonymous, food was recognized as a central element of AA fellowship. On March 1, 1941, when the organization was little more than six years old, the *Saturday Evening Post* provided AA with its first national print media exposure. The organization had grown to include groups in over fifty cities and towns and many hundreds of members. Groups in Cleveland gave "big parties on New Year's and other holidays, at which gallons of coffee and soft drinks [were] consumed" (Alexander 1941, 9). More recently, "some groups have larger spaces, with more seats, and abundantly flowing coffee, [while] other groups may have trouble keeping their finances in order, are often squeezed into a too-small space, with little or no budget for extra supplies" (Rayburn and Wright 2009, 62). In AA, Reich et al. (2008) found food availability to be a vital indicator of AA meeting stability and success.

Thursday night Either-Or meetings at the Ministries were most successful when pizzas, soda, and coffee were available. Comments on the coffee were a running joke of annoyance and appreciation: "So, did you make your crude oil caffeine this time?" was a question often shared to provide a quick laugh among the early arrivers willing to drink the too-strong coffee. Gradually the ancillary add-on of food apparently became an unspoken expectation. Following from Alexander and Reich et al. above, the collective spirit ascribed to the organization is informed by the welcoming appreciation food provides (Alexander 1941; Flynn et al. 2003; White 1996). Consistent with the nutritional resilience the Ministries provided (see chapter 3), for many, the pizza, coffee, and soda may have been the only reliable meal that day and were a symbolic and material invitation to a place of acceptance and healing.

Along with the food came family. Either-Or meetings were open to all. Loved ones of affiliates in recovery often accompanied them. During the early meetings of AA, the family of AA members would gather near the meetings (Laudet 2008), and similar practices continue today. As previously noted, Jonathan would regularly bring his sons after their baseball practice to the Thursday night meetings during the summer. Another affiliate, Joe, often brought his four preteen children, who joined the meeting circle. During these years, Sonja, a Native American–ancestry mother, would often bring her adolescent daughter and teenage son. On Saturday mornings, two young White couples, an African American custodial grandmother of three, and two other young people often brought their toddlers to the meeting. Another couple, a husband in recovery and his wife, who was not, would bring their adolescent son on Saturday mornings. While the father participated in the Either-Or CA meeting, the mother and the son would be in pastoral counseling with Pastor Marshall.

Either-Or CA meetings' family-friendly context also included Jack, twenty years old in 2006, and his father who brought him. While Jack was attempting to sustain sobriety at a young age, his father would sit silently and glare intensely at others during their shares. Jack's father reacted to others with nonverbal moral judgment and an unwillingness to understand his son's addiction. He did not meet anyone's eyes in greeting and did not respond to hands extended to him for a welcoming handshake. If asked to read something, he would respond with a dismissive look away and a loud, pregnant sigh until the meeting chairperson passed him by. His passive-aggressive disapprovals tended to be even more dramatic when his wife attended as well, though her responses were far less hostile. Such palpable hostility in the meetings was muted by the presence and caring diversity of several family inclusions.

Rituals of Celebration and Grief

Wherever they occur, through whatever means, celebrations matter. As Humphreys and Lembke (2014, 14) noted, "The Obama administration engaged in many intentionally symbolic efforts to celebrate recovering people and simultaneously give hope to individuals still suffering from addiction." From the macro to the micro, to enrich a shared mission of healing, celebrations are vital in a social ecology of resilience. They are "actions that create visibility and awareness inside and outside of the [shared mission, and] consistently endorse . . . sustained stakeholder engagement such as speeches and celebrations" (D'Amato and Roome 2009, 426). Celebrations at the Either-Or meetings took many forms and happened regularly.

The sober anniversaries of Either-Or home group members meant a great deal to many. Hearty applause at everyone's sober time announcement, especially for those in their first year of sobriety, was a caring expression of the unspoken sentiment: "Congratulations to you and your spiritual progress. We have been where you are. We remember, and are glad for you and the many miracles your sober time affirms." Most often, the heartiest applause was shared with newcomers or others with the least length of sobriety. Doing so publicly recognized the value that many placed on being in the first, toughest, thirty days of continuous sobriety and how difficult for many those early weeks often are. When people said anything ending in "eleven months and seventeen days" or something similar, a "tick, tick, tick" countdown call-and-response would occur. This recognized the often-challenging process of an approaching sober anniversary.

To enrich stakeholder engagement, on Thursday nights Albert made sure that a cake was present when the sober anniversary arrived. No matter the number of years sober, plastic forks and paper plates were available, along with a knife to cut the cake. "Happy Birthday" was sung with smiles and laughter, either in the traditional way or in the Black folks' Stevie Wonder format (written to commemorate the birthday of Rev. Dr. Martin Luther King Jr. becoming a national holiday). After presenting the person celebrating the start of another sober year with their anniversary coin, attendees shared heartfelt hugs. Sober anniversaries were tracked by the meeting secretary to ensure that a home group member's correct anniversary coin was in the clean time tray when the day and meeting arrived. Prior communication with the sponsor of the home group member occurred so that, if possible, their sponsor could present their coin.

Like sober anniversaries, mourning someone's passing is among the most important dimensions of recovery and the resilience of healing. There is "a wide range" of language used "to describe the deaths of contemporary members of groups to which [one] belongs" (Walter 2014, 69). How one died informs the death's perception in relation to the resilience of others. Periodically, people who had regularly attended one of the Either-Or meetings experienced severe health challenges and passed away. Not surprisingly, a death after experiencing COPD in sustained sobriety was understood and addressed far differently from that of a homicide secondary to an apparent relapse. Yet, regardless of how an affiliate passes, the presence of a critical mass matters in shaping how the group responds to the death.

Major, for example, was an old-timer who regularly attended Saturday morning Either-Or meetings. In his sixties, Major always arrived with an oxygen tank and an air-feed line to his nostrils. He had multiple heart-lung challenges and had spoken openly in the meetings about how his past actions of substance use, which began during his Vietnam War military service, had led to his current poor health. Major's decline was gradual and visible. Many in the CA fellowship supported him along with his family. Several of his family members were members on the church side of the Ministries. With many on the verge of tears or openly crying at the mention of his name, affiliates reacted to Major's passing with profound grief that continued for weeks. He was deeply respected throughout the district CA chapter and in the area (i.e., state level) of CA as well, reflected in the many Either-Or meeting affiliates who attended his memorial service and burial. Cards and condolences from both meetings were passed around and signed by those who chose to and were then sent to his surviving family members. Major's was a "good death," with dignity, honor, and respect on both the church and the recovery sides of the Ministries.

Alternatively, when relapse appeared to have caused someone's death, responses reflected a far greater range. Perhaps the opposite of a "good death" is an ambivalent one. Informed by the perceived fragility of sobriety, such deaths tend to receive a scolding, moralizing response. The suggested topics and the shares that people gave at the meetings following the announced death reflected people's scorn, perhaps indicating a perceived fragility of their own sobriety. Such deaths are understood as soiled or surrendered resilience. Questions are raised about what the now deceased could have, and perhaps "should have," done differently. Denial, anger, and the other stages of grief (Kübler-Ross [1969] 1997) seemed to have an organizational and individual character, experienced as acts of sober affirmation among affiliates, who all share in a relapse risk and "daily reprieve contingent on the maintenance of our spiritual condition" (Alcoholics Anonymous 2001, 85). Anger appeared to be the most demonstrative stage Either-Or affiliates expressed in the aftermath of an ambivalent death, for not having "been there" for the person in a critical time of need, or for not having been called upon by them, or for not having cultivated enough of a bond to warrant any crisis communication with them.

In meeting shares that followed an ambivalent death, anger was often expressed at that person for having made a decision that in some ways seemed to weaken the recovery of others in the fellowship and the meeting's recovery as a whole. Others responded to the relapse and death of an affiliate with a sense of foreboding. Their actions and the life-taking outcome seemed to be a fracture in the resilience of both CA and the Ministries, weakening others' efforts in the meetings, leading some to doubt the group's and organization's ability or power to be of any help, and perhaps to question their own faith and strength to sustain their own recovery. These were uncertainties, anger, and unanswered questions about the credibility of recovery. At the FACTS Ministries and Either-Or meetings, as Berger (1969, 52) noted, "every human society is, in the last resort, banded together in the face of death." This sentiment resonates among health-challenged groups that gather to heal, as all affiliates are engaged in a present risk of death. Whether it was a "good death" or not, most met it with sober empathy as a dimension of shared efforts to abstain from "just one more" hit. When confronted by the difficult process of mourning for an apparently relapse-driven death, core affiliates provided principled leadership during the request for prayers at the beginning of a meeting. They helped ease the devastation of affiliate survivors at Either-Or meetings and of family members who had just lost a loved one with affirmations of their emotions and experiences, co-signed cards, phone messages of support, and other caring follow-ups. Through death or other challenges, unhealed wounds remained.

The Fractured Affiliation of Either-Or Meetings and the Ministries

In 2000, when Pastor Marshall requested that a CA meeting be hosted at the FACTS Ministries, he likely did so as a result of his and the Ministries board's recognition that their efforts to establish a faith-based organization to address substance use and other health challenges with just a storefront building in the 'hood needed something beyond Pastor Marshall's charisma and the predominantly White anchor churches funding his efforts. A 12-Step fellowship—preferably one that was a bit more "roguish" and nontraditional than AA—would provide the Ministries with additional legitimacy as a grassroots health organization worthy of respect to those in the neighborhood and throughout the city. To Pastor Marshall and the Ministries board members, CA was a beneficial option. As noted earlier, among the motives for reaching out to CA was the shared value of healing beyond harm and stigma and Pastor Marshall helping himself and others move from health-compromising active addiction to an empowered collective of active, long-term recovery.

Yet from the very start, their affiliation with each other was, at best, a tempered inclusion, with an "outside" organization being "welcomed with open arms and dealt with at a distance, creating a vocational and spiritual[ly liminal] space" (Price-Spratlen and Goldsby 2012, 55; see also Bricker 1995) of measured affiliation. Of course in any organizational relationship, there are degrees of affiliation. It is unclear the degree to which becoming a partnered collaboration (Gray 1985; McNamara, Miller-Stevens, and Morris 2020) or an "empowered collective" (i.e., an equitable collaboration of shared mission, extending from a sense of respect and mutual appreciation) was ever the goal of either organization. CA is officially a fellowship allied with no one. According to their organizational Preamble, they are "a fellowship of men and women . . . not allied with any sect, denomination, politics, organization, or institution. We do not wish to engage in any controversy and we neither endorse nor oppose any causes" (Cocaine Anonymous 2018, 5). While the Ministries had no Preamble, it was led with a traditional religious oligarchy, perhaps more than most, never having any affiliate leadership structure of any kind. At no time was anything so much as a deacon board ever given any legitimacy as a means to establish even the most traditional form of rank-and-file, participatory leadership. CA's non-allied traditions came together with the Ministries and its leadership to create, in effect, an organizational "marriage of convenience," or an affiliation of muted trust and tempered inclusion. As the years progressed, signs of increasing discord emerged (see table 2).

As organizations and their affiliations change, movement from a relatively flat stability to fluctuation may occur (Beckhard 1969; Lissack and Letiche 2002). Built as it was from a fragile foundation of non-allied traditions (Either-Or/CA) and traditional religious autonomy (Ministries), the quality of their affiliation will inform how the fluctuations are responded to interdependently. The most challenging affiliation fluctuations began in the eighth year of Either-Or meetings. Declining appreciation for these attributes by cutting corners in nurturing and sustaining them were detrimental signals in the CA-Ministries affiliation. Gradually, the enthusiasm, hopes, and resource richness that had marked the Ministries' early years changed. By 2012, changes in the attributes of interdependent flourishing—i.e., true leadership and service, food/family/community, and rituals of sober celebrations and grief—turned these fluctuations to a steady pace of decline. Consistent with Gray's (1985) model of partnered collaboration and the resilience framework of Kumpfer (1999) and Kumpfer and Summerhays (2006), the Either-Or/Ministries affiliation decline was a five-stage process to which all three interdependent flourishing domains of affiliation were subject (see also Bassuk et al. 2016; Bennett and Windle 2015; McNamara, Miller-Stevens, and Morris 2020; Perkins and Khoo-Lattimore 2020). A brief consideration of each of the five domains of fractured affiliation summarized in table 2 follows.

As the first column of table 2 summarizes, compromised credibility was present from the start. Pastor Marshall did not participate in 12-Step sponsorship, which is a core practice among all 12-Step fellowships, including CA. He was public during his Either-Or meeting shares and

Table 2. Processes of fractured affiliation between Either-Or meetings and the FACTS Ministries. Source: Developed by the author for this book.

Affiliation Domains	Compromised Credibility	Uncertain Alignment	(One-Sided) Volatility ---- ---- Intentional Disruptions	Closure/Eviction Endpoint Actions
Leadership and Service Theory Links – Fractured empathy • Affiliation – (re: Gray 1996) *Absent transparency, unexplored options; Unyielding religious oligarchy in perception and practice;* • Resilience – (re: Rudzinski et al. 2017) *Compromised problem-solving, limited process for uncertainty, shared commitments*	• Pastor's Either-Or mtg. participation declines, others follow • Sober homes residents' requirements incrsngly. appear to be policy w/o practice • Pastoral alienations of several of the most steadfast CA members • Uneven attendance, inconsistent leadership, unsteady GSRs	• Reciprocities of service are fractured/less freq. • I'personal resentments increasingly exhibited, presented as humor • Key bridge affiliate reduces their presence, participation; Thu. night ride ripple effects result • Increasingly ambiguous collegiality ("above" and beside)	• Unsettled, secretive funding uncertainties; retreat of private pain (opportunities for shared empathy decline) • Increased autocratic decision-making (re: progrmng., prsnnel, etc.) -- -- • PWT rehearsals increasingly bleed into Thu. night mtgs. • Pastoral disorders incr. • Scheduled overlaps incr.	• Bldg. key return demand from CA key members that remained • Thu. night CA mtg. closure (reasons never shared) • Sat. morning CA mtg. evicted (othering reasoning manufctrd.)
Food and Outreach Theory Links – Fractured inclusion • Affiliation – (re: Gray 1996) *Limited enrichment of external support; muted exploration of (un)shared agendas* • Resilience – (re: Rudzinski et al. 2017) *Muted ecological relations between risk and protective factors*	• Outreach declines (summer anniv. bkyrd. BBQ ends, becomes off-site fundraiser; street evangelizing less regular; mentions of CA mtgs. at lunches declines/ends) • Thu. night food rule adherence more uneven (leading Thu. night food to end) • Fri. night Youth Night ended w/o explanation	• Similar uncertainties as Leadership and Service • Key bridge affiliate reductions have added affiliation consequences (less regular Thu. night food, less "mobile mission" Ministries evangelizing, less trust of mission when a [former] devotee retreats, etc.)	• Ministries donations to CA district ends • Less attendance, less partic. in the CA district monthly 50/50 raffle • Special event partic./ limited availability -- -- • Similar disruptions and outcomes to those of Leadership and Service above • Pastoral disorder behav. esp. challenging (literal and symbolic conseqs.)	• Pizza on Thu. nights ends, attendance overall dwindles • Core CA affiliate partic. ends (alienated away), far fewer newcomers • 2013 Thanksgiving Day meal not allowed • 3rd party org. partic. ends (CCF women and men in Either-Or mtgs, ancillary church volunteers, etc.)
Rituals and Reasons Theory Links – Fractured reciprocity • Affiliation – (re: Gray 1996) *Compromised repetitions of implementation* Resilience – (re: Rudzinski et al. 2017) *Uneven trust cycles, compromised accountability*	• Fewer participants → less shared respect → more doubt of Ministries mission • Fewer cross-references to mission symmetries	• Similar uncertainties as Leadership and Service • Key bridge affiliate reductions have added affiliation consequences (offers of Thu. night post-mtg. rides ended → other consqs.)	• Decline in sober homes residents' partic. • Increasingly brazen refs. by sober homes men to sex industry worker patronage -- -- • Similar disruptions and outcomes to those of Leadership and Service above	• Disruptions become ritualized → soiled trust • CA members largely alienated from the desire to fight • Unshared rituals too insular • Too few attending to mourn their decline

from the pulpit about not having a sponsor and not sponsoring others. While he attended Either-Or meetings regularly, when he began to miss meetings on Thursdays and Saturdays in 2008, other affiliates did the same, further compromising the credibility of Either-Or meeting inclusion. From a modeling perspective alone, Pastor Marshall's signaling of declining attendance informed the level of investment others had in Either-Or meetings, and the level of sober homes resident participation also faltered. Despite the sober homes requirement of full participation in all Ministries activities, including Either-Or meetings, such participation declined, even when residents were not working or getting rest needed to prepare for work, or when no family commitment was present. These changes had been preceded by Pastor Marshall alienating some of the most staunch Either-Or affiliates through a variety of leadership choices. Among those who shared his evangelical fervor, albeit for CA more than for religious adherence, particulars of their departures were never made public. They simply voted with their feet and did not return. These increasing absences among the informal and most charismatic leadership likely led others to do the same.

In addition, on the church side, compromised credibility was reflected in the lack of outreach to the North Lawson neighborhood with food and fellowship. The everyday outreach promoting health-affirming behavior change to sex industry workers declined. Usually done by members of one of two large, predominantly African American churches several miles north of the Ministries, these evangelical appeals would often point them to the FACTS Ministries as a space where they could enrich their faith while also addressing the substance use issue typically underlying their sex industry participation. This was sometimes done in partnership with Ministries affiliates. The eviction of a sober homes resident who was a member of one of those large churches in early 2009 led these street outreach partnerships to weaken. Also, the Ministries ended its annual July anniversary parking lot barbeques in 2007. These events served as goodwill outreach of good food and fellowship, and had a lingering benefit of appreciation long after the end of the meals themselves. While the weekly lunch meals continued, at them, what struck many as an increasingly moralizing tone of condescension toward those who appeared to be homeless and housing-insecure attendees was being presented during the prayer preceding the Tuesday and Thursday meals. Invitations to consider returning to the Ministries to attend Either-Or CA meetings and address substance use issues, relevant to many lunch patrons, were made less often. As these changes occurred, words of doubt were shared among North Lawson neighbors, CA affiliates throughout the city, and others who might otherwise affiliate in some way. Fewer attendees likely led to lesser shared respect for the Ministries mission, less ritual consistency among CA affiliates attending Either-Or meetings, and a more uncertain alignment to many.

The second column of table 2 shows that, as the credibility of the Either-Or/Ministries relationship was increasingly compromised, an alignment of shared mission became more uncertain to many. Simple reciprocities of service declined. As charismatic informal leadership declined and fewer sober homes residents attended regularly, those with a "vested" affiliation willing to chair Either-Or meetings for a month at a time, or simply read one of the readings to begin a single meeting, decreased. There were many of these actions of a shared mission. They could be as simple as a sober homes resident reading "How It Works" as the words echoed off of the Ministries' community room walls: "Rarely have we seen a person fail who has thoroughly followed our path. Those who do not recover are people who cannot or will not completely give themselves to this simple program. . . . If you have decided you want what we have and are willing to go to any length to get it—then you are ready to take certain steps" (Alcoholics Anonymous 2001, 58). When said by a vested Ministries affiliate, these words were especially valued as an act of service. The words of ritual and respect enriched the narratives of a social ecology of health and resilience to a greater degree than when the same reading was read by others. Regular readings by those less vested contributed to a more uncertain alignment between the Either-Or meetings of CA and the Ministries.

Interpersonal resentments born of a fractured trust were more apparent, especially when they were presented with a "humor" that few found funny. "Get Jerry to do it. So long as the driving route takes him by the Crooked Walkway Motel, he'll be good to go." This was said as a joke before a Saturday morning Either-Or meeting by a member of Ministries leadership regarding a volunteer errand by car loudly enough for all in the room to hear. The Crooked Walkway was a motel known for sex industry work and substance use. It was calling attention to a moment of shame in the spiral of active addiction, to which Jerry, a longtime Either-Or affiliate, referred with a humored anguish. While it could be experienced as funny, it was a dig at a place of Jerry's vulnerability. More broadly, it was an effort to mock the validity of the CA program of recovery and the 12 Steps. It did so with an implied yet unspoken sense that "Jerry, like all of you CA recovery people, are a bunch of whoremongers anyway, who wouldn't know how to maintain a stable, caring relationship if you tried." Such unspoken implications, if presented to the Ministries leadership either in the moment or later, would quite likely be quickly dismissed as a hypersensitive overreach, or someone being needlessly and ridiculously thin-skinned. Perhaps those dismissals would be accurate. Perhaps not. Like all examples of this type of humor, it was presented with enough "I was just joking" energy to be veiled as being "all in good fun." Still, the increasing repetitions of these comments, and their seemingly progressively biting, disrespectful undertones, amplified the corrosive effect on the alignment between the organizations. Their cumulative effects eventually led to a tense moment of raised voices in October 2013 between (longtime sober homes resident and Thursday night Either-Or meeting secretary) Albert and Pastor Marshall. Shortly after their confrontation, Albert, a vital, well-respected, and vested bridge affiliate of the Ministries and Either-Or, stopped attending Thursday night meetings. Albert was central to the food donations for Thursday night Either-Or meetings and, perhaps more crucially, gave rides home after meetings to several other vested affiliates. When he stopped attending, reliable access to post-meeting rides declined, and several of those most vested Either-Or affiliates stopped attending the meeting as well, leading the alignment of shared mission to be still more uncertain.

The third column of table 2 summarizes two deeply interdependent processes of fractured affiliation between Either-Or CA meetings and the FACTS Ministries: (1) an intensely one-sided volatility in leadership decision-making, communication, program development, and other aspects of organizational change, and (2) the intentional disruptions this largely one-sided volatility often created as the affiliation fractures between the two organizations grew. When a 2011 decision was being made pondering the move of Millwood Fellowship, the primary funding source for the Ministries, from a city suburb it had called home for decades, into the urban core of the city, information about its possibility and effects of the move on the Ministries itself was mostly unshared. That silence of possible cause and effect was one of many silences associated with the Ministries (see chapter 5). What was apparent to Either-Or meeting affiliates and Ministries Sunday worship affiliates alike were outcomes of increasingly unsettled funding instabilities. These included changes in the stability of sober homes resident staffing and leadership, what appeared to many as an increasingly autocratic and arbitrary decision-making regarding Ministries programming and personnel, and declining expressions of empathy. These actions included the hiring and then quick firing of a musical director for the Ministries, the salary cutting of the sober homes resident manager, fall 2013 statements from Pastor Marshall about "shutting down" one of the Either-Or CA meetings hosted at the Ministries, and other procedural and narrative behaviors of uncertainty. It felt to many that a "divide and conquer" strategy was being initiated by Pastor Marshall to divide the Thursday night Either-Or meeting from the Saturday morning meeting by suggesting that one or the other was to be shut down. Given the quality relationships between key affiliates in both meetings and the role of three affiliates who regularly attended both meetings, any such outcome was highly unlikely. Not understanding his relationship to the Traditions of Cocaine Anonymous, Pastor Marshall did not realize that he alone was not in a position to shut down any meeting of the fellowship for whatever motive.

Other actions of volatility and disruption also increased. These included Pastor Marshall arriving late to Saturday morning Either-Or meetings. He would then come through the back door from the parking lot, most frequently used by Either-Or affiliates, while carrying on loud cell phone conversations. He would then go to his office on the chapel side of the building, and he frequently would call one or more of the sober home residents into his office from the meeting. He often did so by shouting their names from the other side of the building. Doing so added to his disruptions and reduced the leadership, fellowship, and ritual participants in the smaller and smaller Either-Or meetings. These behaviors indicated disrespect for CA protocol by those whose primary affiliation was via the Ministries.

Among the minor disruptions were breaks with CA protocol at Either-Or meetings. Whoever chaired Thursday night meetings began more frequently to go off-script. For example, the portion of the script that asked newcomers to the meeting or to recovery if they wished to introduce themselves was not being read. As the off-script ad-libbing increased, adherence to other meeting protocol decreased as well. Soon, not only were the fewer and fewer newcomers not properly welcomed, brochures for them were not passed around the circle. This incomplete circle led to only a few people in attendance giving their contact information to the newcomer formally. This reduced the salience of the ritual for all, newcomer and longtime affiliate alike, perhaps causing the newcomer to be less willing to trust those who had reached out (i.e., "What does she or he want from me?"). Protocol violations seemed to attract some affiliates and disturb others. A few sticklers for protocol called attention to the relatively minor breakdowns of the group's engagement with traditions. Despite the continued stability of the Either-Or meetings in the early years, however, these slippages signaled a coming uncertainty to many.

More than these minor shifts, for reasons never made clear to those who had been attending Either-Or CA meetings for some time, the Ministries seemed to become increasingly hostile toward individual Either-Or meeting affiliates and toward the hosting of CA meetings at the Ministries (see chapter 6). The Thursday Either-Or meeting was first bled of viable, consistent affiliates willing to return to the Ministries through alienating decisions by Pastor Marshall. These included the increasing presence of unfriendly "jokes" that disrespected background or personal characteristics and were told far too loudly. It also included conversations intended to be overheard that were rife with name-calling and unpleasant innuendo, hiring decisions that were intentionally off-putting (e.g., hiring an ex-cop in 2014 to help supervise the sober homes, whose residents were most often returning citizens with a jail or prison history), and various other distancing actions of authority. These volatile actions also included PWT rehearsals being scheduled such that their endings would overlap and loudly disrupt the start of Either-Or meetings. By tradition, Either-Or meetings were to begin with a moment of silence followed by the collective reciting of the Serenity Prayer. With the sound bleed from the chapel on the other side of a thin wall separating the Ministries' chapel and community room sides, moments of silence were neither possible nor honored as intentional disruptions increased. Such scheduling overlaps, tasks assigned to sober homes residents that demanded their missing Either-Or meetings, and the other actions above led many primarily CA affiliates to vote with their feet and not return. Because Ministries domains were largely siloed (see chapter 3), advocacy by one domain's affiliates for the enrichment, or mere stability, of another domain was not likely. This was a structural leadership decision allowed or perhaps encouraged by the board, embraced by Pastor Marshall, and made worse by the absence of any deacon board or other affiliate leadership outlet. Within Either-Or, these dynamics affected charismatic leadership, the presence and practices of food and fellowship, and the engagement of valued rituals in comparable measure. All suffered, and together these led each disruption to negatively affect another in an interdependent disruptive decline.

As the final column of table 2 summarizes, the fractured affiliation between the Either-Or meeting of CA and the Ministries ended with closures, evictions, and an end to interactions and access of any kind. In early 2014, Pastor Marshall asked for keys to the Ministries building from three longtime Either-Or and Ministries affiliates. The keys had been given to each of them by Pastor Marshall two, four, and seven years earlier, respectively. They had been shared with each affiliate as a ritual of leadership and fellowship that affirmed the appreciation Pastor Marshall and the Ministries board had for the consistent contributions each had made to the Either-Or meetings, to the Ministries, and to the North Lawson neighborhood, through various events and activities across the years. No reasons for the request for the return of the keys were given. The demand for their return was made to each affiliate as if they had taken the keys or otherwise acquired them by deceptive or other unprincipled means. Each affiliate returned their key, as requested. The locks on the building were quickly changed. Other expressions of volatility and intentional disruptions increased.

Then, in April 2015, Pastor Marshall, who by this time rarely attended Either-Or CA meetings on either day, called a Group Conscience for the Thursday night meeting. His goal for that meeting in the 12-Step decision-making process? To end the Thursday night Either-Or meeting. In a Group Conscience, by CA tradition, "every member is heard. The right of each group member to participate is both respected and valued" (Chappel 1995, 143; see also Teo, Lee, and Lim 2017; White, Kelly, and Roth 2014). Taken for granted is the ability of each home group member to make an independent "best fit" choice after considering the information presented to them. Because Group Consciences are the means by which the God as understood by each member speaks through them to further the mission of CA, it is extraordinarily unlikely that they are ever used to bring an end to a meeting. To use a Group Conscience in this way is, in effect, an ultimate betrayal of the primary purpose of CA: "to stay free from cocaine and all other mind-altering substances, and to help others achieve the same freedom. We use the Twelve Steps of Recovery, because it has already been proven that the Twelve Step Recovery Program works" (Cocaine Anonymous 2018, 5). Closing a meeting for reasons never shared, in North Lawson or any neighborhood of concentrated disadvantage that continued to be adversely affected by substance use and the presence and process of drug markets, is contrary to the achievement of that primary purpose. Pastor Marshall was now using participatory leadership in Cocaine

Anonymous—a process that had never before characterized any aspect of Ministries decision-making—to end the CA meeting. He had asked for the CA district's approval to host when the Ministries was establishing its legitimacy fifteen years prior. Many in the CA district, and other Ministries affiliates as well, viewed it as a curious power play of ego and avarice that further fractured the Ministries' affiliation with the Either-Or CA Saturday meeting that remained and with CA in the city as a whole.

Through what in other spheres many would label a "kangaroo court," or a highly unprincipled decision-making process and outcome (e.g., Butler and Maruna 2016), Pastor Marshall all but ensured that the Thursday night meeting's "closure" would occur. Having already alienated to absence all but two of the informal charismatic leadership, and otherwise behaving in unwelcoming ways that led many others to leave as well, his actions led CA district leadership elsewhere in the city to grow weary of striving to save what had become a meeting in an unwelcome and increasingly hostile host site. As a result of the Ministries' work, all but two of the Group Conscience participants were directly beholden to Pastor Marshall for their shelter in the sober homes, for their work through jobs he had helped them find, for their family support he had helped them restore, or for other resources that made any decision other than siding with his position virtually impossible. That Either-Or meeting was attended by only five (of the twelve) sober homes residents, Pastor Marshall, and two other CA affiliates. Devonte, a sober homes resident, bravely abstained. The two other longtime Either-Or affiliates strongly advocated to continue the meeting. Pastor Marshall and all others in attendance voted to end the meeting. Contrary to the mission and intent of what Group Consciences are to be used for, and contrary to the primary purpose of CA meetings, he instead used the ritual and collective leadership the CA Fellowship seeks to affirm in an autocratic way. The vote for the group action to end the meeting passed. The Thursday night Either-Or meeting was ended. The search to find the meeting a new home in the same congregational corridor of Akron Avenue was unsuccessful, as no other outlet was affordable and available on Thursday nights (see epilogue). The soiled trust that resulted led the core Saturday morning Either-Or meeting affiliates to recognize that their eviction was simply a matter of time.

Since the Thursday night meeting was discontinued, a strong feeling among many CA and Ministries affiliates was that only a residue of resilience remains. "True" resilience demands shared resources and trust and a shared respect for principled governance in leadership, values, and practices. Resilient responses to chaos continue in CA affiliate meetings. These everyday expressions of a sustained renewal of one's sober life, despite each week's challenges, have value. A parent's passing is recognized with a call for prayer. When someone loses a job, requests are made for a good word for getting the next job through "whom-you-know" channels the rooms of recovery sometimes provide. The relapse of a valued member is greeted with nonverbal laments and questions of concern for how they are at the moment. Anguish and anger follow, along with post-meeting nods and whispers about how to help in the challenging first days of recovery that begin again. For those few and fewer who had not yet been alienated, these were among the social ecology of resilience remains in the Saturday morning Either-Or meetings at the Ministries.

Saturday Either-Or meetings continued yet felt fragile. Pastor Marshall, a person in recovery himself, virtually never attended them. The new resident manager of the sober homes, the ex-cop not in recovery, did not attend either. Any sense of leadership investment seemed to weaken with each passing week. However, a couple of strong personalities with long-term sobriety remained, with a couple more as irregular attendees on Saturday mornings. Their continued presence is far less than sufficient to move the meeting to a sustained place of well-being. Yet a GSR presence means less when, due to a variety of circumstances, the GSR often could not attend the monthly district meeting.

In addition to leadership inconsistencies and the other challenges of volatility and disruption noted in table 2, Saturday Either-Or meetings suffered from an uncertain affiliation-turned-collaboration between the Ministries and a church two blocks away. Due to this new collaboration, that church scheduled prayer breakfasts to occur regularly at the same time as the Either-Or meeting on Saturday mornings. Multiple Either-Or meetings were then disrupted each month, as the kitchen space to cook the meals was in the small community room of the Ministries. Furthermore, there was a complete absence of any sober home residents or CCF-affiliated men in the Saturday morning meetings, which caused them to shrink even more. Adjustments took place during the Saturday morning meetings as well, be it heating and cooling problems, replacing carpet in the chapel, carpentry hammering in the pastor's office, or adding a second door in the wall between the chapel and community room sides of the Ministries. These various activities often required sober homes residents to help out in the (free labor) management of that work. Like a death by a thousand cuts, there was a growing, largely unspoken sense that the one remaining meeting's impending end seemed inevitable.

Given all of these factors working against the Saturday morning Either-Or meeting, an apathy toward this meeting increased among CA affiliates attending other meetings elsewhere in the city. While difficult to distinguish the precise mix of apathy and the alienations largely brought on by Pastor Marshall, a viable CA meeting in the deep 'hood appeared especially vulnerable. Still, more than a residue of resilience remains.

Conclusions

There is a very long history of mutual aid societies exchanging resources with organizations for improved health and other shared benefits. How they share those benefits has varied a great deal. Over time, some form of collaboration to achieve shared ends has challenged adverse circumstances and improved the quality of life in many communities. The willingness of these organizations to do so often extends from an environment of shared support, or a collective ethos, to strengthen the ethnogenic thread. Since 2000, the relationship between the FACTS Ministries and the local chapter of Cocaine Anonymous is a valuable recent example. As this chapter shows, the collective ethos of the ethnogenic thread is quite fragile. Despite the strong historical foundations noted above, organizational affiliations on any scale are often uncertain and volatile. Among the uncertainties are what affiliation means to each participating organization, how to maintain and enrich resources most valuable to their shared mission, and how affiliation dynamics change with time. For several years, a quality affiliation for good health was shared by the FACTS Ministries and CA. Their affiliation flourished and helped many to move beyond short-term programming and treatment options to sustain long-term support systems and organizational relationships. Their resource sharing improved chances for resilience and health success among affiliates of both organizations. The CA mission and the rituals and other activities extending from it, in the city and in Either-Or meetings, changed very little. While "collaborative efforts presume that [collaborators] are one among many stakeholders whose activities are truly interdependent" (Gray 1985, 915; see also Hodges and Hardiman 2006), when previously shared motives seemingly diverge in ways that leave many alienated, that affiliation and potential for sustaining an organizational interdependence are compromised. This becomes more likely when divergent actions are repeatedly and erratically displayed from one side of the affiliation. When too many of the fragile critical mass of informal, charismatic leadership abandon the affiliation, old fractures seem to get worse and new fractures appear. The alienations and the lesser allegiance resulting from them lead more affiliates to "vote with their feet" and stay away.

As noted in the introduction, resilience is a framework of beliefs, organizational patterns, and communication "processes that can reduce stress and vulnerability in high-risk situations, foster healing and growth out of crisis, and empower [persons] to overcome prolonged adversity" (Walsh 2003, 67). Best-practices analyses of peer-based addiction recovery support emphasize the importance of having a broad-based approach that implements peer support from multiple perspectives (Madras 2018; White 2009). The unique contributions they offer to help sustain resilience and health are important since behaviors can often be properly examined, diagnosed, and treated when understood in the community and the societal context where they occur. This is especially vital in neighborhoods like North Lawson. At the Ministries and at Either-Or CA meetings especially, a resilient ecology existed. In it, a host site shared its mission of sobriety and its goal of providing multiple health services.

As organizational relationships proceed, "perceptions of continued dependence on each other for resources will motivate stakeholders to formalize their normative order [and] increase interorganizational communications which, in turn, [lead] to formalization of relationship[s] among health care agencies" (Gray 1985, 928; see also Hodges and Hardiman 2006). Other alternatives may also occur. The conditions described above in the flourishing period of the Either-Or meetings reflect what is valuable about an affiliation between a meeting and a host site being mutually beneficial. Increasingly, there has been a visible reduction of treatment center clients directly participating in outside 12-Step meetings—even as those meetings are taking place on site in the treatment center itself. Multiple, interdependent macro shifts may occur, further weakening collaborative sustainability. There is also a shapeshifting focus of media, health care, and recovery research toward pills, crystal meth, heroin, and other opioids; and there is an apparent decline in 12-Step affiliations overall and in local chapters of CA in particular (Best and de Alwis 2017; US Surgeon General 2016). This may help magnify an apparent, and perhaps even growing, hostility from among those who have long ago disaffiliated with all recovery in the 12-Step model. Coupled with the dynamics considered above, these and other macro factors well beyond Either-Or meetings at the Ministries have further compromised the ecological sustainability of the meetings as a "cocaine and all other mind-altering substances" recovery oasis in the North Lawson neighborhood. Growing uncertainties in their organizational affiliation were associated with declines in other health resource access at the Ministries (see chapter 6).

The ethnogenic thread reflected in the legacy of collaborations nurtured by the National Negro Health Week and related efforts early in the twentieth century remains. Like all organizations, at the FACTS Ministries, organizational processes and their related organizational affiliations changed over time. For growth to happen, a reciprocity *must* occur between evolution and revolution, or between stages of crisis and growth (Lissack and Letiche 2002; Morell 1996; White 2009). It is unlikely if not impossible for any organization—especially a small, religiously anchored one, operating in a challenging neighborhood environment—to do so without the support of, and engagement with, informed others. Within and beyond challenging moments, leaders can span organizational boundaries and pull resources together to sustain a resilience for shared missions to flourish. Relationships between these processes were considered in the context of faith, health, and collaboration at the Ministries. What follows in chapter 5 is a discussion of how individual and group differences inform organizational silences that make the FACTS Ministries' social ecology of resilience and current dilemmas more uncertain.

Chapter 5

Silence in Our Midst

(In)Visibility and Voice at the Ministries

> In the cause of silence, each one of us draws the face of her own fear. . . . [In] the transformation of silence into language and action, . . . what is most important to me must be made verbal and shared, even at the risk of having it bruised or misunderstood. . . . The speaking profits me, beyond any other effect. . . . We all share a war against the tyrannies of silence.
>
> —Lorde 1984, 40, 41, 42

Few things compromise a collective ethos more than toxic silences. In the intentional weaving of the ethnogenic thread, even in a nontraditional environment of resilience and support like the FACTS Ministries, silence that reinforces oppression is much more than the absence of sound. At its best, silence can be a peaceful and sacred moment two people in communion share without judgment or discomfort, or that a congregation shares preceding a faith-informed collective activity. Silence can be affirming, as in the silence after a sigh of satisfaction. It can also be understood literally as not speaking for a good reason: the right to avoid incriminating oneself, as suggested in the standard Miranda warning, which begins with: "You have the right to remain silent. Anything you say can and will be used against you in a court of law." At its worst, silence can be an act of denial, such as an act or speech that intentionally circumvents what is apparent and detrimental, screaming between the lines yet left unspoken. Silence can thus be a disempowering tyrant. In that silence is the recognition that risks are real, consequences are unpleasant, and a reserve of a strength of spirit is vital for anyone who wishes to stand her or his ground and resist corrosive silence. As Audre Lorde suggests in the above quote, one can win "the war against the tyrannies of silence" only by transforming it "into language and action" (Lorde 1984, 42). This chapter discusses ways in which FACTS Ministries affiliates were silenced and how many fought to transform those silences.

Consistent with Lorde's statement, Betancourt and her colleagues (2013) associate silence with secrecy and stigma, both understood to be harmful to health outcomes. They equate "disclosure and openness . . . [with] resilience and self-efficacy, [and] silence, secrecy, and stigma . . . [with] feelings of self-hate, anxiety, hopelessness, and confusion" (Betancourt et al. 2013, 432). For those in recovery from addiction, confronting those tyrannies is vital to sustaining "a daily reprieve contingent on the maintenance of our spiritual condition" (Alcoholics Anonymous 2001, 85) and the health-affirming benefits of that spiritual maintenance (see Dossett 2017). At the FACTS Ministries, depending on the Ministries' domain, event, or ritual, many types of silence were expressed. Each opposed, rather than enriched, an environment of support for health and well-being.

Whether the motives for silence are financial, "moral," or personal, it can be used for many reasons and in many ways that inform organizational outcomes on several levels. When misused in spaces of recovery and resilience, it acts against both. Misguided silences marginalize their recipients by muting the beneficial "scrutiny of acts, identities, practices, relationships and desires that are illicit and illegitimate, proscribed and hidden . . . making silence the enemy of comfort and communitas" (Reid and Walker 2003, 85, 87). Vital to any social ecology of recovery and resilience, communitas is "a majestic sense of community . . . transcending particular ethnic, religious, gender, and class lines to reveal humanity as an unstructured and free community" (Turner 1974, 169; see also Boyd and Stahley 2008) in which people are equal. However, when associated with secrecy and stigma, silence thwarts health and healing.

Through silence, members of an organization "suppress concerns about difficult or troubling personal as well as organizational issues. . . . Fear, embarrassment, narrow conceptions of ethical responsibility, implicated friends, lack of opportunity for voice, and lack of organizational political skills are factors [that] cause silence" (Beheshtifar, Borhani, and Nekoie-Moghadam 2012, 275). The impact of these factors is often more uncertain in religious settings in general, and even more so in predominantly African American religious settings, where "tension between religiosity and the body stems from the manner in which various forms of Black religion, such as the Black Church, understand the body as representing desires and needs that harm one's ability to maintain a proper attitude or posture toward the divine" (Pinn 2004, 5; see also Johnson 1998; Lorde 1984). The religious need to manage the body in relation to differences of gender, generation, sexual identity, and class can lead to a risk-averse reduction in the ability of diverse groups to transform silence into language and actions of visibility and healing. These tensions are magnified when affiliates of an organization with these identities are voiceless. As a result, the recovery and resilience mission of the organization may suffer.

In contexts of resilience, silence can be a growth process or an artistic expression. For example, in describing jazz musician Charlie Parker's music, someone once remarked that his genius was between the notes. The way he enacted silence was an essential expression of how his artistic grace helped others heal. Whatever the implication of this observation might be for Parker's audiences, silence has a potentially beneficial role when it is used as a necessary pause in music. In other contexts, however, suppressing self-expression can give rise to uneven or otherwise problematic behavior. Audre Lorde's need to transform silence into language and action was in her experiences as a Black, lesbian cancer survivor. She recognized her own need to share in the collective healing of many women, who were both similar to, and different from, herself. For example, she refused to wear a post-mastectomy prosthetic, thereby transforming breast cancer survivors' silence, which reflects a caving in to beauty prescriptions for women, often set by males. Collective silencing can also be oppressive. As Taylor, Gilligan, and Sullivan (1995, 3) observed in their research at an urban public school, many female students engaged in

> a fight for relationship [and] often became dispirited as girls experienced betrayal or neglectful behavior and felt driven into a psychological isolation they readily confused with independence. . . . [This] included their experience of having no effective voice, [which] regularly preceded overt manifestations or symptoms of psychological trouble.

Taylor and her colleagues found that, for these girls, not having an effective voice impaired their resilience and other resources for health and beneficial change. They wrote, "Having a 'big mouth' often got [the young girls who were described as having one] into trouble, but silence, the slow slipping into a kind of invisible isolation, was also devastating," stunting their growth and development (Taylor, Gilligan, and Sullivan 1995, 3; see also Annamma et al. 2016).

Being silenced in an organization where one heals can be especially devastating. The wounds of silence may feel more severe in spaces where a warm acceptance of shared resilience is what is wanted most. In his poem about visibilities, inclusion, and psychosocial health, Essex Hemphill (1991, 75) noted, "I will always be there / When the silence is exhumed / I am always there for critical emergencies / I am the invisible son." In blood family and other intimate ties, a person experiencing stigma returns to their environment of support, even in the face of being muted in and by that environment. In Hemphill's case it was regarding invisibilities of his sexual identity as a Black gay man at family gatherings. In a social ecology of resilience, affiliates hope that silence is not alienating and, instead, is expressed most often in health-affirming ways. However, too often at the Ministries, silence inhibited resilience and undermined affiliates' healing. One might suspect that silence toward a stigmatized part of one's identity might be less painful when experienced in an environment where it is essential to embrace one's unhealthy, addictive past. Being willing to engage in fellowship with others striving to recover from the same addiction was vital for affiliates of the FACTS Ministries. Similar to "identity amplification" in social movement building (Snow and McAdam 2000), in a predominantly African American, faith-based space of health, affiliates may feel a need to mute differences, to amplify an "I am normal" identity for self-perception.

Although the Ministries was never presented as part of a social movement toward a more radicalized recovery (Morell 1996; White, Kelly, and Roth 2014), identity amplification—or "heightening the salience of an existing identity" (Snow and McAdam 2000, 58; see also Best et al. 2015)—can reinforce one's investment in a resilience organization. This process is reflected in the chapter 1 profiles of FACTS Ministries affiliates, in the health domains of the Ministries explored in chapter 3, and in the resources when the Ministries' collaboration with Cocaine Anonymous flourished, as discussed in chapter 4. When opportunities to engage in identity amplification are denied, more or less aggressively, silence may help to normalize while also undermining the capacity to heal. Taking actions that "exacerbate[e] silence is a feature of conflict-ridden, tense,

[and] fragile societies" (Reid and Walker 2003, 85; see also Canetti 1984; Ferme 2002). As Brinsfield, Edwards, and Greenberg (2009, 4) have noted, "The juxtaposition of voice and silence [can reveal] a great deal about organizations and the people in them." A tense silence can impair healing organizations like the FACTS Ministries.

This chapter examines silences at the FACTS Ministries to explore how unacknowledged issues magnify stigma and harm the health of affiliates who do not fit conveniently into the narrowing mission of a centrist faith-health organization that was incrementally imposed on the Ministries community by Pastor Marshall and the Ministries board. There are "intricate and vital connections [in] the interaction[s] of trauma, addiction, and spirituality" (Morgan 2009, 5). The five silences considered in this chapter are among the harmful effects on recovery, on the social ecology of resilience among affiliates, and on the FACTS Ministries as a whole. To add detail to the "hurts" resulting from decline in organizational affiliation considered in chapter 4, this chapter explores the silencing of women, youth, race-class differences, LGBTQ+ affiliates, and social justice themes.

The Silencing of Women

There are known and well-understood differences in the active addiction, incarceration, reentry, and health of women and of men. Using the best near-representative sample of past drug users, the Drug Abuse Treatment Outcome Studies (DATOS), Wechsberg, Craddock, and Hubbard (1998, 97) stated, "Men reported more alcohol use while women reported more daily use of cocaine [and] more problems related to health and mental health. In addition, women reported much greater proportions of past and current physical and sexual abuse [and] greater concerns about issues related to children" (see also Greenfield et al. 2007). At the FACTS Ministries, with few exceptions, there was a stark invisibility of female leadership and women-centered initiatives. Among those exceptions were the (2007–13) Friday Youth Nights during the summer. Programming was traditional and family-centered, with Youth Night volunteers providing a few hours of summer evening day care. Again assuming traditional roles, from 2008 forward, women provided critical leadership in food preparation, service, and cleanup at the community lunches on Tuesday and Thursday afternoons. During these lunches, women provided nutritional counseling and made meal services and other food bank resources available.

Among its special events, the Ministries hosted a Women of Faith and Wellness luncheon in 2009, which was attended by women from throughout the city's faith and recovery communities. At that luncheon, the pastor of another church in the neighborhood was recognized for her long-standing contributions to a North Lawson civic association, and the luncheon initiated a women's faith-health group (see chapter 3). In its health programming, a longtime member of the Either-Or CA home group was one of the two co-facilitators of the Ministries' relapse prevention workshops. Her workshops considered issues of women's health and recovery differences identified in the DATOS data and other prior research. At Either-Or CA meetings hosted at the Ministries, women-centered participation and leadership informed every meeting activity including chairing, doing meeting readings, suggesting and speaking on topics for discussion, and leading the meetings in prayer. Women's participations informed each of the health service domains central to the Ministries' health and resilience mission and each aspect that allowed the CA-Ministries affiliation to flourish (see chapter 4).

Still, women were silenced in many ways. Limited leadership by women was especially true on the church side of the Ministries. There was an implicit expectation of women on the church side to be submissive, which caused many affiliates to experience "the literal silencing of women in spiritual communities" (McGuire, Cisneros, and McGuire 2017, 187). Very few Ministries affiliates attended the Women of Faith and Wellness luncheon, and the women's health group it initiated was not sustained. Though pledged as an annual event, after 2009 no women's luncheon was organized again. Pastor Marshall perpetuated traditional role models in sermons by frequently and proudly repeating that his wife did not work outside of the home and that she was comfortable with, and in fact preferred, it. However, his wife Cheryl herself felt silenced enough never to say anything on the topic either way. Yet she was the one with a college degree (not her husband), she had been sober longer, and she had single-parented their children, working outside of the home while her husband was still in active addiction. Cheryl's behavioral silence and Marshall's repeatedly calling attention to her current stay-at-home status reified the Ministries culture of upholding traditional gender roles in the family.

At no time during the nearly fifteen years of research for this book did a woman share a message from the pulpit—neither at Sunday sermons nor at Men's Prayer Breakfasts, neither during the anniversary parking lot tent revivals early in the Ministries history nor at later fundraising

Partnership Dinners. Yet, occasionally, male guest speakers were invited to present a Sunday sermon. There were no women-centered health discussions, and the pastoral counseling for both women and men was done only by Pastor Marshall. The offertory prayer of tithing was always given by male members. Consistent with the Ministries' resistance to any internal leadership development, no usher board, elders circle, or other mechanism of traditional churchwomen's leadership and voice was ever initiated. Female participation and leadership took the form of Cheryl and the Marshalls' youngest daughter performing in the Praise and Worship Team during Sunday service or some women affiliates sharing testimony during the "open mic" period of church services. In addition, as presented in the prologue, contrary to Terra's hopes for support from Pastor Marshall and Ministries leadership for a women's faith-based sober housing, no such initiative ever progressed. As he stated in a 2013 guest sermon, Pastor Marshall believed that, like Cheryl, women were "the most exciting thing on this earth," without whom men would "have good reason to exit stage right." However, expressing that excitement through establishing and sustaining everyday leadership roles among women of the Ministries was almost entirely absent.

A respected women's leadership is vital, as "womanists call for a process that work[s] for the healing of everyone [and] considers the health and wholeness of the entire community" (Cummings 1995, 61). As Lorine L. Cummings (1995, 61–62) notes, central to any faith-health mission, "implicit in the womanist perspective is the idea that African American women have something to offer the community that has been heretofore overlooked or dismissed. . . . The essence of womanist thought is the healthy affirmation of African American women so that the entire African American community can thrive." The FACTS Ministries would not have been sustainable without the affiliation and diverse contributions of women. Still, the limited leadership opportunities for women reduced the health resources available in the community. No formal outreach occurred beyond occasional referrals to nearby women's and children's clinics. Other than the women's luncheon, no women's wellness workshop was ever proposed or held. No regular women's 12-Step or (the generally more women- and family-centered) Al-Anon meetings were ever proposed or hosted. Alienating lesbians (see "The Silencing of LGBTQ+ Affiliates" below) also furthered the silencing of women in the Ministries. Though it was not absolute, it compromised health and well-being both at organizational and individual levels.

Race-Class Silences

Socioeconomic status was among the silences of the FACTS Ministries. Class awareness was apparent through both omission and commission. During many Sunday services, Pastor Marshall combined a prosperity ministry narrative with what multiple Ministries affiliates described as an “uncomfortable aspiration” or a “megachurch envy.” He frequently referred to T. D. Jakes, a successful prosperity minister in the Dallas, Texas, area, with a derisive appreciation—not exactly a malicious envy, which “includes some form of anger, hostility, or ill will” (Harris and Salovey 2008, 335). His references to Jakes were more of a longing for an idealized outcome to which Pastor Marshall was striving. The social distances (of location, mission, membership, etc.) between a more than ten-thousand-seat megachurch in Texas and the eighty-five-seat storefront chapel of the Ministries were far greater than the geographic distance between them. Lee (2007, 228) noted:

> The prosperity gospel is a central part of word-of-faith teachings and suggests that God wants all believers to prosper financially and will bless them according to their faith. The timely spread of the prosperity gospel in the 1980s resonated with millions of Americans [and] consumer culture of the Reagan era and the explosion of wealth inflamed by the rise of Wall Street. Black neo-Pentecostalism procured a facelift through business-savvy prosperity preachers like Creflo Dollar, I. V. Hilliard, and T. D. Jakes [who speak] about their million-dollar portfolios and lavish lifestyles. Almost every city has at least one megachurch where middle-class and wealthy African Americans worship and network.

Prosperity teachings allow religious leaders, Lee (2007, 228) cautions, “to enjoy their wealth and consumerism as their rightful inheritance as God’s faithful children. . . . [This] teaching asserts that Christians have the power to control their physical well-being and financial fortunes through their faith [and that] God’s ‘hands are tied’ from blessing many Christians who lack faith and misappropriate biblical principles” (see also Gilkes 1998). Prosperity teachings explain that the reason some Christians are not experiencing healthy, prosperous lives has to do with their own lack of faith. Pastor Marshall appeared to have bought into this explanation. However, in the opinion of many Ministries affiliates, his prosperity ministry seemed misplaced. Often, his prosperity narratives received dismissive, nonverbal pushback from many in attendance, with some rolling their eyes or huffing in annoyance. However, those who seemed not to share Pastor Marshall's sentiment only spoke in nods and whispers. There was no platform where they could have their voices heard. Pastor Marshall or other Ministries leadership never acknowledged any discontent with his words or disconnect between him and the congregation.

Exacerbating many affiliates' sense of alienation from himself, Pastor Marshall made frequent comments about his commute to his family home in the suburbs, financed by the anchor benefactor church. He made references to the costly construction going on at their home. His prosperity repetition from a storefront pulpit in the disadvantaged neighborhood he grew up in was coupled with a very limited structural analysis. References to poverty were rare and most often linked to individual decisions and personal weakness. When neighborhood poverty was mentioned, he associated it with active addiction and the role of choice. He offhandedly explained away North Lawson being a high-poverty neighborhood by saying that there were "too many addicts not strong enough in their faith" to sustain their sobriety; that he sees that truth "repeated over and over again at the Tuesday and Thursday community lunches." For Pastor Marshall, prosperity's possibilities were available and a product of individual initiative. This narrative style and examples of a living faith were a reach, given the largely working-class neighbors, the returning citizen (i.e., recently released former felon) sober homes residents, and the uneven sprinkling of largely White, anchor church members in attendance on any given Sunday evening service. Pastor Marshall did not appear to have considered the incompatibility of his chosen ministry rhetoric with Christ's teachings against structures of inequality or His empathy for the most marginalized as being the most in need of compassion, not criticism.

In a 2013 guest sermon at a larger, wealthier, predominantly African American church in a different part of the city, Pastor Marshall preached the following:

> It's been a challenge. Anytime you do ministry in the inner city, Amen? Some of the things that you see and experience just make you shake your head. . . . *Sometimes I can't believe that people like being stuck.* I just don't believe that people don't want to prosper. But over the years I've learned that *what you eat, don't feed me.* So if I give you what sayeth the Lord and what the Bible says, and you don't apply it. Now, I'm

> not talking about this Ministry. . . . Some people just want to ride in on your coattails. Ride in on your prayers. Ride in on your meditating in the Word. . . . It behooves us to stand firm for the prize of the high calling in Christ Jesus and not look back or turn back. Because *many people are giving up. They're going back*. . . . There's a longing that goes on inside each one of us for that house that is from Heaven. (public presentation, January 2013)

For Pastor Marshall, many persons in poverty "like[d] being stuck" or had "given up." Too often "stuck" people would "ride in on [his] coattails," too irresponsible to put in the necessary work. He added Darwinian individualism: "What you eat, don't feed me." This and similar tropes emphasized independence over interdependence and denied the many structural truths that informed the lives of neighbors and affiliates of the Ministries. "Inequality" was never stated, and discrimination was a vague force rarely acknowledged. There was very little consideration of health disparities or mass incarceration, and when mentioned, these topics were almost exclusively presented in terms of individual deficit. Inner-city class marginalizations appeared to him to mean that those addicted were too entangled in the affairs of this earthly world or had given up and were "going back." The near-complete omission of class acknowledgment at the Ministries was a crippling limitation, given the location and post-prison reentry prevalence in the area and among Ministries affiliates. It is impossible to quantify in detail the consequences of race-class silences. How could one measure the affiliates' losses from health volunteering that ended, reduced-rate medical and dental care that was no longer offered, pastoral counseling unsought, nutritional outreach no longer made, and fewer people choosing to attend 12-Step meetings hosted on site? What was apparent over time were declines in these resources of the Ministries' health mission largely due to declines in the organizational affiliations which helped sustain them.

The Silencing of LGBTQ+ Affiliates

Beyond the silencing of women, youth, the working poor, and survivors of mass incarceration, the limited recognition of lesbian, gay, and other LGBTQ+ affiliates' voices also constituted an uncomfortable silence at the

FACTS Ministries. As in most organizations (see Schilt and Westbrook 2009), there was a tacit assumption at the Ministries that heteronormativity ruled and would define the behavior of people in everyday interactions. This assumption projected onto the affiliates in various ways, marginalizing lesbians and gays. Many at the Ministries behaved in ways consistent with heteronormative beliefs, as in many other organizational settings of the African American community. Regarding reciprocities of sexual identity and religiosity, Irene Monroe (2004, 122), an African American lesbian feminist, suggests, "My struggle in fully coming out and being accepted in the Black community, as the Exodus narrative calls for, is inextricably tied to the liberation of all my people. Because when and where I enter the struggle for Black liberation both within my community and within the dominant culture is where the whole race enters with me." It is unclear how the Ministries perceived the "Exodus" narrative in terms of identity and health. However, alienating actions of heteronormative omission and commission contributed to eroding the Ministries' health mission.

As Alton B. Pollard (2004, 326) recognizes, "the Black Church is at a dangerous and foreboding crossroads . . . [and] now struggles to accept many of its own, [given] the sexual politics of the church." From 2005 to 2015, three African American lesbians—Marla, Claretta, and Dawn—regularly came to Either-Or CA meetings. They were silenced by what appeared to be a homophobic omission. Not vested in typical expressions of femininity, they attended the CA meetings wearing ties, men's khakis or shorts, no makeup, and gender-neutral or more "boyish" haircuts. They carried themselves with what struck onlookers as a masculine demeanor. In a health setting, where the most vital recovery capital is the longevity of one's sustained sobriety, Claretta and Dawn had significant sober time. Claretta was approaching twenty years of sobriety and Dawn had well over ten years. They "worked a good program," were active in CA at the district level, taking on various roles of service, and were informed students of recovery. They could comfortably, and without pretense or ego, relate passages from the Big Book of Alcoholics Anonymous to suggest topics in an open-topics meeting format. They consistently did so, more often than the heteronormatively behaving males with generally far less sober time behind them. For many Ministries affiliates, these women deserved respect for their long sobriety and CA fellowship service. Yet there was very limited acknowledgment of their sustained sobriety, and little effort was made, beyond the perfunctory, at including them as affiliates of the Either-Or meetings and the Ministries. Those in attendance seldom spoke to them after the meetings. Like too many others, they were not invited to participate in other Ministries domains, and little effort was made to develop opportunities for a broader inclusion of them.

In addition to the longtime CA members who occasionally came to Either-Or CA meetings, other women who also did not adhere to heteronormative gender expectations came from the women's Community Correctional Facility (CCF). How these soon-to-be returning citizens experienced the Ministries' silencing of LGBTQ+ people is unclear. Though this was one among many potentially alienating silences they likely would have experienced at the Ministries, all CCF affiliates, whether the women who came on Thursday nights or the men who came on Saturday mornings, discontinued their Ministries participations after their CCF incarceration ended.

The experiences of Dorren and Martell also demonstrate the heteronormative responses to sexual identity at the Ministries. Dorren affiliated through the musical circles of the Ministries' Praise and Worship Team (PWT), a local, highly competitive Christian musical performance "circuit." In summer 2014, the board hired him to head the musical ministry and unceremoniously introduced him during a Sunday service. Dorren never made his sexual identity public, though he displayed what to many were "clockable" characteristics. To easily be "clocked," or recognized as gay, can be "a constant threat" for some gay men and lesbians (Fields et al. 2015, 124). His professionalism as a musician, appearance (always in a three-piece suit), shy, measured speech, and visible depth of faith reinvigorated the PWT and Sunday evening services. He brought a quality of musicianship that made it easier to appreciate. However, this peaceful period of Dorren's directorship was brief. Stigma leads to both individual and organizational management strategies of spoiled identity that reinforce a normative ideal (see Goffman [1963] 1986). Soon, a dispute of some kind occurred between Dorren and Pastor Marshall. After two months, Dorren left the position and the Ministries. Given a distant, external board and the absence of any internal leadership, like all decisions of staff and program development, circumstances of Dorren's removal were never disclosed to affiliates. His case exemplified discussions of Pollard (2004), Fields et al. (2015), and others, that despite one's beneficial contributions, removing someone to reduce a stigmatized visibility is one strategy of reducing organizational tensions and making silences louder still.

A year prior to Dorren's brief Ministries affiliation, Martell was a twenty-two-year-old resident in the Ministries' sober home next door to the Ministries building. After living in the sober home for two months in the summer of 2013, he made the brave choice to question his sexual identity publicly at a Thursday night Either-Or CA meeting. Various personal aspects are often expressed when an affiliate feels that a particular piece of information is relevant to one of the topics being discussed and to one's overall recovery. Valuing the meeting as a healing space worthy of a stigmatized visibility, Martell likely hoped for empathy and publicly stated his truth. After he did so, an unusually long silence followed. Then two affiliates who spoke after Martell referenced the "management of sin" as a necessary task in sobriety. A person sitting next to Martell got up for coffee and then sat down in a different chair at the opposite end of the room. These clear expressions of discomfort were followed by less subtle, disapproving words of judgment from Pastor Marshall. He loudly and "jokingly" asked Martell after the meeting "when was the last time [he] had had a girlfriend," a long-standing trope of heteronormative imposition. Another affiliate openly questioned the sexuality of Martell's two female friends who came to the Ministries with him, wondering aloud if one of them was his girlfriend. In the meetings soon after Martell's brave call to action and inclusion, a few affiliates displayed the motion of hand wipe-offs after shaking Martell's hand or walking by him minutes prior to the meeting without greeting him (i.e., "Even though I see you, if I ignore you, are you less here?").

Though many Ministries affiliates were "passively neutral," doing nothing, a few were not judgmental and offered support in informal conversations with Martell after that meeting and prior to the next. Three affiliates, one male and older, the others in their thirties, much closer to Martell's age, had ten and more years of sobriety and were known to be working good programs of recovery. They spoke to Martell with caring support. They appeared to respond to him without bigotry and encouraged Martell, with no agenda ("If I can be of help, or if you just want to talk, just give me a call"). Other than these three welcoming affiliates, what stood out were the everyday alienations of upholding a heteronormative status quo. These more and less veiled hostilities—conveyed in tight-faced smiles or uncertain and insecure behaviors of sober home co-residents and other affiliates directly toward, and indirectly about, Martell—were among the Ministries' loudest silences. Together they comprised an ambient sense of rejection that likely influenced Martell's mental breakdown just two weeks later, with police officers being called to the sober home next door to the Ministries; and less than two weeks after that, Martell was evicted. Police had been called to the sober home many times before because of other sober homes residents with mental health breakdowns. In a split among Ministries affiliates, several felt that far too few knew they had been complicit in silencing Martell after his disclosure and too many seemed unaware of the direct impact of their behavior toward him.

Years prior to the Ministries' short-lived affiliations with Dorren and Martell, from fall 2006 to summer 2010, Mason—a tall, thin, White, and effeminate thirty-something man—came to the Ministries after having been referred by his suburban treatment center. During his shares at Either-Or CA meetings, Mason made direct reference to attending meetings at Stonewall, an LGBT-affirming social service agency in the city. Soon after first attending these meetings, Mason brought his partner Tyler, who was also in recovery. They made it clear to all that they were in a relationship. They spoke about their house, their friends, their cats, and the challenges of recreating a social circle that no longer includes the frequent presence of substances and the repetitions of active addiction. The information they disclosed about their life together was received generally without overt judgment but with barely marginal inclusion. Their silencing was palpable. Whenever one or both of them attended and spoke, no one sneered, and no catcalls or other disruptive actions were notable. Nevertheless, often in the meeting shares that followed, other men would make apparently intentional pronouncements of "liking pussy" and recount escapades with female sex industry workers. At other times, there were nonverbal actions of othering as well, such as an affiliate slowly scooting their folding chair further away from Mason or Tyler and other microaggressions. The silencing of LGBTQ+ affiliates was in these behaviors, as though their very presence were a threat to them individually and to the legitimacy of the Ministries.

While Mason and Tyler were attending on Saturday mornings, Jess attended for a little over a year on Thursday nights. Jess was a sixty-something, short, White, bald man who could easily be "clocked" as gay. At Either-Or CA meetings, he spoke of "the club scene," poppers (an addictive, inhalant drug associated with gay men), and orgies he had participated in. He said these were a part of his "active addict past" while referencing Atlanta, Georgia, where "years back, things were real, real wild down there." Jess's silencing was seen in his choice to stop attending Either-Or meetings after a physical threat to him was made at the end of one meeting.

Taken together, Claretta's and Dawn's tempered inclusions over the years, Dorren's brief tenure as musical director, Martell's self-disclosure and mental breakdown, the undercurrent of hostility in the responses to Mason and Tyler, and the threatening end to the short affiliation of Jess exemplified a pattern of problematic silencing and organizational shaming. Regarding the potential for the "radical inclusion" of lesbians and gays, "gay-inclusive ministries, whether heterosexual or homosexually led, are often inspired by a variant of liberation theology [and] take place within black political churches that see political action for social justice as a part of their religious duty" (Shaw and McDaniel 2007, 138). However, responding to these and other apparently LGBTQ+ affiliates with compassion and without judgment in this place of faith, health, and healing was done by only a few longtime affiliates. They were the exceptions, as so few welcoming words and actions occurred. By omission or commission, apparently lesbian and gay affiliates were far more often alienated than accepted in the slow erosion of a healing environment at the Ministries.

The Silencing of Youth

Another disturbing silence at the FACTS Ministries was the treatment of youth and young adults. Several affiliates reacted with concern to the overt, alienating actions and limited consideration of their needs. Prior research has asked, "How did systems of shared information between Sacred and secular settings . . . and exchanges among persons borne of different eras matter in nurturing sanctuary [i.e., a social ecology of resilience]?" (Price-Spratlen 2015, 7; see also Flores 2013; Taylor, Gilligan, and Sullivan 1995). At the Ministries, it is difficult to know the answer because of the intergenerational silencing that often occurred. Pastor Marshall seldom engaged well with the few preadolescent and adolescent youth who attended services. A few millennial twenty-somethings would come to a service or two at the most, but they would quickly disappear. Not surprisingly, research has found that "institutional responsiveness to millennials improves their perception of, and involvement in," an organization (Waters and Bortree 2012, 200). However, a careless neglect characterized the Ministries' approach to youth.

An example is Pastor Marshall's words in spring 2014 to Jaleel, a twenty-year-old African American man from another part of the city. The pastor's words reflected little compassion in response to the young man's bravery and willingness to speak out. Jaleel spoke about trying to get his dad to stop drinking. In his early fifties, his father was already beginning to display "elderly" problems secondary to long-term alcoholism (e.g., hand tremors, incontinence) and was not employable. Pastor Marshall responded with an impatient sigh, saying, "The touch of the Lord's healing is not promised to all." Pastor Marshall quickly returned to glad-handing others rather than responding to Jaleel in his moment of need at a sermon's end. He seemed to display a limited awareness of how to support Jaleel as a concerned son and how doing so could in turn support the father and their family. Such an effort could also have strengthened the Ministries' outreach to a neighborhood on the other side of town, where Jaleel's family lived. In a time of dwindling affiliate numbers and unspoken organizational crisis, this apparent lack of recognition was striking.

This type of moment, of not being able or willing to meet young people where they were, occurred with some frequency. Such seemingly dismissive choices toward young men like Jaleel highlighted a lack of engagement with youth in recovery and in the North Lawson neighborhood more generally. Though it cannot be confirmed, Pastor Marshall's indifference likely had everything to do with Jaleel's growing disaffiliation and eventual departure from Sunday services and from the Ministries altogether, as with the departures of other young affiliates. The boxing club hosted by the Ministries engaged young boys (see chapter 3). Still, several situations of similar stunted responses to youth who were serving as leaders in their families occurred during the years of observing Sunday services. Call to the Altar moments for young people occurred a couple of times each year. During them, Pastor Marshall would call to the front of the chapel "all young people in attendance who wanted to be recognized and celebrated in the name of the Lord." This Call to the Altar ritual struck many as much more of an act of keeping up appearances than of inclusion of young people's input and affiliation. With no youth council or other means of leadership and voice, the altar recognitions did little to engage children and young adults in the development of their faith.

Another instance of the silencing of youth was far more detrimental. On a Sunday in early fall 2013, a young man around eighteen or nineteen years old attended the Ministries' Sunday evening services for his third visit. During his previous two visits, with slumped shoulders and no eye contact, he had seemed to be attempting to make himself as invisible as he could. Yet he returned. During this third visit, he had his toddler daughter sitting on his lap, perhaps to give him strength when he spoke. Pastor Marshall requested testimony as usual: "Who would like to share experiences about how their faith had served them during the week?" The typical long pause of tentative silence followed. Perhaps no one would choose to say anything that particular week. Finally, the young visitor bravely stood up with his toddler daughter in his arms and stepped to the mic stand at the center of the chapel:

> Just got to say. Don't know 'bout all this church and whatnot. But I know that I been standin' even when dudes I know been fallin'. They been fallin' hard, for real. Gettin' bullets in 'em no how. In the game. Out the game. Not sure it much matter, for real. [Brief pause.] They just been fallin'. And I been holdin' out. I been standin'. I been able to come back daily to pick her up [*now holding his daughter above his head*]. Share a hug wid' her. You know. Make a face or two, or whatnot, to make sure she smilin' some. Change a diaper or whatnot, for real. You know. Let her know I'm here, for her, for real. Been a good week, yep.

Despite his apparent nervousness, the young man's words were calm and caring. A long pause followed. There was a notable shift in mood and quality of attention. Everyone in attendance was riveted. The usual sidebar conversations in a loud whisper stopped. Adjustments of the soundboard and other movements in the chapel's back corner came to a standstill. No one fidgeted in their chair. No one coughed. Blithely unaware of how he had captured the room, the young man continued:

> And my baby mama; she and me. We gettin' good, a'ight, for real. She gettin' to know that I'm gon' be here for my daughter. We not so good, she and me. But I'ma make sure my chil' got all what she need, for real. [He paused, now apparently near tears.] She ain't never gon' go without, no way. And that's all wa's up. And I be glad for the week, for real. True 'dat.

It was a thoughtful, deeply heartfelt moment of profound power. Throughout the multiple pauses and sincere words pouring out of the young man, several people attending were moved to tears. "All right, young brotha. Welcome," someone was heard to say. Then one church elder said, "Um, hmmmm," amid a couple other Amens and caring smiles. The appreciation of his words and his courage to speak them was palpable. There was power in the young man's vulnerability. After an uncomfortable pause that felt too long, Pastor Marshall, visibly agitated, stood and, nearly shouting, angrily said:

> I don't know what's goin' on here. I said I am inviting folks forward for testimony! Everyone hear that?! Testimony! I 'on't know what folks got up to say. That means talkin' about living a life of Christ. Speaking about the lamb of God. That means talkin' about the way the Savior's been workin' in your life during the week that was. Anything else does not have a place here! So I'm lookin' for someone to share a testimony tonight!

A stunned silence followed. Pastor Marshall's words, spoken at the edge of anger in a scolding tone, had shattered the possibility for healing from this youth in the simple form of a heartfelt willingness to listen. The young man quickly walked out with his daughter. He never returned. Longtime affiliates who witnessed the Sunday service exchange were aware that a fruitful opportunity had been spoiled. At the very least the moment and an empathetic response to his words could have contributed to this young man's and his daughter's healing. Such a response could have signaled support for other teen parents and young adults in the room that day. Pastor Marshall likely did more damage to young adult inclusion that evening than with any other single decision he ever made.

Young adults' access to the value of the Ministries in the North Lawson community was silenced further when Friday Youth Nights were discontinued (see chapter 3). From 2007 to 2013, this program had been available for three hours each Friday evening during the summer, from the end of the city public schools' school year to just before Labor Day. In summer 2013, it ended—the coloring books, finger painting, children's Bible study, G-rated movies, and more—and affiliates never knew the reasons for this change. It was not because families were not dropping off their children with regularity. There were plenty of principled and trusted volunteers to supervise. Like many other Ministries decisions, it was yet another seemingly random act, void of any affiliate leadership input. This end marked the beginning of a repeated pattern of abrupt endings without explanation, with no associated plan of action, and without replacement.

In their seminal work on African American churches over a generation ago, Lincoln and Mamiya (1990, 310) noted that "two major challenges . . . confront Black churches: the problem of identity among young black children and the issue of the growing sectors of unchurched black teenagers and young adults." Yet at the Ministries, consistent with its pattern of undoing rather than creating and initiating programs, precious little was done to be supportive of the young, young men in particular. Little was done to engage twenty-somethings at the monthly Men's Prayer Breakfasts. Four young men came virtually every month. Another three or four would rotate through irregularly. Very little was done before, during, or immediately after each gathering over breakfast to acknowledge, value, or present these young men with opportunities to contribute. There was also very limited interaction with young persons from the CCF who came to the Either-Or CA meetings. Through their shares during Either-Or meetings, and in conversations after the meetings, many of these young men seemed to be in search of mentoring and mission. They often seemed unsure of how to ask for the support of people who could help them move their lives forward after their CCF incarceration ended. These few means for children and young adults to participate and to lead were only minimally improved with the highly compartmentalized programming of a summer youth Bible camp that began in 2014 after the Friday Youth Nights ended. Taken together, these and other smaller organizational actions silenced the possibilities for enriching a more youth-centered mission at the Ministries.

Social Justice Silences

The most surprising silence at the FACTS Ministries was the very limited consideration of social justice issues, considering this was a "House of God" extending from a foundation of challenging the stigmas of substance use and other health disparities. Many African Americans see "religion as crucial to public life . . . [and] tend to believe that there are structural causes of poverty, rather than only individual-level causes" (Sager 2007, 475; see Lincoln and Mamiya 1990). However, Ministries leadership never addressed structural causes and their relationships to the North Lawson neighborhood or to the faith of affiliates. Opportunity, equity, or any other consideration of fairness in organizational relationships or by the state were virtually never mentioned. They were only discussed at a distance with rank-and-file Ministries affiliates when a break-up occurred between the Ministries and its founding anchor church (see chapter 6). Even then, the prosperity narrative, along with a tone of disappointment, was frequently expressed. Actions of charity (e.g., the free lunches) are ministry's fixtures.

Yet collective empowerment or capacity building were never considered. As previously noted, the Ministries was resistant to any traditional participatory leadership, like the formation of a deacon board or an usher board. Consistent with the sentiments of his 2013 guest sermon excerpted above, in pre-meal prayers for the lunches, Pastor Marshall "jokingly" but regularly judged frequent lunch patrons as being "lazy" and "unwilling to do what it takes." No volunteers overtly challenged him publicly on his diminished compassion. Missing among Ministries leadership was even a minimal public acknowledgment of the rich legacy of the Black Social Gospel (Dorrien 2016; White and Hopkins 1975).

The Social Gospel movement "called for the fulfillment of Christ's promise . . . through expansion of human cooperation and the creation of a collectivist society that would abolish poverty" (Simon 1994, 54). Rejecting ideas of the marginalized poor as an immutable group, "it challenged Social Darwinism by asserting broader public responsibility for problems created by economic injustice and by identifying social helping with religious ethics of caring and service" (Tangenberg 2005a, 198). Yet, at the Ministries, overt animosity toward the poor was frequently displayed, as though associating with them would bring oneself down, more so than expressions of any Christian model of social justice. These challenging choices of organizational narrative were especially glaring in a faith-health ministry focused on substance abuse recovery and resilience. This was made worse, given that it was led by a returning citizen who was raised in the neighborhood, and who was himself in recovery after having spent the greater part of his adult life, with a wife and six children, in active addiction.

Consistent with Du Bois (1903), Lincoln and Mamiya (1990), and others, African Americans have historically used their churches as their chief source of community cohesion and political activism (Barnes 2005; Pattillo-McCoy 1998). However, when a shooting nearby presented an opportunity for a conversation about crime, poverty, and opportunity and the lack thereof, and about where these realities can often lead, no such discussion was initiated. In the early morning hours before the start of a Men's Prayer Breakfast on a Saturday in fall 2013, a homicide took place just a few houses east of the alley behind the Ministries parking lot. As the men coming to the breakfast walked, biked, or pulled up in their cars, the victim's body was still on the ground with a tarp draped over it. Yellow caution tape had cordoned off the crime scene. Several of the younger men did not enter the chapel for the breakfast until after they had gathered information about who others thought it was on the ground, what the circumstances of the shooting had been, and other relevant details. Clearly, that was a teaching moment for the men at the breakfast that morning. Whether the shooting was drug-related or not, despite no one from the Ministries being directly involved, some consideration beyond veiled symbolisms seemed warranted.

However, though the neighborhood shooting had taken place just seventy feet away from the Ministries' back door, Pastor Marshall barely acknowledged the apparent shooting. He made what struck many as a dismissive remark from a place of superiority over the shooting victim. First, the guest pastor who was visiting that morning made a reference to "the chaos down the block" before swiftly moving on to speak about his hopes and plans for his own church and its future. Next, when Pastor Marshall spoke following the guest pastor, he remarked how "the distance between you and evil is never very far." The only follow-up at the Ministries acknowledging the shooting was the posting of a flyer on a community room refrigerator announcing a community march one month later. As with other neighborhood shootings, the posted flyer was the full extent of Ministries consideration of the crime. Recovery-related discussions of it occurred at Either-Or CA meetings, with no Ministries leadership in attendance. At the end of a Saturday breakfast attended by twenty-two mainly African American men across three generations, many of whom had had near-death experiences, men commented that they had expected a more formal acknowledgment of the shooting. Yet again, even this loss of a human life nearby was met with near-complete silence. This was consistent with a larger lack of attention to matters of social justice that appeared to be beyond the topics the Ministries was willing to undertake.

The most striking justice silence of all was that Pastor Marshall consistently personalized the process of incarceration. In essence, he repeatedly blamed the victims for their inadequate individual relationship with the glory of God. Although he was an ex-felon himself, at no time did he use the term "prison system" or anything else that acknowledged mass incarceration. He repeatedly held each reentering citizen personally responsible for their success (or its lack) in recovery from addiction and the health outcome that ensued. While these beliefs are consistent with the sentiments of recovery management and the 12 Steps (e.g., Achara-Abrahams et al. 2012), a prison reentry outcome is contingent on much more than personal effort alone. An empathetic recognition of how structural practices inform incarceration and its related disparities, or resource constraints that shape many individual outcomes, can affirm many returning citizens in their fight against addiction. During Ministries events, Pastor Marshall never mentioned any civically engaged faith leaders like William Trotter, Rev. Dr. King, or James Cone historically, or Bishop Yvette Flunder or Rev. William Barber more recently. These women and men of faith, in the past and today, take contexts of societal oppression into consideration in their activism and arguments.

Beyond CCF attendance at Either-Or CA meetings and Pastor Marshall's occasional visits to state prisons to speak, there was no apparent formal resource sharing with any criminal justice entity. No Ministries-led, co-sponsored workshops or regular prison activity facilitated by the pastor or by Ministries volunteers were offered at the CCF facility. Neither was a letter-writing campaign, inviting currently incarcerated persons soon to be released to a sober new beginning, ever proposed. Typically, the residents in the Ministries' sober homes were returning citizens. Their valuable presence and experiences could have contributed to the Ministries' assets to flourish, but they were never more formally recognized. Affiliates' participatory leadership was denied the simplest affirmation of a nod, a smile, or a thank-you. Whenever he mentioned having recently visited and spoken at a prison from the pulpit, Pastor Marshall never acknowledged the contribution of any Ministries sober homes residents who had gone with him. In effect, these justice silences may have been more than an omission of a modern Social Gospel. They may have been informed by organizational funding considerations (Sayer 2012), given a perceived need to sustain a more individualized narrative for health practices and outcomes and for socioeconomic circumstances.

Conclusions

Consistent with the compromised affiliation explored in the previous chapter, this chapter has analyzed ways in which organizational silences were apparent to, and experienced by, many affiliates of the FACTS Ministries. In the early years of the Ministries, the rooms of recovery from addiction provided beneficial silences, a pause of healing, and a moment's unexpected experience of Grace. Silence was almost exclusively a means of shared faith across religious differences, a neutral, valued absence of tension and sound. In later years, too often silence became a "tyranny" (Lorde 1984), an act of denial through reduced access to respect and resources for healing. Its uncertain benefit and generally adverse effects on the Ministries' mission made it increasingly clear how individual affiliates experienced the phenomenon of silence. Group dynamics and leader actions play a central part in silencing. Organizations struggle with "the potential consequences of silence [and] must gain a deeper understanding of how group and [leader] behaviors elicit silence and/or encourage voice" (Bogosian 2012, v). In an environment of shared stigma, a health ministry provides distance from the marginalization of normative society. However, having one's identity silenced in such a place—where someone who already feels vulnerable expects to feel safe and receive mutual respect—can further distance a person from a sense of self-respect and self-care. Subjects who are kept silent are led to suffer even greater shame and even more intense alienation by experiencing virtually the same worthlessness and inadequacy from which the safe space of recovery had promised to heal them.

Rebecca Sager (2012) suggests that what an organization does and does not give voice to may be informed by the politics of its funding. However partially, many of the what appeared to be detrimental silences at the Ministries may well have been financially pragmatic. The Ministries' founding and flourishing occurred during the period of rising social insecurity, ongoing declines in the priorities of social welfare, and "the crafting of the neoliberal state" (Wacquant 2010, 197), whose "most central feature is the primacy given to the interactions between the individual and markets [and where] the availability of socioeconomic (health) resources are either blocked or muted" (Siddiqi et al. 2013, 196; see also Hackworth 2010). These silences were likely informed by a centrist, more risk-averse, and conservative leadership wedded to a religious "benefactor charity" funding model. The leadership was unwilling to act "against" anything that could be perceived as threatening to the predictable reciprocity of dependence on the suburban, White, evangelical anchor churches funding it and with which the Ministries and the anchor churches felt most comfortable.

The silences were consistent with "the compressed welfare state [and its] individualization of risk [where] social cleavages are more pronounced, reducing the sense of belonging, citizenship, collectivity, and social cohesion" (Siddiqi et al 2013, 196; see also Kawachi and Berkman 2000). The White House Office of Faith-Based and Community Initiatives, a legacy of the second Bush administration, restricted and reconfigured resources for faith-based initiatives to address addiction. This included those resources available to faith-based community organizations (Sager 2012). Given the reduced autonomy that resulted from this restructuring, any justice mentions could be regarded as a danger to an organization's funding stability. The funding base of the Ministries likely made Pastor Marshall and the board cautious about justice themes, lest they risk altering their funding circumstances. Proposals by longtime affiliates for enhancing the autonomy of Ministries funding were repeatedly rejected. Consistent with Sager's findings, little in the Ministries events, programming, or symbolism ever attempted to explore the boundaries of funding politics. Not doing so likely contributed to the compromised potential of the Ministries' health-promoting domains.

Silences that many affiliates experience as oppressive are deeply entrenched in the organization. They compromise the presence of the ethnogenic thread and the equity-affirming, collective ethos associated with it. Larger factors of influence beyond the organization itself are likely to influence how they matter as well. The resilience of recovery can be heartily and repeatedly enriched through "a daily reprieve contingent on the maintenance of [one's] spiritual condition" (Alcoholics Anonymous 2001, 85). That daily reprieve can be maintained and strengthened in a setting like the FACTS Ministries. But it may be interrupted by a silence of denial, expressed in a variety of ways. Silence plays a role in both the healing reprieve (e.g., the solitude of prayer in the company of others) and in the compromised resilience (e.g., the "tyranny" of disrespected difference, or public shaming). The daily reprieve may become more unsteady when silences compromise resilience in spaces of healing. Environments of support for health and resilience can be fraught with expressions of trauma and other stigma-related silences. Given the importance of respect with others in a health-promoting setting, ending Either-Or CA meetings at the Ministries is indicative of fractured resilience at the Ministries. Ending the meetings displays its own form of silence that was problematic, if not devastating, to many. New affiliates dwindled, and the term "former affiliate" grew in number as many felt and acted on the need to retreat. These silences were an especially egregious limitation in an organization intended to provide a safe space for healing.

Muting opportunities of FACTS Ministries' affiliates to benefit from its many assets of people, places, and things—its diversity of affiliate backgrounds, identities, and experiences—mattered. Doing so had resilience-compromising consequences "on decision-making and processes of change by blocking alternative views, negative feedback, and accurate information, perpetuating the façade of a singular, unproblematic commitment to the organization" (Beheshtifar, Borhani, and Nekoie-Moghadam 2012, 280). These silences never allowed potential benefits from the affiliate leadership of a deacon board or some similar form of input to exist. The collaborative potential of enriching the Ministries' relationships with CCF or a nearby homeless shelter or the behavioral health center in the neighborhood were never explored in any way that was apparent to affiliates. Potential innovations including a program for young fathers, the "radical inclusion" and visibility of LGBTQ+ affiliates, or a workshop series on mass incarceration as a faith/public health issue are just some of the many unrealized initiatives.

Pastor Marshall acknowledged and often celebrated only identities and behaviors with little or no stigma attached to them. When it came to stigmatized identities and behaviors, he at best tolerated them. At the FACTS Ministries, expressions and consequences of the unspoken often seemed to be products of "the social construction of stigma and secrecy as a site of shame . . . [because] silence and secrecy threaten the structure of social relations and the social order itself through the disintegration of communitas" (Reid and Walker 2003, 87; see also Flores 2013). These silences contributed to the disintegration of the ability to sustain an ecology of health and resilience by communing with others in an environment of equity and shared respect. As Morell (1996, 309) noted, "Whether thought of as God or as the vitality that results from communing with others, spirituality can inspire and sustain people to move beyond external and internalized oppression [and toward] radical recovery." Instead, the Ministries silenced women, youth, race-class differences, and LGBTQ+ affiliates. Worse, it silenced any hope for thoughtfully addressing social justice. With these silences, it categorically muted, and definitely did *not* sustain, "vitality" or any health-promoting "radical recovery."

Any one of these silences alone would have been compromising to the Ministries. Together, they signaled a lack of organizational introspection and any willingness to allow for decision-making transparency. Welcoming, instead of rejecting, an opportunity to consider how the politics of funding informed these and other organizational silences would likely have made a profound difference; but lack of transparency itself became a compromising silence. Less autonomy due to more restrictive access was a concern regarding FACTS Ministries' funding stability. Instead of willingly addressing these challenges, the Ministries' silences fractured its potential for resilience, which then only grew louder still. The silences could have been used strategically to help further the potential for an organizational resilience of growth and change. Instead, the organization's trajectory was compromised. How the Ministries itself declined over time is the focus of chapter 6.

Chapter 6

Change Gon' Come

The Flourishing and Decline of the Ministries

> The dynamic nature of sustainability raises questions about the contextual meaning of "evidence-based practices" for improving health. . . . Many churches participated in health fairs, but we have no information about the evidence base for those additional information sources or their outcomes. The multi-faceted processes involved in this type of community participatory project means that the evidence behind their sustained delivery cannot be closely controlled.
>
> —Scheirer et al. 2017, 8

Introduction

The FACTS Ministries experienced a great deal of organizational change during the years of the research project. Consistent with Scheirer et al. above, the multifaceted processes of the Ministries' expressions of the ethnogenic thread have contributed to the health and resilience of its affiliates and to the North Lawson neighborhood. In the preceding chapters, the people (chapter 1), places (chapter 2), and things (chapter 3) (i.e., health resources of the organization's faith-health mission) are among its primary evidence base of hope. Challenges of an often uneven affiliation between the Ministries and the local chapter of Cocaine Anonymous (CA) (chapter 4) and the incessant silences of intentional omission or callous inattention (chapter 5) are among its evidence base of resilience-sacrificing hurts. Beyond the Ministries' process of affiliation fractures with CA, its pattern of organizational change over time and eventual decline have not been analyzed. The trajectory of any ecology, or environment of support, is an essential aspect of how its impact can be better understood. Understanding an organization's change is essential since "true health resilience must derive from stronger health and health care systems . . . and the capabilities to sustain . . . healthy individuals and communities amid large-scale changes" (Wulff, Donato, and Lurie 2015, 364). This chapter explores the large- and small-scale changes that shaped its mission. Its physical appearance and contents were among these many changes. For much of the Ministries' first eight years (2000–08), the chapel held three rows of large ten-person pews. During these years, there were sixteen such pews in a floor space that could barely hold twelve. As in most churches, the moving space between the pews was too small for comfortable motion, and the wood seating made sermons seem longer than they were. This crowded chapel is where the recovery-informed sermons and the Bible studies took place. From its Sunday sermons and Tuesday morning prayer sessions to the faith messages while blessing the food prior to the Tuesday and Thursday lunches, the Wednesday night Bible studies, and the Men's Prayer Breakfasts, chapel pews were where those receiving their food sat as they ate and where the mission of the Ministries unfolded. Other special events periodically took place in it as well, including the Ministries' early anniversary celebrations. Curiosities of the Ministries' social ecology of resilience inspired this research project, which began at its third anniversary celebration in 2003. During its first three years, it appears that activities undertaken at the Ministries occurred at a steady, slow pace. A group from both anchor churches was consistently coming, and together with North Lawson neighbors, Sunday services often had forty-five to fifty-five people. The sober homes resident attendance was nearly 100 percent on most Sundays. By 2003, the third anniversary celebration of the Ministries had arrived.

The Early Years: "We're Still Standing!"

July 12, 2003, was a hot and sticky day in the city. The Saturday morning Either-Or meeting of Cocaine Anonymous had just begun. During announcements from the floor, though a CA meeting and its host are autonomous and kept separate, all were invited to attend a special event scheduled to take place in one week. The Sixth Tradition of CA states, "A C.A. group ought never endorse, finance, or lend the C.A. name to any related facility or outside enterprise, lest problems of money, property, or prestige divert us from our primary purpose" (Cocaine Anonymous 2018, 7). Still, the relationship between a CA meeting and its host site is often collaborative, as was the case at the FACTS Ministries. The upcoming July 19 anniversary announcement was made in celebration. A strong sense of hope and possibility was dripping from every word. Albert (see chapter 1), one of the Ministries' core affiliates, stood up proudly and with a broad smile nearly shouted to the other affiliates at the Either-Or CA meeting:

> I just want everybody to know that next weekend the FACTS Ministries will be celebrating its third anniversary! Everyone is welcome. Tell your friends. Bring your family. There's going to be good food and games for the kids. Good fellowship and quality speakers. Did I mention there's going to be lots and lots of good food? We'll be celebrating all weekend, with the Call to Worship and barbecue that will begin next Saturday at noon. Please be sure to come! Hope to see everyone there.

The Ministries' third anniversary was a powerful demonstration of how the Ministries understood itself at that moment. The cover of the four-sided event program handed out as the festivities began said, "We're Still Standing." This phrase appeared below an image of an individual walking across a bridge. Symbolically, the program cover's message appeared to be that recovery is a walk of faith. In that walk away from one's active addiction past, the Ministries affiliate stands with the God of their understanding, moving in a new life of recovery toward the sober and sacred side of the bridge. The event answered vital questions of presentation to, and celebration with, a neighborhood still getting used to the Ministries' presence so vividly displayed behind two large words, FACTS Ministries. The building's availability made it the perfect time of one church's end for another to begin and a perfect place to address recovery, with trap houses all around it and public drug sales always nearby. The importance given to organized religion among residents of a neighborhood nearly 90 percent African American and the unique appeal of providing a public visibility to something often associated with anonymous shame made a faith-based organization for recovery and resilience with a church's name a good fit. The program cover image suggested Ministries affiliation was a bridge beyond stigma's shame, to a new understanding of sustaining their sober self. As volunteers helped to set up for the celebration, scheduled to begin at noon, there seemed to be something unspoken that informed this welcoming, though unsettled, place. Did it have something to do with the unspoken presence of trust among strangers in this religious setting? Was it a result of being a stone's throw from two dope houses, where people were likely getting high at the very moment anniversary preparations were taking place here? There were histories to be healed: individual, organizational, neighborhood, and other faith/health uncertainties for the Ministries and its mission. Whatever it was, an energy and tension of various contrasts was palpable that day.

The two large charcoal barbecue pits in the parking lot were covered in pork and beef ribs, hot dogs, and hamburgers. All of them were cooking with a loud sizzle. A fifty-something African American man was tending to one of the pits, while two White men in their sixties were tending to another. The men were sharing the language of friendly competition. With more meat cooking, the already-cooked, ready-for-the-plate meats were stacked on the grills' resting level to keep them warm. These along with the food that was being stocked in the community room led one to wonder exactly how many people were expected at this event? A hundred? A hundred and fifty? More? All that meat seemed both excessive and inviting. It reflected a caring sentiment that "all who come are our neighbors and all of our neighbors are welcome to eat and eat well." These unspoken words were acted out in an inclusive manner, giving the celebration more of a feel of a family backyard barbeque than a charity event of a religious or health/recovery mission.

The Ministries' third anniversary engaged people of all ages. Children-centered games and play were a priority throughout. Cross-sticks, Hula-Hoops, board games, and cotton candy were among the child-friendly options, leading a joy in the innocence of faith to be apparent and celebrated. Some happened upon the event while walking down the alley next to the parking lot. Others had been longtime Ministries affiliates and volunteers and had helped plan activities of the day. Regardless of one's relationship to the spectrum of engaged faith, secular recovery, or other domain of its health mission, true to Albert's invitation the week before, it offered a simple pleasure of good fellowship and good food. The turnout from the neighborhood was strong and seemed to indicate a moment of equitable and caring triumph for the Ministries, one that was seldom if ever equaled in celebrations to come.

That third anniversary celebration was among the best of what the Ministries did right. In tone and tempo, with the possible exception of the keynote speech, it was outreach-oriented and affiliate-centered. The words and activities were a caring and welcome invitation to strangers unfamiliar with the Ministries and its mission. A motive for fellowship and reason to belong was apparent to all who attended. The smiles of those already affiliated seemed genuine and reinforced a sense of resilience and possibility rooted in Christian mission. The day's activities nurtured a discovery of self without substance(s) and of a self within Christ. Evangelical appeals were presented as a caring possibility for healthy change, instead of a judgment of sin and flaw and a shouting down of an incomplete self.

As preparations for it began, affiliate differences became increasingly apparent, as people presented a stark divide in the subgroups of the more than 150 people there during the hours of the celebration. Those who came because of a direct, neighborly appeal were largely African American, younger, with small children, who had walked to the celebration from the neighborhood. Those who were volunteering were mostly White, middle-aged or older, and arrived without children. They had driven in from outside of the neighborhood and were more overtly evangelical when they spoke. The third group consisted of a mixture, including those who attended the Either-Or CA meetings and those not conveniently reflective of the other groups there. They appeared to not be interested in the religious trappings of the event and were there for the fellowship and the food. Some of them were White nonlocals of an apparent higher-class standing. Others drove older-model cars and included people of various races, ethnicities, and backgrounds.

As the food on the grill was cooking, conversation included those with a substance use history speaking openly without concern for judgment or condescension. This mixture of strangers made for cautious, yet genuine, small talk as the afternoon proceeded. At first glance, visible, unspoken tensions of neighborhood, affiliation, and others were among the most apparent elements of the Ministries' anniversary. Still, the event had the feel of a backyard barbecue. Improving the lives of persons living in concentrated disadvantage, often among the most addiction- and prison-affected neighborhoods, has long been one of the more vital projects of African American churches (Bakken, DeCamp, and Visher 2014; Cheney et al. 2014; Freeman 2001). The most recent generation of mass imprisonment has heightened both the corrosive effects and the related urgency of creatively and constructively responding to these challenges. The FACTS Ministries third anniversary celebration did so with a caring familiarity.

During the first six years (2000–06), a steady division of faith labor and health mission developed between the northern church side of the Ministries, which had the chapel, the pastor's office, and the men's bathroom, and the community room side, where the community room, kitchen area, and women's bathroom were located in the building's southern side. During the third anniversary celebration, much of the activity was in the gentle tempo and flow between the two sides of the building. Only a thin, paneled wall was between them. As various tensions grew over time, the wall between the two areas of the building came to feel five feet thick.

That steady division of labor seemed to also mark distinct aspects within particular domains of the Ministries. It was sustained between the Thursday night and Saturday morning Either-Or CA meetings and was strengthened by a stable level of diverse affiliate participation. Albert was ready to offer pizza before and during, and a ride home from, Thursday night meetings. On Saturday mornings, Jerry was enthusiastic about his CA district fundraising 50-50 raffle and his weekly donuts donation. A professional salesman, he used that sales enthusiasm when promoting tickets for the CA district fundraiser and in other activities of his informal leadership. During these years, on the church side of the Ministries, a small and consistent Praise and Worship Team (PWT) was sustained. Both its membership and musicianship were strong. The entire musical dimension of the Ministries lost a great deal of its momentum when, in late 2004, Arnold, the lead guitarist for the PWT, relapsed and returned to active addiction. A couple blocks south of the Ministries' front door, he was shot and killed during what appeared to be a drug-buy gone wrong. This was the first death of a regular Ministries affiliate since its opening. Because Arnold was one of the few who regularly attended both Either-Or CA meetings on Saturday mornings and the Sunday worship on the church side of the Ministries, his sudden relapse and death was especially unsettling, and few knew how to cope with it.

Still, by 2004, even after Arnold's untimely death, the Ministries continued its healthy trajectory as an "outreach ministry" of the anchor churches that funded it as their "inner-city" urban mission. The funding paid for Pastor Marshall's full-time salary and assisted the Marshall family in purchasing a suburban home. The Ministries' slow, gradual growth made possible the purchase of the first two sober homes in the FACTS Ministries' name. With them, the Ministries was able to house up to eight men as they developed a sober homes program. The following year, the Thursday night CA meeting was becoming popular in the city and the numbers rose from ten or fifteen regular attendees to more than thirty. The number attending Sunday evening services increased, as eight to ten Either-Or CA affiliates were open to, and interested in, a house of worship and services presented in a nondenominational, Black Baptist–tinged tradition. By the fall of 2005, the Ministries was listed among possible host sites for a CA citywide party to ring in 2006 in sober celebration with others also seeking a place to share in the holiday without alcohol or drugs. In a spirit of collaboration, CA district leadership chose the Ministries as the host site for its New Year's Eve gathering, and Ministries leadership agreed. This selection strengthened the relationship between the Ministries and the citywide leadership of CA. Still, even after this event success and a collaborative pathway forward, the dynamic nature of the Ministries' sustainability was affected when it formalized as a nonprofit organization.

The Nonprofit Begins

In 2006, the FACTS Ministries secured and finalized its 501(c)3 nonprofit status. Efforts that had begun in late 2004 were now reality. No one knew exactly what this change would mean and how the mission of the Ministries would be impacted. It is unclear how much consideration and what planning occurred in anticipation of this change. What would becoming nonprofit mean for the board, both in terms of tasks and who was on it? How would this affect Marshall's pastoral role? What organizational affiliations were to be prioritized and maintained? How would individual affiliates on the chapel side and the health/community room side of the building's middle wall be impacted? Amid these and other uncertainties, it was clear that various changes would occur, and they began almost immediately. The first shift was one of organizational perception and neighborhood niche. The annual anniversary celebrations changed immediately. The Ministries' annual parking lot barbecues were no longer held during a long Saturday in July. There were no more barrel pits of barbeque, and no more cotton candy and old-school games for neighborhood kids. There was no more direct outreach to the neighborhood in a tent-revival atmosphere mixed with a Southern cookout, and no more on-site walk-through folks with their mac-and-cheese and greens and dripping pork ribs as they sat in the chapel pews.

These accessible, "down-home" communal celebrations of 2001–05 were replaced with what was euphemistically called the "Partnership

Dinner." Beginning in 2006, Partnership Dinners were, in many respects, everything the on-site celebrations were not. They were held off-site, at a small, cloth-napkin-and-white-tablecloth banquet space owned by one of the FACTS Ministries board members. These dinners changed from the familiar, come-as-you-are of the parking lot next to the alley, during a hot and sticky summer afternoon, into overtly "upscale," formal, invitation-only events. The ability to be fluid with the call-and-response of a storefront church service was replaced by chefs, a professional waitstaff, reserved table service, and a more rigid program led from behind a solid podium at the front of a banquet room. The value of the "call-and-response interaction lies not only in the possibility of realizing concrete results from particular supplications, but also in the *cultural* familiarity [as] a common language that motivates social action" (Pattillo-McCoy 1998, 768; italics in original). One of the most visible expressions of that common language for communal resilience was now gone. Where the anniversary parking lot barbecues had been warm and welcoming, with a true North Lawson neighborhood religious familiarity, Partnership Dinners were stiff, formal affairs. Gone were the alleyway walk-up people who happened by to share in a good meal, replaced with a (by 2012) $50-per-plate minimum or $400-per-table required donation. The shorts and flip-flops of summer were replaced with the shirt and tie formality of a winter banquet. Fittingly, the warmth of the summer outdoors was replaced by the off-putting cold of February evening and the need for an artificially heated interior.

In addition to the nonprofit status and the Partnership Dinners, the third transformation during the 2006–07 period was a noticeable reduction in the nurturing of internal leadership. Instead of using the newfound nonprofit status and autonomy to develop longtime affiliates or North Lawson neighbors, it seemed that the board began to get fragmented. On the one hand, the anchor churches were questioning whether to continue to fund the Ministries at its current level and location. On the other hand, some board members were beginning to assess possible new sites the Ministries, or perhaps even the anchor churches themselves, could move to. Meanwhile, vital questions of how actual Ministries affiliates could participate in the development of new initiatives, networking with other organizations in the neighborhood and city, or other capacity-building efforts were never raised. The neighborhood's largely African American working-class residents, who had regularly come to the celebrations, and many of whom returned to visit during Sunday service or an Either-Or CA meeting, were replaced by almost entirely White, evangelical, and corporate table-purchasing donors who only came to this single charity event. With these changes the often uneven, "Who are *those* people in *that* place?" relationship between the Ministries, the surrounding blocks of North Lawson, and other organizational collaborators became more unstable.

During this period of organizational change, one of the annual events that endeared the Ministries to the neighborhood, both for its food-centered resources and its health mission, was the annual Thanksgiving meal that took place before, during, and after the Thursday night Either-Or CA meetings during the final Thursday of November. In the years 2005 through 2008, Thursday night Either-Or meetings were held on Thanksgiving night. Keeping the Ministries open during this time allowed those who might not otherwise have a holiday gathering to attend to join the small group of dedicated CA members who prioritized this meeting and were there after being a part of their family or other commitments. These Thanksgiving night Either-Or meetings were smaller than the other meetings during the year. And for those who came, they seemed far richer. The potluck format felt more intimate and allowed those who came and contributed to be more self-revealing. Memories of private, despairing "war stories" of active addiction were shared about the drunk and drugged holidays that those who were there were now grateful to no longer be living. They expressed their appreciation of a sober holiday with the strong bond of Ministries and CA affiliates more than they did at any other meeting. Though this arrangement changed in 2009, these testimonies of sober healing often led to tear-filled breakdowns where authentic expressions of sober resilience replaced the remorse of prior holiday debacles in their lives.

Still, the seeming absence of a structural rationale and shared action plan to guide change became apparent when resource changes of any kind were initiated. Whether it involved cutting a second door in the wall between the chapel and community room, or funding the purchase of a car for Ministries use so that donations for the community lunches could be picked up more conveniently, or changing the third sober home next door to the Ministries to be the host site for an expanded youth ministry, no clear markers of necessity or plans for strengthening demand seemed to warrant these changes. Silences were a product of many things, and perhaps central among them was the complete absence of an affiliate leadership apparatus of any kind. No men's deacon board was ever initiated. No women's usher board ever existed to value women-centered input. No youth leadership, nor church elder circles were developed. Repeatedly, material, process, and structural resource changes occurred with seemingly little forethought and with no affiliate input of any kind. These decisions were having sustainability consequences as Pastor Marshall made himself available for an interview during the summer of 2007.

The Interview

In July 2007, with its nonprofit status now one year old, the author interviewed Pastor Marshall to explore his experiences of the first year. An excerpt of that interview appears below.

Author [AU]: What is the institutional relationship of the Ministries to any other church? Is there a sponsoring organization or other formal relationship that is a part of the Ministries' foundation?

Pastor Marshall [PM]: Ya, that would be Millwood Christian Fellowship, along with Christ Faith Church. They are our two anchor churches. We're currently in the process of seeking two other anchor churches. They kind of oversee [related activities] and are part of the board.

AU: Have you developed a relationship with any of the [churches] immediately adjacent to you? Are there any parishioner or church leadership relationships you are cultivating nearby?

PM: I don't know that it would be immediately. [Laughs.] [We've been] ignored. I don't think anybody really takes us seriously. Because they don't know who we are. They don't know what we're doing. And so therefore, I think there's a fear there. Of it being a cult, or you know. Seeing that we've been here for these [seven] years. I don't see the rush right now. [More laughter.] But I will take the initiative to contact some of the leaders in the area. Because I think we're in that season as a Ministry, that we can go and introduce ourselves. And maybe, dare I say, even take the first step to allow other leaders to know what we're doing. You've got the whole 12-Step thing going. You know, and people are just . . . like that. And when you don't know, you become afraid. . . . So, I think they'd just rather stand there and not know.

AU: Has that changed over time in any way?

PM: Not with any other normal churches. It doesn't matter whether they're in the suburbs or the inner cities. It will change when they have people in their ministries that need our services. That's the only way that we've made these connections because we have something they need. Or that they don't know how to deal with [addiction]. So they say, "Well, maybe that's what they do." And they find out about us.

AU: Regarding Ministries affiliation, do you have members?

PM: No. None.

AU: Why not?

PM: Because we were never geared to be a church. We were geared to be an outreach ministries around a residential [drug treatment] facility. And we're trying to stay—I don't know how we can—as far away from looking like a church [as possible]. . . . I told someone last night at Bible study, we are getting a makeover, a new face. And so, how all of that looks, I really don't know. I think that God has allowed us to get our feet wet. To know what we're in for. There's not really a challenge. I think there's a redirecting, continuing to lay a foundation to help the type of people we want to help. . . . A redirection from being a revolving door to a place where people can call home. I think it's relational. If we're able to connect people with longevity [i.e., long-term sobriety], it's going to be better for their recovery. We haven't had the personnel to do what it is I think we need, to do it better. So, that's where we are, trying to better what it is we've done. . . . If we were to have a plan of action with the action items, and setting the goals, I never had any outcome I was really reaching for. If it's more geared toward the outcome, I think we're going to get a better return.

AU: What is your vision for the Ministries' institutional success?

PM: It would be [having] a residential facility where 50, to 75, to 100 people could be housed on the campus with a worship center in the heart of it. And to have other recovering people actually operating it. And to be able to release people from recovery. Maybe after a year, or 18 months. And then they, in return, continue to come back. And to give back. Through service work. Or through whatever means they have gotten involved. . . . l wouldn't say that I have a timeline. So, my whole goal is to get comfortable in what I do. I don't want it to be an Ellwyn thing. I want it to be a God thing.

A Tension Arrives

Shortly after the interview, a board meeting changed this trajectory and timeline. Pastor Marshall understood it as one thing, yet it quickly became something else. From the start of the FACTS Ministries' nonprofit status, an informal board position of oversight was created. Ostensibly, this position was to assist Pastor Marshall in the fiscal and personnel management sides of the Ministries, so that he could focus on building a formal pastorate. Calvin Sandorn had the means and interest to serve in the half-time position. A longtime member of the anchor Millwood Fellowship Church, Calvin had been an ex-officio board member from the establishment of the Ministries' board. A few months later, in early 2008, he was hired by the board to be the operations manager in a salaried position of thirty-five hours per week. Before he began, Pastor Marshall resented Calvin's hiring as an imposition. Almost immediately, Pastor Marshall's resistance and the tension between the two men were palpable. They made some effort to define a clear division of labor. Yet they did not overcome the unspoken passive-aggressive tension between them. Pastor Marshall was African American, high school educated, and had spent much of his adulthood enlisted in the military, in active addiction, or in jail. Calvin was White, college educated, and had experienced professional success that allowed him to retire in his early fifties. Marshall was a person reared in the Black Baptist tradition; it was while he was incarcerated that he had found his Calling; he was now a "jackleg" preacher and often spoke in the CA meetings about "not being much of a reader, for real." Calvin was a schooled student of the Bible and of the Protestant Christian tradition. Calvin was a man of means who lived in the suburbs, while Pastor Marshall had limited means, had grown up in North Lawson, and was much more salary-dependent on the anchor churches' urban mission. These differences between the two men's backgrounds could have been neutral or even beneficial. However, their net effect had a corrosive impact on the Ministries.

Soon after hiring Calvin, the Ministries created a more formal sponsorship component. Individuals, churches, and other organizations were solicited to become Ministries sponsors, with four monthly contribution levels of support, from $50 to $500 per month. Identifying a third church willing to take on the responsibility of serving as another "anchor" church remained elusive. Funding was needed for the salaries of Pastor Marshall, the operations manager, and an on-site resident manager for the sober homes, as well as for building maintenance costs. Other donor forms were identified and sustained, including restaurant donations, which allowed the Tuesday free lunch program to expand to Thursdays. These and other outreach initiatives more than doubled the number and amounts of donors and donations to the Ministries. Despite the contentious relationship within the leadership, progress continued as the Ministries flourished.

The Ministries Flourishes, 2009–12

Despite the ongoing leadership tensions, 2009 to 2012 marked the Ministries' most successful years. In 2009, a professional grant writer and member of one of the anchor churches volunteered to work with a board member task force to secure grant funds to further the Ministries mission. The fruits of these initiatives included selling the bulky, wooden pews, which were replaced in the chapel by a set of plush, movable chairs. This improved the flexibility of room arrangements for the different health domain activities in a given week. The more consequential benefit of access to a professional fundraiser was the first large local foundation grant for $10,000 being secured in 2010. This grant and the means through which it was secured seemed to magnify an already palpable prosperity ministry envy toward select megachurch pastors. With increasing regularity, Pastor Marshall spoke in his Saturday morning Either-Or CA meeting shares and in his Sunday sermons about family vacations he had recently taken or was about to take. His references to these vacations included mentioning the settings they had been in, the people they were vacationing with, and other opulent markers. However, such remarks contributed to a growing tension between him and the most frequent Sunday service affiliates. Among the factors that contributed to this period of sustained success were stable numbers across each health service domain and respectful interactions with affiliates during them. A quality diversity of Sunday evening service attendance helped, as did successful special engagements during the holiday season, along with the Ministries' sponsorship of special events of Christian mission and resources extending from the local foundation grant.

By 2009 attendance at Sunday services was consistently fifty to sixty people, sometimes approaching the eighty-five-person capacity of the storefront chapel. The mixture of those attending was healthy, including affiliates from both anchor churches, longtime friends of the Marshall family who lived nearby, a few other persons from the neighborhood, faith volunteers who prepared and served one or both of the free lunches, and residents of the Ministries' sober homes. The ten to fifteen people who regularly attended Wednesday night Bible study and the three or four evangelists who were members of one of the large African American churches a few miles north and did street outreach to sex industry workers along Akron Avenue also regularly came to FACTS Ministries' services. Most had a home church different from the Ministries and used the evening services as their late Sunday second service. A few people who regularly attended one or both of the Either-Or CA meetings also attended. Together, these affiliation diversities were a product of those who prioritized regularly attending services that began at 6:00 p.m. on Sundays to help further the health resilience and capacity building of the Ministries' mission.

Pastor Marshall was energized by the consistent numbers, reflected in an improving consistency in the quality of his sermons. He often used humor and self-deprecation that included making fun of his own struggle with weight and fast food, disagreements with his wife, and the challenges of his children's choices that, in their missteps, often reflected what he described as a "spiritual immaturity." When speaking of the challenge of temptation, instead of always referencing substance use "triggers," he would sometimes reference the challenge of driving by his favorite fast-food restaurant, saying:

> For me, a trigger can be the image of a double-cheeseburger floatin' by. [While holding his stomach] You see I don't make a habit of missin' many meals. Matter fact, I think I'ma end this sermon early and find my way to a drive thru. [Loud laughter.] No. Naw. Oh ya. My responsibility to further my faith is addressing the backsliding choices I do NOT make. Amen? Yes. Let me remember that next time. Maybe I need a safe word for my own stomach's grumbling. 'Cause it's gotta be about much mo' than just sayin' no. Oh, y'all did not come to hear a sermon tonight.

Knowing laughter, a call-and-response of "Ya know?!" and "You betta preach, Marshall, yep, yep," and the like were accompanied by an empathetic recognition to which many could relate well. During this time, though he did not work a 12-Step program of recovery himself, Pastor Marshall consistently made thoughtful links to the recovery process and to the 12 Steps. Pastor Marshall was commonly dismissive at CA meetings toward working the 12 Steps, but this was in part a product of his first sponsor having relapsed and returned to active addiction just six months into Pastor Marshall's sobriety and period of working with him. That weakened the credibility of the 12-Step program in his eyes. Still, during these flourishing years, his sermons effectively referenced addiction as an example of one's wayward past and recovery as the example of one's faith-informed, resilient present and possible future through sustained Ministries affiliation.

The Ministries' growing success was reflected in its health programming (see chapter 3), sober homes, food, and welcoming faith fellowship. The purchase of a third sober home property in late 2009 briefly intensified the participation of two more predominantly White anchor churches: Green Street Fellowship and Worship Faith Ministries. Volunteers from both churches refurbished the duplex next door. Relationships among the now four anchor churches, and between them and Ministries affiliates living on nearby blocks, were strengthened due to greater frequency of engagement, duration of projects that were shared in equitably by North Lawson neighbors and nonresident volunteers, potential links to further resource relationships, and on-site, collaborative recognition of both the religious and the (spiritually grounded) CA fellowship recovery sides of the Ministries and its mission. During this time resource relationships included what proved to be temporary collaborations with college student volunteers from local religiously affiliated colleges and student Christian fellowships on secular state and private campuses nearby. At this time, Pastor Marshall was also speaking regularly at the county jail and state prisons.

During this 2009–12 period, admission into the Ministries' sober homes was determined by a collaborative assessment. Pastor Marshall, operations manager Calvin Sandorn, and sober homes director Isaac H. participated in the screening interviews. A paper application for residency was required and used in the interviews. If approved, the applicant's willingness to sign an Agreement of Residential Ministries Affiliation formalized their admissions process. They then entered a probationary residency period that could last up to ninety days, in which a relapse or any other potential violations of house rules could result in automatic eviction. On-site resident peer monitoring strengthened a transitional relationship among new residents, where they could value the balance between the rather strict rules of the sober homes program and the caring empathy of co-residents. These practices enhanced adherence to the house rules, including full participation in all Ministries events and activities unless working, preparing for work, or participating in a family commitment; being in house by the 11:00 p.m. curfew; hosting no unapproved house guests; random drug testing; and attending regular house meetings.

Residents from sober home #3 next door took leadership of the monthly Men's Prayer Breakfasts. Their leadership added to demonstrations of resident successes through the formalized resilience of social role expectation (Cheney et al. 2016) of having a place to be, getting to and being there, and sharing in service and something beyond providing access for many to a warm meal. With breakfast being served at 8:00 a.m. each third Saturday of the month, their early Saturday wake-up and meal preparations communicated a committed end to a "sleeping off" or "coming to" after a Friday night's active addiction. Sober homes resident success flourished when several interdependent types of outreach came together, including regular outreach to those attending services and activities at the Ministries (e.g., men attending Bible study). Both newer and more long-standing residents partnered to reach out to people on the street. They handed out flyers and the new glossy Ministries brochures. They shared with others, including men who had recently attended and graduated from Salvation Army programming and others who rested their heads at a homeless shelter a few miles away. Nearby pastors of churches along the Akron Avenue congregational corridor were also contacted. Speakers with a quality message to share and an appealing delivery added to the value of the breakfasts. They included former local athletes, longtime FACTS Ministries affiliates, and local leaders of faith-based organizations with a comparable health and resilience mission.

Other than the Sunday services, the free lunches were the cornerstone of the Ministries during the flourishing period. As the volunteer team and food contributions grew, a second Thursday free lunch was added to the Tuesday lunches that had been running since 2005. Many of the elements that enriched the Men's Prayer Breakfast successes were also a part of the successes of the now twice-weekly lunches. During this time, with uneven success, the Ministries also prioritized outreach to the largely female sex industry workers on Akron Avenue. The goal remained encouraging them to understand themselves and their choices beyond the "edgework" soliciting interactions that often included prospective clientele among Ministries lunch attendees. In his pre-meal prayers during these years, Pastor Marshall sustained a more empathetic tone. He reduced what many viewed as the less empathetic "Get a job!" moralizing. In these brief faith offerings before the meal to come, he shared hopeful passages of a resilient new self. His more caring words were a small, important part of a fragile balancing act among these many Ministries successes.

The Decline of the Ministries (2012–Present)

In the book's introduction, the social ecology of resilience framework of Bennett and Windle (2015) presents a conceptual model founded on communal interdependence. Centered in the community domain, the framework emphasizes the social as a key modifier of support, cohesion, and participation. When the social is replaced by silences that are interpersonal, procedural, and programmatic, the social subsides, and the organization and its mission suffer. Few organizations fall all at once. Far more often, as these silences grow, a process of decline proceeds at an uncertain pace. The decline of affiliation and related declines in shared resources between Either-Or CA meetings and the Ministries, analyzed in chapter 4, were indicative of similar declines at multiple levels of the Ministries mission. From its origin, and especially during the 2009–12 flourishing period, the Ministries was "an enabling place [with] resources such as a sense of belonging and social support, an understanding of the self in terms of illness and death, and self-discipline regarding alcohol [and other drug] consumption [coupled with other health-affirming organizational practices, together] provided the conditions for contemplating a different future" (Evans et al. 2015, 123; see also Boeri 2018; DeVerteuil and Wilton 2009). As those enabling social resources were fractured, the potential for establishing and sustaining resilience also fractured, and the decline of the Ministries began.

In 2011, St. Priscilla Evangelical Church just two blocks south of the Ministries finally closed. The church had been struggling to keep its doors open for several years. Its pastor, Alethia Banton, had tried many things to sustain St. Priscilla's place in the Akron Avenue corridor and religious marketplace. It was the second-largest building in the immediate area. Questions initiated after its closing intensified growing discontent and friction at the FACTS Ministries. The denomination leadership that had jurisdiction over St. Priscilla had recently opened a much newer, larger, and predominantly White church in a nearby suburb. That newer church was led by a younger, White, more visible pastor. Despite its century of history and possible neighborhood consequences of its much more civically minded, charitable mission, St. Priscilla's closure made economic and religious sense to its denominational leadership.

Extending from the mixture of the Ministries' charity model anchor church funding, prosperity narrative dreams, and entitlement wishes, the closing of St. Priscilla initiated both a space and mission change dialogue among leadership of both the anchor churches and the Ministries. At that point, Pastor Marshall appeared to use his gradual annoyance with the presence and operations oversight of Calvin Sandorn to intensify a power struggle between the two men. It appeared to have been done to refine the mission and direction of the Ministries, though the true motives were never made clear. Pastor Marshall became increasingly public about what he perceived to be growing faith mission differences between the anchor churches and the Ministries. As a result, adding to his long-running tensions with Calvin, tensions also grew between Pastor Marshall and the anchor churches over these same issues. A potential move into the St. Priscilla building and its related dialogues were also associated with many other possible changes. If a move occurred, would it be just for the Ministries? Would the Ministries continue as the "satellite" urban mission while more than tripling its chapel space and overall square footage? With the move, would Millwood Fellowship and the FACTS Ministries merge and share the new space? If so, who and what portions of what mission were to be included? What leadership role and labeling changes would be made? If a merge occurred, who would be lead pastor and who would be associate? Who should maintain actual access to, and displays of, on-site power and how? Pastor Marshall and Calvin's apparent inability to engage in any dialogue beyond terse hellos in passing made the fragile balance of tensions between them even more unsustainable.

By the end of 2011, the relationship between Pastor Marshall and Calvin had grown to be openly tense. Specific circumstances of their tensions were never made public. Expressions of it were apparent to many affiliates as they danced a dance of passive-aggressive annoyances. When their paths crossed during Ministries' events (e.g., while hosting the Saturday morning Either-Or CA meetings), they often passed each other without speaking or even acknowledging the other. Each was seen and intentionally overheard pulling a trusted Ministries affiliate to the side to share a thinly veiled criticism of the other. These were said in a "Well, you didn't hear this from me . . ." tone, while being presented loudly enough for others to overhear. As with a pending divorce, the two men were seldom at the Ministries at the same time. When other changes occurred, the Ministries' mission and social ecology of resilience suffered as a result. The primary anchor church, Millwood Fellowship, was considering a move from the suburbs into the urban core. With all but two (of the eight) Ministries board members also being Millwood members, questions arose about how such a move would affect the Ministries. Those questions of the Millwood move and its sustainability consequences for the Ministries were never presented to affiliates as the decline of the Ministries began.

In late 2012, the board approached Pastor Marshall with what was both an opportunity and an ultimatum. Millwood was selling their suburban church site and building and were going to move their predominantly White, suburban-resident member church somewhere in the North Lawson neighborhood. Their move was being done, he was told, for a variety of reasons, including the desire to expand the outreach of their urban ministry. The FACTS Ministries was to soon merge with Millwood and would no longer be a distinct ministries. With the merge, Pastor Marshall would become an assistant pastor. He would continue leading services at the new ministry on selected Sundays. This status change would come with a salary increase, a platform increase, and increased resources for enhanced visibility of Marshall's personal ministry beyond the Ministries itself. The primary "sacrifice" was that the Ministries would no longer be a stand-alone organization. The "or else" of the ultimatum was withdrawal of Millwood's support as the funding anchor for the Ministries. Pastor Marshall said, "No." His choice was to take his nonprofit status of the Ministries with him and become an autonomous organization. While his decision in many respects made sense, he made it without engaging in any form of enrichment of an internal leadership and seemingly little consideration of possible resilience-compromising consequences.

When Pastor Marshall finally walked away from the original anchor church affiliation, he did so with no sustainable safety net, no Ministries affiliate participatory leadership structure, no internal grant-writing experience, and no funding innovation beyond anchor church charity. Furthermore, for many years, he had responded in a hostile manner to the suggestions for growth and change that had been made to him by longtime affiliates. Among the suggestions affiliates had proposed were creating an affiliate board similar to the deacon or usher board of a church, establishing a young adult faith outreach grounded in the leadership of the previously "unchurched," furthering a woman-centered health collective in affiliation with the family health clinic nearby, and establishing a grant-writing affiliate group for fundraising. Meanwhile, the Ministries' most consistent affiliates were left unaware and almost entirely ignored, which furthered fractures leading to the organization's decline. Pastor Marshall had been unwilling to enrich, or even respond respectfully to, any participatory leadership initiatives, or to begin to consider any alternative model to the Millwood-led anchor church collaboration to sustain the Ministries. With Pastor Marshall having not prioritized a functional backup plan, the decline of the Ministries continued.

In late 2012 and throughout 2013, the monthly, third Saturday morning Men's Prayer Breakfasts began to be canceled with more regularity. Cancellations were announced abruptly, occurred often for two months in a row, and always for reasons that were never shared. No more Men's Breakfast promotional flyers for neighborhood outreach were made. No more breakfast invitations were extended to current Ministries affiliates of other health domains—including those who did not attend Sunday evening services. No more youth outreach was available to the many young men of the neighborhood in their early twenties, now increasingly alienated from the world of work and in search of a purpose and affiliation to value, religious or otherwise (Barnes 2005; Flores 2013; Mooney et al. 2018; Western 2018). Very little outreach was extended to women affiliates to encourage men they knew to attend. There never was any focused outreach to the men's homeless shelter just over a mile south or to Salvation Army clients whose schedules allowed for their off-site attendance at events of Christian mission. There was no consistent outreach to other sober homes affiliated with churches just blocks away from the Ministries. Instead of enriching an "All hands on deck!" sensibility of shared mission, each of the health domain silos (see chapter 3) seemed to become more emboldened in their isolation. Only the most collaborative, donation-driven Tuesday and Thursday community lunches and the most autonomous, externally led Either-Or CA meetings seemed to be able to maintain any semblance of stability. All the while, these interdependent fractures of affiliation leadership remained largely unspoken, yet they were as apparent and collectively damaging as a loud, highly visible unkept secret.

At the start of 2013, the formal break with Millwood that had been underway for months finally took place. With it, both the pace and depth of the Ministries' decline increased—not because of the break with the anchor church per se, but due to lack of any apparent effort toward developing a fiscally sound, collaborative leadership. Different people familiar with the Ministries and its mission had approached Pastor Marshall over the years to discuss funding and other possible resource changes to enhance its strength and stability. Yet neither he nor the board had even remotely taken seriously any alternative. Despite questions regarding whether he had the authority to do so, Pastor Marshall fired Calvin as operations manager. He then assigned Calvin's duties to a friend who was volunteering at the time. Pastor Marshall's choice to do so was a power play in keeping with the toxic silences and autocracy that had long characterized much of his leadership (see chapter 5). Perhaps his doing so was the final action that led Millwood Fellowship and its now former urban outreach health initiative to part ways. Any "settlement agreement" or formal change in the resource relationship between the two was not shared with longtime Ministries affiliates. Prior to a Thursday night Either-Or meeting in February 2013, Pastor Marshall was heard saying to one affiliate,

> They [Millwood leadership] were trying to treat me like their "boy" [i.e., disrespecting him in a racially insensitive, socially distancing way]. Assistant this, and part-time that. Even with that salary raise, it was clear they were taking away *a lot* more than they were sharing with me. And that was just too much. So glad those [local foundation] funds are going to be available for the coming fiscal year. We'll just have to see what's next.

Quite consistent with Christian mission, anchor church leadership seemed often to be driven by an almost colonial framing of "their" urban Ministries, which it largely was (Sager 2012). Pastor Marshall became quite comfortable with the health domain silos of the Ministries, no on-site affiliate leadership infrastructure, and the autocracy and board sign-off he had access to, until a shift and forced collaboration led to the sequence of fractures analyzed here. Still, however accurate Pastor Marshall's experience of the exchange with Millwood leadership may have been, his and the board's choice to be dismissive of every form and proposal to develop an affiliate-anchored, participatory leadership was especially damaging. Now, with tensions mounting and ties worn thin, resilience-compromising changes at the Ministries continued.

Toward the end of summer 2013, the Friday Youth Nights were ended. As Pastor Marshall put it while sharing with one longtime affiliate, "The Ministries [was] no longer willing to be a free babysitter for crackhead mothers in the neighborhood. They ain't gonna be walkin' the street on our dime anymore." Confirmed by multiple sources, curiously, this immensely unempathetic "free babysitter" sentiment was alleged to have first been fueled by Cheryl, Pastor Marshall's wife. In that dismissive sentiment, any questions of relevant factors that informed those mothers' realities, however "true" it was, never appeared to have been raised. Engaging any proxy of an opportunity of critical awareness of Black Womanist insight regarding gender, addiction, and African American families (e.g., Cheney et al. 2016; Gubrium 2008) never occurred. Ending the Friday Youth Nights furthered multiple Ministries declines of mission, affiliation, and administration. They occurred in a way where family and gender mattered. Ending the Youth Nights reduced the Ministries' neighborhood-oriented collaboration and interaction down to Sunday services, Tuesday and Thursday free lunches, and Wednesday night Bible study. Many also included Either-Or CA meetings, though they were viewed by most as a "liminal resource" more than a "true" Ministries outlet. When "all that Ministries drama" was increasingly referred to in one way or another at other CA meetings in the city, the number of those attending Either-Or meetings at the Ministries continued to decline. Pastor Marshall began periodically floating the idea of "canceling" one of the two CA meetings hosted at the Ministries. Being unclear about CA Traditions and meeting autonomy, he did not realize that cancellation could only be done by the chapter of CA (Cocaine Anonymous 2018). Still, with increasing regularity, Pastor Marshall repeated the language of possible Either-Or meeting cancellation. Predictably, this was not received well by regular Either-Or affiliates who remained. At that time there was still a critical mass of affiliates Pastor Marshall respected who attended both meetings often enough that he did not carry out the decision then. With what appeared to several affiliates as motives of insularity and ego, efforts to end one of the Either-Or meetings had been sowed.

As 2013 proceeded, desperate adjustments and further alienations extended from Pastor Marshall's largely autocratic leadership style and seemingly increased paranoia toward all attempts at engaging him in possible changes to improve the Ministries and to better serve its larger mission. In 2008, one affiliate, Richard, wanted to expand his small custodial business. Richard proposed to Pastor Marshall the possibility of a service contract or day-work agreements to provide short-term employment opportunities with new residents of the Ministries' sober homes. This "temp service" opportunity was quickly rejected for reasons both Richard and Pastor Marshall were unwilling to share. In 2010, another affiliate, Edward, worked with a solicitation firm and proposed a similar service contract arrangement for sober homes and community lunch patrons as well. This initiative was also not given the opportunity to succeed. Sometime in 2011, among multiple proposed funding streams a few longtime affiliates became aware of, a possible restaurant arrangement with another faith-led recovery organization and a formal agreement with a restaurant chain that regularly donated food for the community lunches were also presented and rejected. With no affiliate leadership structure of any kind, any collective consideration of them never took place. These opportunities and the reasons for not allowing them to proceed were never shared.

Then, as the 2013 holidays approached, Pastor Marshall told a few affiliates that, with an uncertain budget (and for other reasons not shared), the Ministries would not be hosting a Thanksgiving Day meal. As noted earlier, the success of the Thanksgiving Day meal, begun in 2005 when Either-Or CA affiliates chose to potluck for their Thursday night meeting on Thanksgiving night, led Pastor Marshall and the board to make it a Ministries-sponsored event. The Ministries had previously been closed and did not serve their regularly scheduled Thursday community lunches on Thanksgiving. From 2009 to 2012, these holiday meals continued during the day. When Either-Or CA affiliates became aware of this 2013 Ministries decision, several said that they would willingly take up the funding, cooking, serving, security, and cleanup responsibilities. All that would be necessary is for someone to open a door of the Ministries the morning of. Pastor Marshall and whatever Ministries board members remained said no. With no responsibility beyond an open door, making meals available on a day when many in the North Lawson neighborhood, and throughout the city, would otherwise go without one was turned into a nonstarter. Fractures to the Ministries' sustainability grew.

The instability of the sober homes program increased when, without explanation, Pastor Marshall cut Isaac's salary as sober homes manager in half. Predictably, Isaac resigned his position and moved out of the sober homes soon after. Within this same period, tensions grew between Pastor Marshall and his staunchest ally and longtime friend, Albert (see chapter 1). Albert had skills, enthusiasm, and calm devotion consistent with those of an assistant pastor or some similar title and role. Now, with Pastor Marshall's high-strung personality further stressed with the uncertainties of the post-Millwood break, his relationship with Albert became another casualty. Albert grew increasingly annoyed with Marshall's reticence, as he had seen many others (e.g., Calvin, Isaac, Raymond) come and go as hired, paid personnel. Albert's contributions to the actual day-to-day operations of the Ministries' functioning was comparable to, or greater than, that of any other person, with the possible exception of Pastor Marshall himself. Rides home from Thursday night Either-Or meetings, computer repair and other technology supports, lending his personal cars to Pastor Marshall's adult children, running the sound board and audiovisual so the PowerPoint slides for lyrics and sermon excerpts during Sunday services were in sync and properly displayed, and being Pastor Marshall's most reliable advocate were among the acts of unpaid labor Albert willingly shared with the Ministries for years. Yet no such well-earned symbolic, non-salary position or title, nor any consideration for a paid position of any kind, had ever been presented to Albert.

Further undercutting the sober homes and Ministries stability, Pastor Marshall made what appeared to many to be a series of desperate residential screening choices for the sober homes. With personnel turnover along with Pastor Marshall's unwillingness to call upon any longtime affiliates to assist him, only a limited, often non-collaborative, screening of potential residents was carried out. Prioritizing financial incentives over residential makeup and program stability, Pastor Marshall allowed people with significant mental health challenges into the houses, not for the first time but with less on-site and co-resident support than ever before. This destabilized the sober homes and magnified their limited supervision and incomplete programming (e.g., less adherence to house rules, less participation at all Ministries events, less time with sponsors or other sober programming and affiliation, less leadership of the Men's Prayer Breakfasts, less calling to account when these lesser actions were not done).

With financial support more uncertain than ever, Pastor Marshall's desperation grew. He proposed to simultaneously launch five distinct Ministries initiatives: a young men's outreach and ministry, an on-site children's church, grandparenting support for custodial grandparents, faith-based tutorial support, and a women's ministry. He developed persuasive, professional posters for each. Yet he was unwilling to test-market these initiatives with anyone. By ending the Ministries' relationship with Millwood Fellowship, he had relinquished access to their grant writer and her skills. Periodically, after Either-Or CA meetings he was attending less frequently, Pastor Marshall mentioned that he was trying to continue to rely on grant money while also appealing to various large, White churches who he hoped were in search of an "urban" social mission. In this environment of dwindling resources and silent desperations, he increasingly used a prosperity narrative in his sermons. He began to engage in a faith-healing type of call to the front of the church and a laying on of hands, seemingly to broaden his evangelical appeal. He attempted to engage large African American churches through the few most evangelical members who attended Ministries' Sunday evening services. In the face of fewer consistent affiliates, increasingly strained organizational collaborations, and ongoing funding challenges, as the Partnership Dinner approached in February 2014, these uncertainties reduced the stability and effectiveness of each of the Ministries' health services (see chapter 3, table 1).

Meanwhile, attendance at Sunday evening services, the flagship event and activity of the Ministries, had been declining since early rumblings of the break with Millwood began. No words were openly spoken to anyone about the break, and people took the convenient action of simply voting with their feet and quit coming to services. The few members of the anchor churches still willing to travel the miles of geographic (and the far greater social) distance into North Lawson to attend the FACTS Ministries' services on Sunday evenings dropped, during a short period, from thirty-five or forty to twenty or twenty-five—just a few people beyond Pastor Marshall's immediate family. These significant declines further reduced the Ministries' resilience and stability.

In what struck many remaining affiliates as a desperate move, Pastor Marshall abruptly announced the Ministries' intention to change the Sunday service from a 6:00 p.m. start time to 10:00 a.m. Sunday mornings. "Now we'll be just like a real church," he repeated on several Sundays through the summer of 2014, always with a chuckle. Poorly conceived and problematically executed, on National Back to Church Sunday in September, the FACTS Ministries held a 10:00 a.m. Sunday service for the first time. Sober homes men had been asked to help with parking the cars on the grass plot just north of the Ministries building. A few women had been recruited to present a pleasant, welcoming face at both the Akron Avenue front chapel west door and the eastern back door by the parking lot off the alley. With the promise of food afterward, suggested by the barbeque pit and the plastic picnic tables and chairs poised for setup in the parking lot, there was a rich mix of people in the chapel that first Sunday morning. Those attending included families from the neighborhood, sober homes residents and their family members, longtime church-side-only Ministries affiliates, and a few from the Either-Or CA meetings interested in supporting the Ministries' new effort. Notably absent that morning was the handful of people from the anchor churches who still attended in support of the Ministries' original mission. Also absent was the small yet critical mass of evangelicals whose home church was one of the large, predominantly African American churches a few miles north of the North Lawson neighborhood. They were among the Ministries' most vocal supporters, active in the call-and-response central to many services and vital to the tempo of the Ministries' and Pastor Marshall's preaching style.

More than sixty people attended that first Sunday morning service, including a strong family presence with many small children. In the weeks that followed, the numbers quickly dwindled. Soon, the only attendees were a couple of residents among the twelve men living in the sober homes, a few members from two neighborhood families that had long supported the Ministries, and a few people from the CA meetings who were looking to engage in a religious practice to supplement their program of 12-Step recovery. Within weeks, the start time was changed from 10:00 a.m. to 11:00 a.m. This change did little to alter the numbers of those in attendance, as fifteen or fewer people were there on any given Sunday morning. Few services can survive with little more than a pastor's family members in the pews.

As 2015 began, the Ministries experienced further changes that reduced access to its resources, on both sides of the wall between the chapel and the community room. The Men's Prayer Breakfasts had been held in all twelve months of 2012 and ten months of 2013, then had dropped to seven months in 2014. When only one was held in March 2015, and not again for months with no word given as to why, it signaled what was never formally announced: The Men's Prayer Breakfasts would no longer take place. In April, again providing no reason for doing so, Pastor Marshall announced that the Ministries would no longer host the Thursday night CA meetings (see chapter 4). No rules had been violated. No incidents had occurred. The small Thursday night meeting numbers, largely brought about by various alienating actions of Pastor Marshall toward CA affiliates, coupled with the declining critical mass and collective apathy of CA affiliates toward the Ministries, meant that no collective resistance to the meeting's end occurred. Most CA affiliates had grown ambivalent about both the pastor and the Ministries. Discontinuing the Thursday Either-Or-CA meeting hurt the women of the county's community correctional program. They relied on this approved, off-site recovery meeting to enrich the resilience of their community supervision. Its end also removed any possible, more formal collaborations with the community correctional program that served as the county's drug court. Potential momentum toward enriching or establishing any other organizational collaborations was never supported, and any other progress in the Ministries' possible sustainability declined.

Conclusions

Over the years, the FACTS Ministries provided, and contributed to, a social ecology of resilience for many. It enriched a process of positive adaptation in the context of significant adversity (Luthar, Cicchetti, and Becker 2000; Ungar, Ghazinour, and Richter, 2013; Werner and Smith 1982). In location, prior uses, and present possibilities, the Ministries building contributes to bouncing back. The history of the building has a spiritual quality that informs its current use. Its place memories reflect North Lawson's bygone era of greater stability and are as much a part of the building as are its years of vacant dormancy. Following from the Bennett and Windle (2015, 23) resilience framework, "the environment/context is an important aspect of positive development and subsequent resilience." The content and function of these contextual factors must be enriched by the social cohesion central to their framework. Tensions that test that cohesion may lead to fractures and the organization's decline. Symbolically, the Ministries reflects a paradox of tensions with other religious and secular leaderships within the neighborhood. From a collaborative standpoint, it has embodied many resource exchanges: White, suburban anchor church funding; restaurant and grocery store food donors for the community lunches; the Either-Or substance use recovery meetings of Cocaine Anonymous and related recovery services provided by CA affiliates; nutritional counseling, periodic free health screenings, and other health-care services provided by on-site volunteers; and health-care providers willing to offer reduced-rate services available for some Ministries affiliates, both prior to and after the Affordable Care Act began. As the Ministries' reputation of being accessible and consistent grew, Christian recovery organizations also shared their time, event participation, referrals, and other resources of shared mission. For example, a person from the leadership of A Tranquil Place sober home was a keynote speaker at one of the Ministries' Men's Prayer Breakfasts. The Ministries was an approved site for the women's and men's community corrections facilities, and both the nearby homeless shelter and the Salvation Army had informal referral relationships for much of its history.

The Ministries' decline demonstrates ways in which organizational resilience has its limits and the key events and threshold fractures that remained unhealed. Fewer consistent affiliates, strained or broken organizational affiliations, ongoing funding challenges, and no openness to affiliate-initiated input destabilized the Ministries and its five health service domains. The Ministries' many silences had a corrosive effect on its fragile social ecology. Its fiscal secrecy constituting the most pronounced silence of the Ministries and its mission. Affiliates never knew how the mortgage was paid or how the lights stayed on. Social justice issues were rarely discussed. References to those incarcerated were characterized only as violators of the law in need of a Christianity-anchored personal responsibility. No critique was expressed about mass incarceration. Little more than lip service was paid to the shootings that all-too-regularly occurred in the neighborhood. No political literacy was encouraged before or during the Obama presidency. No civic engagement was undertaken to further a sense of "the personal is political" or the potential benefit of exploring addiction recovery as a health choice and a political act. There were never deacon boards or usher boards, nor any formal mentoring beyond the sponsors that many Either-Or affiliates had and used in the working of their 12-Step programs. From among the many expressions of resilience through the living legacy of the Black Social Gospel (e.g., Lincoln and Mamiya 1990; Price-Spratlen 2015), none of this affiliate leadership appeared to ever be thoughtfully explored or even mentioned to Ministries affiliates.

During a Saturday morning Either-Or CA meeting in June 2016, Pastor Ellwyn Marshall spoke with a somber tone in his share: "I just don't know any more," he began. The meeting was smaller than usual that morning, with three longtime affiliates, three sober homes residents, and the pastor himself. The quality of fellowship was still strong, despite the pastor of the Ministries not having attended them from beginning to end for many months. Pastor Marshall continued:

> Right now, things are a challenge. And knowin' what to do next doesn't seem to be too comfortable for me. Who do you talk to about your kids? Who do you talk with about where the Ministries is going? And what is up with the rest of my life? I mean, I'ma come up on sixty [years old] soon enough. And the challenges of that being what it is and all. Then with this Ministries. [Looking out the window, he took a long, deep breath, seeming to be on the verge of tears.] Just don't know where we goin' and all. . . . And with the kids what they doin' and all. I

> mean, my eldest daughter just came back into the house again. [Looking at the carpeted floor for a long pause, searching for the right words.] Now, she gon' act all grown and say she can do whatever and whatnot. Then, things go wrong where she at, and she gettin' hit on again. And I just want her to not be harmed anymore. And my son, even after the shooting and all. He got a long way back, still he wanna talk kinda crazy, and all. And then with my wife, and, you know, we still got some kids not yet in high school?! So it's gonna be a longtime gone and all. The whole what to do kinda thing just rides ya, 'cause you just don't know. So, ya. Makin' the days count? Ya. That's the topic? Ya. Well, doin' that and keepin' things movin'. That's what I'm tryin' to be about, 'cause just don't know what's next. How to make all this work. That's the thing. Tryin' to make that time count and all, day-by-day. I pass.

Pastor Marshall's uncommon openness surprised all in attendance. He presented himself with humored self-assurance, perhaps to the point of arrogance. Now to be willing to show his vulnerability and expose his anguish—this spoke volumes. What did it mean to be so unsure about his life's direction and with his lifework on unsettled footing? How much leadership could one person assume, while accepting so little help from collaborating affiliates, before the burdens were too much to carry on one's own? What could "collaboration" truly mean in the religious marketplace of a poor neighborhood's congregational corridor? The Ministries was "a body of doctrine, a system of values and beliefs, a set of myths and symbols . . . which provide group members with a common vocabulary for understanding their world" (Gecas 2000, 98). Given the mix of alienations and increasing uncertainty, fewer and fewer people were willing to share in the common vocabulary of the Ministries. As in many affiliations, its threshold of potentially beneficial tensions passed and the collective assets of resilience that remained broke down. Little was left besides Pastor Marshall's anguished lament as a leader beginning to finally acknowledge his own agency in the actions and outcomes central to the Ministries' decline. How he had been enabled by the content of his relationships with Meadowbrook Fellowship, unwilling to even consider any other options beyond the benefits and strictures of their charity, was in the unspoken of his insight. Along with what worked well when it flourished, considering key aspects of its fractured sustainability is also helpful. Best practices and policy implications that emerged from them are explored in chapter 7.

PART 3

HALLELUJAH!
HOW HEALING HAPPENS

Chapter 7

Faith-Based Best Practices

How a Fractured Ministries Can Heal

> Stereotype[s] of the faith-based concept and motives behind partnerships involving public health do not map onto the longstanding history of collaborative work between religious and public health agencies. . . . The potential for good is considerable. The faith-based sector has much to offer public health, yet it remains underused.
>
> —Levin 2014b, 130

This book explores how a faith-based health organization helped to enrich and successfully maintain a social ecology of health and resilience in an urban neighborhood of concentrated disadvantage. The social ecology is at the core of the African American ethnogenic thread where faith-based leadership addressed public health dating back to the early twentieth century (Du Bois 1906). Previous chapters explore what happens when lines of communication are compromised and when challenging leadership decisions and actions work against sustained affiliations of shared mission and lead to organizational decline. When a spiritually grounded, 12-Step fellowship (Cocaine Anonymous) affiliates with a faith-based, community health organization (FACTS Ministries), together they can effectively address substance use recovery and other related disparities. They contribute to the health and resilience of their affiliates, the neighborhood, and the larger community. The decline of the organization and its affiliations with others were largely a product of leadership and process fractures and of the resource-compromising outcomes that resulted from them. Within-community leadership can be an uneven terrain. The unstated yet apparent assumption of a culturally competent leadership foundation emerging from that "from within" empathy is not enough to avoid toxic outcomes and may, in fact, instigate many of those outcomes. Still, consistent with the call to action of Levin's quote above, best practices to further a beneficial social ecology in a high-poverty neighborhood emerged and are considered here to close this chapter and book.

More than two decades ago, Imani Woods "admonished drug policy makers on the outside who 'parachute in' to African-American communities in an attempt to implement imported programs in the absence of community input. It is critical to match the harm reduction message to the population you are working with" (cited in Marlatt 1996, 782). An organization can only succeed when it harnesses its affiliates to contribute collaboratively toward achieving a shared mission. It equips all affiliates to lead and all to follow, all to contribute well to an ecology of expertise and all being ready to step in when necessary. Led by an African American US Army veteran, a returning citizen and person in recovery who returned to the neighborhood he was raised in, the organization flourished before fissures became fractures. This book has demonstrated how this organization's services, silences, and affiliations with mutual support groups and health service agencies contribute to improved health and well-being. An affiliate's health and well-being can be strengthened when "groups provide individuals with a sense of meaning, purpose, belonging (i.e., a positive sense of social identity), positive psychological consequences" (Haslam et al. 2009, 1), and many other beneficial outcomes.

As Levin (2014b) stated in the opening quote to this chapter, the faith-based sector has much to contribute to public health, yet it "remains underused." Having analyzed how "collaborative work between religious and public health agencies" is sustained, this book has also shown what can happen when challenges of change are not addressed effectively, when leadership limitations exacerbate fractures more than they heal them, and when silences of stigma and shame are left to fester. However fragile the relationship may be between faith-based and health services organizations committed to a community's ecology of health and resilience, the need for collaboration is clear. In the case of substance misuse, as much as 90 percent of those in active addiction in the US population do not receive any treatment, and nearly 60 percent of all who receive treatment get it through mutual support groups (Lipari, Park-Lee, and Van Horn 2016;

SAMHSA 2015; Tagai et al. 2018). The FACTS Ministries, working with health services agencies, supports individuals in recovery from addiction by providing ongoing individual, family, and community health services across its five domains (see chapter 3) for neighbors and all who come into the community for the resources and resilience it provides.

Given the level of unmet need, community organizations who affiliate with mutual support groups are an important pathway to address substance use and health concerns, including the current opioid crisis. This analysis of the FACTS Ministries has shown an instance of how, in this era of neoliberal decline and state constraint regarding citizen well-being (Hackworth 2010), the potential for the faith-based sector's contribution to public health is being realized. It has demonstrated how resilience as a social ecology enriches the faith-health relationship at affiliate, organizational, and neighborhood levels. The health and resilience mission of the FACTS Ministries is being met despite the "synergy of plagues" (Wallace and Wallace 1997, 789; see also Drucker 2011) that characterize North Lawson and other neighborhoods like it. The Ministries helps confirm the 2016 US Surgeon General's report, *Facing Addiction in America*, which stated, "People in recovery, their family members, and other supporters are banding together to spread the message that people do recover [in and through] the growing network of recovery community organizations" (5-1). At this time of increasing urgency, the people of collaborative institutions with the FACTS Ministries exemplify how this growing network of community organizations is doing so.

As presented in the introduction, social reconstruction and social recovery to further the health of marginalized groups have a long history in the United States. At the twentieth century's turn, Du Bois ([1899] 1967, 309) focused on a "mighty influence to mold and make the [African American] citizen: the social atmosphere which surrounds him." To further the relevance of the social atmosphere, Du Bois "crystallized the conceptualization of social conditions as a cause of poor health status among Blacks" (White 2011, 288) and linked those local area disparities to health disparities. A few years later he recommended "the formation of local health leagues among colored people for the dissemination of better knowledge of sanitation and preventive medicine" (Du Bois 1906, 110), practices for improved health and well-being. Following from Du Bois's focus on the social atmosphere—the family, organization, and community—of African American well-being, along with other research, this book recognizes resilience as vital to health and has explored it as a relational and ecological trait, operating across multiple, interacting levels, after the repeated (personal, family, and community) trauma and alienations of active addiction. Prior chapters have shown that to enrich this social ecology, "individual factors interact with family and community factors to bolster well-being [and] secure the cultural and community resources necessary for health while addressing the problems of stigma and alienation" (Ungar 2011, 7; see also Bennett and Windle 2015; Teo, Lee, and Lim 2017). Following from Du Bois (1904, 1906) and Ungar (2011), the resilience framework of Bennett and Windle (2015) (see introduction, figure 1) summarizes the interacting factors which bolster well-being and secure those resources necessary for health. The framework's components, with their largely unspecified tensions and uncertainties, are the social ecology of resilience characteristics that enrich the health and well-being of FACTS Ministries affiliates and many others. An alternative framework that more accurately explores those resilience tensions emerged from this project and analyses. These chapters have provided a better understanding of the often complicated dynamics of engendering and sustaining a beneficial *collective* environment of support that works together toward individual, organizational, and social change. As noted earlier, outside of discussing large populations' recovery from natural disasters, too often, the sociology and urban health literatures do not explore resilience as a relational ecology. This book has helped fill that gap toward sustaining a social ecology of resilience. Despite its struggles and structural fractures, the FACTS Ministries has persisted since its founding in 2000.

Unhealed Fractures

One of the fractures that informs the current state of social services and health care in the US is the reduction of state participations in all manner of human well-being. Over time, there has been "an undeniable shift in emphasis away from many forms of collectivization and state welfare provisioning. . . . [As a result,] beginning in the 1970s, and accelerating in the 1980s . . . policies and institutions at various scales have been destroyed" (Hackworth 2010, 750–51). This has hurt vulnerable populations the most given the many means by which the most privileged can still flourish from state actions in periods of supposed retrenchment (e.g., tax breaks for the wealthy). For the unwealthy, the "welfare state, marked by universality, de-commodification and escalating benefits, has been eclipsed

[by] a 'hollowed out' welfare state, generally hostile to redistribution and universality, magnifying rather than offsetting inequality [ostensibly to] break the 'cycle of dependency' fostered by existing programs [that] devolve 'knotty problems' to the local level" (DeVerteuil and Wilton 2009, 464). When partnered with institutional actions of a carceral logic including mass incarceration, the racialization of the "War on Drugs" (see the introduction), and prioritizing related criminalization over health interventions, these welfare state retreats can be recognized as not only hostile but in fact cruel. Rife with their own contradictions, faith-based organizations today provide increasingly more services and resources to help address this growing need for a functional welfare state (see Sager 2012).

As has been the case at the FACTS Ministries, limitations within faith-based organizations damage their ability to contribute to improved well-being and the realization of their mission. Although the FACTS Ministries contributed to the sustained recovery and improved health of the North Lawson neighborhood and of its affiliates throughout the city, many unhealed fractures characterize its service delivery, including: (1) leadership, (2) staffing and programming, (3) collaboration and communication, (4) mission and vision, and (5) lack of self-assessment and innovation. Before specifying best practices to help them heal, the next sections provide the lessons learned from the preceding analyses of these five fractures.

Leadership

Leadership becomes fractured when a leader makes consequential decisions unevenly, with uncertain motives and unclear projected outcomes, and which are surprising even to the most committed longtime affiliates. Such decisions can lead to alienation and disaffiliation as affiliates view their loss as being much greater than gains from the surprise decision. Repeated displays of this non- or even anti-collaborative process contributed to the FACTS Ministries' decline. Pastor Marshall made frequent references to off-site mentoring from trusted others, when he could have also prioritized opportunities for input on site (e.g., a deacon board or an affiliates council). Organizational leadership gets fractured when a leader does not allow affiliates who express interest in furthering the organization's mission to have a voice. At the Ministries, further decline became inevitable when that fracture was not given the opportunity to heal through, for instance, a biannual workshop on spiritual mentoring and health, or a peer-to-peer, youth-led wellness gathering on reducing gun violence and the drug markets associated with them, or any number of other such initiatives to enrich and diversify affiliate leadership.

At the FACTS Ministries, the potential for even the most traditional religious leadership (e.g., deacon board, usher board, youth council) was dismissed. Suggestions for a more participatory affiliate council were repeatedly rejected. The only means of affiliate leadership participation was when the very few people who spent time regularly at the Ministries beyond Sunday service, and were apparently perceived as having "proper" class standing, were asked if they would be willing to join the board. However, when opportunities for internal mentoring are minimized or completely denied, or are presented only to a select few by asking them to join the entirely off-site board, the potential for enriching bonds among diverse affiliates playing various roles is lost. For example, longer-term sober homes residents can mentor shorter-term residents. Holding meetings, or just a social gathering, for the 12-Step CA sponsors of sober home residents and their sponsees could bring together affiliates who play multiple roles. Encouraging sponsors to meet with their sponsees at the Ministries could also enrich both interpersonal and organizationally collaborative leadership between mutual support- and faith-based organizations.

Staffing and Programming

In all organizations, rewards of various kinds play an important role in improving organizational productivity. Well-led organizations recognize that "motivating factors that can be used to reward have the awesome power to positively transform the entire work environment" (Spitzer 1996, 46; see also Perry, Hondeghem, and Wise 2010). Extending official titles to less-dedicated affiliates, while passing over more-dedicated others, fosters resentment and alienation, and the organization may suffer as a result. When short-term hires made for visible positions, which could enrich the organization's primary mission, are followed by the quick firing of the new employee before even short-term benefits can be realized, the mission is compromised. When visible hostilities are sustained without being addressed in any clear way toward improvement, the potential for nurturing resilience is compromised.

Fractured staffing bleeds into programming, when rules for sustained affiliation (e.g., sober homes resident rules regarding curfew, 12-Step meeting attendance, and on-site visitors and their behavior) are unevenly adhered to or get entirely ignored. These compromises weaken the value of affiliation for many. For example, when sex industry workers frequent community lunches and then maintain a consistent clientele of organization affiliates, the organization's other programming may be less respected, detracting from its health mission. When a faith-based organization with willing, skilled volunteers and other affiliates is unwilling to at least periodically sponsor health fairs carried out in collaboration with nearby congregations or health services agencies, it denies resource enhancement and trust among the organizations. Programming suffers and the mission and organizational ecology are compromised.

Collaboration and Communication

Like all potential for growth toward a sustained, equitable collaboration, affiliation must be practiced well in order for it to flourish. When an organization has limited or uneven faith, business, and health interactions with the leadership of organizations with which it shares resources, those resources will likely suffer. Following the Ministries leadership's outreach in 2001 to Cocaine Anonymous to host a CA meeting, the Ministries' participation in any formal CA collaboration was extremely limited. The Ministries was the host site for the local CA chapter's 2006 New Year's celebration, and its leaders attended the CA annual summer picnic the following year. No other invitations for resource sharing from CA and several other health organizations were responded to favorably. As much as field observation allowed, it appeared that from 2004 to 2017, the Ministries did not participate in any of the nine recovery events in the city organized and hosted by the local CA chapter. These included district (i.e., city-level) anniversary celebrations, area (i.e., state) conventions, tristate and regional conferences, and other recovery and health symposia. The Ministries did not provide personnel or space to support the multi-fellowship, international recovery community's annual Rally for Recovery in the city. The Rally was sponsored by a local collective of advocates that began the same year as the Ministries. This was another lost opportunity that could have helped reverse flagging affiliate participation and strengthened organizational bonds.

These collaborations could have established aspirational networking with a number of drug treatment and other participating health professionals and organizations. Co-organizing an event with another group listed in the local Christian Recovery brochure was never pursued, despite suggestions and plans of action to do so from multiple Ministries affiliates over the ten years the brochure was published. Participation of evangelical affiliates in selected Sunday services was limited, and the potential for enriching formal connections with their larger, well-resourced home churches (one of which had a sober home a few blocks from the Ministries) was never realized. When Sunday services at the Ministries ended in 2016, attending affiliates were encouraged to attend services at another small congregation two blocks south. The structure and value of this organizational relationship was never made clear to Ministries affiliates. How the health mission was to be maintained or to change was never addressed. This made equity within the partnership that much more unlikely, and another opportunity for enriching resource sharing with a nearby congregation was lost. Throughout, alienating silences toward multiple subgroups were increasing (see chapter 5). The lack of inter-health domain affiliate interactions furthered silos that reduced lines of communication within the Ministries.

Mission and Vision

The Ministries' literature stated, "Our mission at FACTS Ministries is to respond to God's call to set the captives free." However, when an organization is itself captive to an autocratically rigid, and largely off-site, leadership structure, meanings of that promised freedom are unclear, and self-rule is compromised without an affiliate leadership body. Four years before the FACTS Ministries was founded, Morell (1996, 310) suggested, "African Americans addressing addiction may provide a model for radicalizing recovery. Spirituality, along with African American history and communal values, is an indispensable tool for . . . innovative recovery program[s] that combine individual healing and social change." When an organization maintains a faith-based health agenda that refuses to recognize how recovery in an impoverished, predominantly African American neighborhood is itself a political act for social change, it cannot be open to anything approaching radical recovery in events and programming. As a result, its vision and mission remain restricted, and efforts toward that mission will be resisted.

In April 2014, with the Ministries already in decline (see chapter 6), a group of longtime affiliates approached the pastor with concerns and suggestions for assessment and possible change. After an informal consult with one of the remaining Ministries board members, the small, critical mass of affiliates made their collective appeal in a cautious, clear, and respectful letter. Representing the voice and contributions of multiple domains, the letter requested an open forum for affiliate discussion with Ministries leadership. The signatories hoped this forum would be a step toward considering a sustained affiliate leadership of some kind. Weeks later, they received a dismissive letter from Pastor Marshall. In its impersonal voice and tone, the letter appeared to have been drafted in legalese by someone other than the pastor. In part, it stated:

> In this non-profit the rights you are requesting are vested only in the CEO/President and in the Governing Board of said entity and are derived and spelled out in the governing documents of said entity, FACTS Ministries (FM). No such provision you have requested for a group or one-on-one meeting with me is in or a part of our policies of procedures of FM, nor mandatory as such. . . . All complaints, criticisms, grumbles, gripes or accusations must be within the context as a violation of the FACTS Ministries by-laws to be heard. However, I will continue to offer counseling to everyone who seeks it and have an open-door policy that is discretionary and based on the issues at hand.

The response letter concluded by stating that a suggestion box would be set up for affiliates to share concerns anonymously. The authoritarian content of the letter (e.g., stating that he was CEO and president seven times in four paragraphs) showed little willingness on Pastor Marshall's part to consider any dialogue to address affiliate suggestions. His response led to the opposite of what affiliates had intended: it was followed by volatile, threatening face-to-face confrontations between Pastor Marshall and two of the affiliates who had signed the letter.

At a moment of organizational uncertainty, when a group of longtime affiliates formally reached out to address what appeared to be a growing momentum of organizational decline (see chapter 6), the pastor's response to the collective was to invalidate its concerns. By inference, affiliates who expressed concerns needed counseling. That need was to be met with individual pastoral therapy, to be led by the individual at the center of the concerns. When affiliates are not provided with a means to contribute to strengthening the organization and when collective efforts to do so are obstructed with hostility, the infrastructure for organizational sustainability suffers (e.g., Sager 2012; Sittig, Ash, and Singh 2014). If the leadership had a strategic plan for FACTS Ministries, it was unclear to longtime affiliates what that strategy was and which outcomes it was intended to produce. Following from Morell (1996), using communal values as indispensable tools for innovation, healing, and social change demands some means for an affiliate-informed mission and vision. When such pathways are silenced, fractures persist.

Self-Assessment and Innovation

Within an organization, forms of self-assessment are helpful in clarifying what reaches affiliates, what they value, and what appears to be working less well. Despite challenges and lack of "a validated assessment of organizational capacity specific to faith-based organizations" (Tagai et al. 2018, 714), such self-assessment would be helpful as a means to enhance transparency and lines of communication, while improving services and achieving the organizational mission. Once decisions are made regarding how an assessment should be completed, "information for *continuous quality improvement* . . . would be more likely to achieve outcomes" (Wandersman 2014, 100–101; italics in original). Affiliate leadership can then help clarify directives that emerge from the feedback. Programming and innovative strategies for sustaining affiliate interests can then be tried out to "build system resilience . . . which continuously prevents, detects, mitigates, or ameliorates hazards or incidents so that an organization can bounce back to its original ability to provide care" (Sittig, Ash, and Singh 2014, 419). When this is not done, the potential for resilience and innovation is compromised.

Managing these changes well requires cultivating several resources, including assessment and data collection from affiliates about their experiences and how they value them. How affiliates feel about the services and activities matters, and respecting that constitutes a valuable asset of organizational change. In a small organization, with just a few domains of service and affiliate engagement, this process of self-assessment toward innovation can be managed quite efficiently. Still, much more is needed than a suggestion box on a wall. People provide the most observable indicator of what is and is not working by voting with their feet and simply ending their affiliation. For growth, or even stability, to occur, regular organizational assessment and an affiliate-centered means to assess feedback, as well as taking the recommended steps toward possible change, are needed.

Best Practices

The five primary organizational fractures discussed above were not given a chance to heal within the FACTS Ministries. Yet from them, best practices for a faith-based health organization can be specified. These best practices are associated with its health- and resilience-nurturing assets—people, places, and things—that can enrich affiliates, the organization, and the larger community. In figure 3, a conceptual model of these components illustrates best practices and related policy alternatives associated with them. For a social ecology of resilience in North Lawson and other neighborhoods like it, this model conceptually grounds recovery and health. Prior research has shown ways that churches, including some in the very neighborhood in which the FACTS Ministries is located, have addressed faith-based community health care (e.g., Cheney et al. 2014; Levin 2014b; Price-Spratlen 2015). Figure 3 summarizes ways in which each domain of the model helps heal affiliates by informing aspects of care to realize their resilience potential.

Valuing People

People-centered opportunities are a first best practice for faith-based health organizations dependent on voluntary affiliation. When moving from active addiction to sustaining long-term recovery and health, "challenges faced by people whose addictive behaviour has led to the dissolution of their recovery capital, in terms of financial security, positive family and community relationships, self-esteem and self-efficacy . . . diminish when responsibility is assumed and resulting issues are addressed practically" (Dossett 2017, 943). To address organizational fractures, diverse groups of people contribute to a health and resilience mission with shared respect. As exemplified by Brother Hasten and others (see chapter 1), such an environment is more conducive to both individual affiliation and organizational sustainability. Hasten did not drink or use drugs, yet his life has been affected by the addiction of loved ones and by the prevalence of addiction in the neighborhood in which he grew up and never left. Tribble (2005, 96, 116) emphasizes the importance of "strategies of congregational adaptation [including] the shift from the tradition of pastor-centered leadership to shared transformative leadership that transforms the pastor and followers." Such leadership would allow for a balance of roles and affiliate voices in an environment of shared respect and give new meaning and motive to "affiliation."

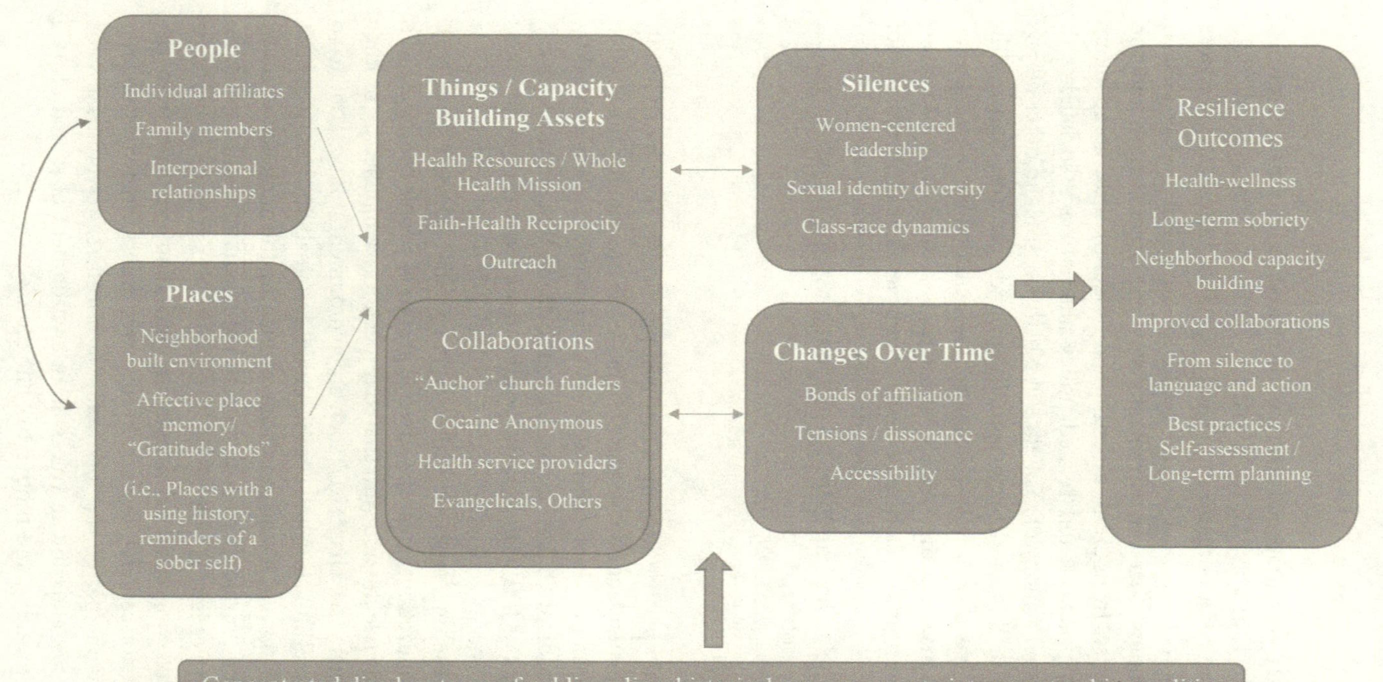

Figure 3. Conceptual model of healing fractured faith through a recovery-focused health organization. Source: Developed by the author for this book.

Another people-centered best practice of a faith-based health organization is to "provide an organized way for people to give back to their communities through volunteer and paid service to others seeking recovery. [They] work with allied organizations [and] offer recovery support services . . . and broaden public understanding of the reality of recovery while remaining accountable to the recovery community" (Faces and Voices of Recovery 2012, 6). Briefly profiled in chapter 3, volunteers with the Tuesday and Thursday lunches give back to the community. Several are in recovery and empathize with challenges of sustaining an environment of support for persons struggling to turn their lives around.

When affiliates can give back to the organization as active peer leaders who contribute to program development, one can imagine the kinds of beneficial women-affirming or young adult and youth-centered programs and related activities that could be implemented and carried out. For example, what could Men's Prayer Breakfasts become? What could happen in one short hour between the breakfasts' end at 9:00 a.m. on the third Saturday of each month and the beginning of the Either-Or CA meeting at 10:00 a.m.? An "In Your Own Words" shop talk where everyone in attendance speaks? A neighborhood photovoice session (i.e., shared empowerment with pictures taken and narrated by an affiliate to enrich the interactions between choice, art, and social justice)? A neighborhood health walk? A discussion on a men's health issue across generations? By broadening the reach of affiliate stakeholder diversities and strengthening the means through which multi-domain affiliation matters, a faith-based community organization can be an environment of equity and resilience. Organizations marked by the "centrality of relationships and interpersonal connections [in] the virtuous circles of human connectivity" (Putnam and Feldstein 2003, 269, 270) place value on diversities of people, identities, and personal histories. This value on diversities can become the means through which a broadened cohesion occurs, even among affiliates of different primary health domains (e.g., youth initiatives and substance use recovery affiliates coming together to explore substance use prevention and dynamics of recovery as a family disease).

Nurturing Places

Sustaining place-based health initiatives that enrich neighborhoods marked by severe health disparities, addiction, and other aspects of concentrated disadvantage (see chapter 2) is another best practice. By definition, a social ecology of resilience is anchored in place. After their extensive review of community competence and capacity literatures, Norris et al. (2008) identified eight attributes to achieve community resilience. Among them are (1) connectedness, commitment, and shared values; (2) critical reflection and skill building; and (3) communication and effective management. All communities have these attributes. Where they are limited, community organizations can play a key role in developing them.

Tensions of recovery are simultaneously internal, existing within any given individual seeking to recover from addiction, and external, informed by all things outside of the individual in recovery that can affect how someone engages their resilience through long-term recovery. By reputation and reality, North Lawson is an "abstinence-hostile environment" (Cleveland et al. 2007, 13; see also Laudet et al. 2014), where people inclined to participate in potentially health-compromising behaviors can readily find the means to do so. At the same time and within the same neighborhood, there exists a congregational corridor of religious concentration (Duck 2015; McRoberts 2003), as well as multiple health outlets. Tensions between these characteristics make North Lawson and neighborhoods like it ideal environments for a faith-based health organization focused on addiction recovery to take root. Recovery is partially, though not entirely, about access. In addition, it is informed by the means through which people engage in their "daily reprieve contingent on the maintenance of [their] spiritual condition" (Alcoholics Anonymous 2001, 85). For those engaged in a medically managed program of recovery, "the disruptive effect of a dosing schedule necessitates daily trips to clinics that are often located in impoverished and drug-infested neighborhoods" (Coombs 2001, 91). However, these tensions of place can enrich health assets.

"Abstinence hostility" can be an asset of "recovery capital" and resilience (Bliuc et al. 2017, 111; see also White 1996). Abstinence-hostile environments are those which heavily promote substance use or where a great deal of substance use takes place. The use of the term has been status driven, with a focus on college campuses (e.g., White, Kelly, and Roth 2012) because of the prevalence of binge drinking and other substance consumption. The phrase also has applicability in neighborhoods like North Lawson. When it flourished, the FACTS Ministries was a place where the best of the ethnogenic thread was present, was readily available, and challenged any such hostilities. It did so by meeting affiliates where they were and sharing resources with them that were about much more than substance use, or any single health challenge alone. Because of their contributions as environments of support and resilience for sustaining health-promoting behavior change, "community-based initiatives are gaining popularity as evidence of their success increases [because] their goal is more than drug abstinence [and] they are more aware of the social, economic, and cultural problems than are treatment clinicians and social workers from outside the community" (Boeri 2018, 180). Community health organizations valuing tensions of place in the opioid crisis means acknowledging the largely underpublicized yet devastating effects of the crisis in African American neighborhoods (James and Jordan 2018). An open-air drug market is across the street from the FACTS Ministries, it has multiple trap houses as neighbors, and drug use behaviors and paraphernalia are quite visible throughout North Lawson (see chapter 2). Yet in a neighborhood environment of abstinence hostility, the Ministries and other organizations like it are in a beneficial location as nurturing places of support for social resilience.

Capacity-Building Assets (Things)

A coherent balance of services and resource access is a vital best practice for a faith-based health organization. Trying to do too much with too little can be a recipe for inefficiency and disaffiliation. Creating and sustaining an environment of shared respect may be the most vital best practice, reinforced by each affiliate's repeated contributions to it. In order for such an environment to contribute to the health and well-being of its affiliates, resources available must enrich "health promotion professionals and churches [who] can be dynamic partners to promote health and wellness in light of our diverse society and health needs" (Peterson, Atwood, and Yates 2002, 401). Staffing and programming are essential aspects of any service delivery system. Who the staff members are, how they behave, and what programmatic resources they use to contribute to the health and well-being of affiliates become all the more important when the staff is small and volunteers are an essential aspect of service delivery (see chapter 3). Tagai and her colleagues (2018, 716) identified staffing as one of the "three major categories of structural organizational characteristics" central to the successful promotion of sustained behavior change among faith-based organizations. Their "bedside manner" is essential as the means through which quality health services can flourish by "combin[ing] the appropriate application of knowledge and technical skills with acknowledgement of and respect for the emotional, social, and cultural needs and preferences" (Weissmann et al. 2006, 662). That value remains and can increase the health and resilience of individual affiliates, the organization, and the community. Demonstrating respect, addressing emotional responses, building personal connections, and sustaining nonverbal communication are among the "soft skills" central to an environment of support for improved health (Weissmann et al. 2006; see also Bliuc et al. 2017).

Another capacity-building best practice is prioritizing health and resilience as a multilevel and multidimensional focus that all persons in touch with the organization can value and to which they can contribute. To strengthen this multidimensional character, periodic self-assessment is vital. Doing so clarifies how the organization can most effectively address substance misuse and related health challenges among traditionally underserved populations (Boeri 2018). As reflected in the health services analyzed in chapter 3, these are among the strategies to promote health services integration. This is done by providing individuals with service options in a single organization—including prevention, recovery support, acute intervention, and others based on need (Faces and Voices of Recovery 2012; SAMHSA 2015; US Surgeon General 2016), which is severe in neighborhoods like North Lawson. As much as their faith-based charter will allow (Sager 2012), advocating for access to Affordable Care Act legislation and universal health care more broadly can communicate with nearby agencies related to health, health care, and health disparities. This can demonstrate the importance of community organization contributions to public policy participations that can improve individual, family, and community health.

Technology can also enrich health access consistent with a faith-based community health mission and practices. An organizational footprint includes the website, Facebook, newsletter, a podcast, and other social media presence. Long before the onset of the COVID pandemic, online participations were among the means through which recovery and resilience can be enriched, and they still are. Technological innovation, as Bliuc et al. (2017, 111) stated, "enable[s] a variety of ways of communication, [and] the ways in which social support in recovery is delivered and received has expanded to include online modes." Given current challenges of privacy and surveillance, related innovations would need to be managed with great care and forethought. Again, volunteer affiliate leadership could be, at the very least, a useful asset, and at most an essential best practice. Regarding the current opioid crisis, either proposed or in development are "new technologies [that] range from wearable devices that sense respiratory depression to alert the user, or automatically inject naloxone . . . or wirelessly report a looming crisis to a first responder. Also included are apps for wireless electronic devices to function as behavioral coaches, to reduce pain, or increase compliance, among others" (Madras 2018, 945). Whatever their form of delivery and engagement or manner of data storage and access, these technologies can enrich the "brick-and-mortar" on-site interactions and related interpersonal resources of such organizations.

Sustaining Collaborations

As discussed in chapter 4, organizational affiliations, whether or not they become formal collaborations of a similar mission, enrich human and material resource sharing and are a vital best practice. Such interdependence follows from a long history of similar faith-health initiatives. More than a century ago, in his seminal work *The Negro Church*, W. E. B. Du Bois (1903, 78) wrote of a necessary "evidence of great cohesion and skilled leadership" in order for African Americans to flourish within and beyond their houses of worship. As noted earlier, just three years later, Du Bois (1906, 110) championed "the formation of local health leagues among Colored people for the dissemination of better knowledge . . . and preventive medicine." In the years to follow, "black health professionals . . . churches, and civic organizations cooperated in a variety of efforts to improve the health status of black Americans" (Quinn and Thomas 2001, 45). Within the next generation, Lindeman (1921) emphasized the importance of affiliate decision-making and participatory leadership as essential aspects of a "community involvement" model and the critical necessity of affiliates having a voice and a means for that voice to be heard and valued. Then and now, sustaining healthy collaborations can enrich the quality of care discussed above. "People of shared mission" can mean cohesion and bonding across differences and collective decision-making despite those differences. The recent "social reconstruction and social recovery model" of Miriam Boeri (2018, 172) builds on this foundation, as do other recent works on the special importance of health collaborations (e.g., Lanier, Schumacher, and Calvert 2015; Mayo and Woolley 2016).

As one part of this collaborative process, an important best practice for a small-scale storefront church is learning how to value and make use of tensions that arise in unexpected ways. When faith-based community health organizations like the FACTS Ministries accept and work with tensions with their collaborative partners, they can be in fellowship with, rather than in opposition to, other local area organizations and businesses. When tensions between two organizations are wisely maintained, together they are at the mission-driven and literal intersection of community clinics and churches, consistent with the "local health leagues" legacy of Du Bois and others from more than a century ago. Given the instabilities of the ACA and related efforts toward universal health-care coverage, and the very high prevalence of limited care opportunities for substance use disorder more broadly, this consistency remains vital and can enrich each of the collaborating organizations' shared and unshared missions. Whether through affiliation or the more formal collaboration, their shared mission can include the use of "social marketing to de-stigmatize addiction recovery" (Lavack 2007, 480; see also Boeri 2018) and potentially much more with technological innovation.

What could a "sister church" relationship look like when the organization initiating the collaboration is at the urban core of concentrated disadvantage and when it bridges suburban Whites and Blacks, Appalachian Whites, impoverished Blacks, and others in a shared mission of health and resilience? There is a growing recognition of the need to no longer "obscure the fact that the opioid crisis has particularly affected some of the poorest regions of the country, such as Appalachia, and that people living in poverty are especially at risk for addiction and its consequences" (NIDA 2017, 1). Collaborations between faith-based and secular organizations with similar health missions can help to overcome tensions of interregional and interracial resource sharing. Though "the opioid epidemic has also profoundly affected communities of color . . . non-white victims of the opioid epidemic are conspicuously absent from political discourse" (James and Jordan 2018, 404). Faith-based community health organizations of the urban core, like the FACTS Ministries, are in a unique position to bridge race, class, and regional differences in the current opioid crisis through collaborations of shared mission. If a sister church relationship is unwieldy or otherwise undesired, perhaps site visit exchanges, or some other resource exchange that is shorter-term and event-driven, could take place. Finding an event-specific common ground (e.g., a co-sponsored, jointly volunteer-staffed "Faith and Addiction Recovery" event) could nurture an interregional social ecology of resilience that could then become a longer-term commitment. This sentiment is shared by a growing number of people associated with the addiction and recovery process (e.g., Boeri

2018; Boyer 2021; James and Jordan 2018; US Surgeon General 2016). It is consistent with what the present moment demands.

The neoliberal funding landscape is an uncertain one. Faith-based organizations like the FACTS Ministries "have been integrated into an effort to reduce reliance on traditional Keynesian forms of delivery in the United States [and are] increasingly called on to deliver [such] services that were 'rolled back' through cuts [to state funding]" (Hackworth 2010, 752; see also Hackworth 2019). As a collaborative best practice, via the ACA and other similar legislation, faith-based organization service delivery can and should be partnered with policy advocacy that expands all forms of health-care access. In his meta-analysis of relationships between service organizations and congregations, Polson (2008) found four characteristics of these relationships, including interdependence and a high level of interaction between those involved. Such interdependence recognizes that "communities stand to benefit the most from the establishment of thick, durable ties of partnership" (Polson 2008, 59; see also Madras 2018). Especially amid neoliberal uncertainties and other funding constraints, affiliate leadership is an important, if not essential, best practice to further these thick, durable ties of partnership. Collaborative best practices are sustained through exchanges of shared respect and appreciation in both the perceptions and behaviors of those involved.

Resisting Silences

To help heal fractures in an organization, resisting silences is an essential best practice, and striving for a high degree of transparency and information sharing is important. Consistent with the best practice of forming collaborations noted above, visible, respected information sharing produces "social mechanisms such as emerging relational structures, heightened awareness of others and working together to tap into existing interpersonal networks to enable organizational health" (Teo, Lee, and Lim 2017, 137). Such information and power sharing can help move beyond "early definitions of silence [that] equated it with 'loyalty' and the assumption that nothing was wrong if concerns were not being voiced" (Bagheri, Zarei, and Aeen 2012, 49). Following from chapter 5, resisting silences means "being able to engage and involve people with diverse cultural, economic, gender and other backgrounds, and should be a goal for groups. Organizations that value the recovery and life experiences of all enrich their ability to serve and to advocate" (Faces and Voices of Recovery 2012, 17). Bonds of affiliation can be enriched when identities are known, visible, and valued, and when the behavior and narratives of stigma and alienation for being "different" are challenged or, best yet, entirely abandoned through a sustainable equity. Prior research has demonstrated the value of voice and "a strong and negative relationship between organizational silence and organizational citizenship behavior. . . . The higher the level of voice, the higher the level of organizational citizenship behavior" (Cinar, Karcioglu, and Aliogullari 2013, 320). Consistent with Cinar, Karcioglu, and Aliogullari (2013), in addition to traditional inspiration and inclusion, to show respect across differences, organizations like the FACTS Ministries could host a workshop on disability and difference in recovery, on youth in recovery, or on LGBTQ+ people in recovery, perhaps in collaboration with a youth social service or an LGBTQ+-affirming health organization.

Such collaboration could be reflected in co-sponsoring "Loving the Family We Are: A Workshop on Faith, Health, and Recovery," which values multiple family roles while placing recovery at the center of an intergenerational and intersectional health and resilience. A dialogue of faith and the 12-Step model could consider the intersecting challenges of addiction as a family disease. A Men's Prayer Breakfast could feature a women's health professional facilitating a women's focus group at the center of the reconfigured chapel. Men would be there primarily to listen and support. This, or something similar, could, in Audre Lorde's (1984, 41–42) words, help "transform silence into language and action" while thickening durable ties of partnership.

Equitable responses in everyday interaction are among the most inclusive means of transforming silence in an organization and can go well beyond mere tolerance. As Lorde (1984, 111) clearly stated, "Advocating the mere tolerance of difference is the grossest reformism [and] a total denial of the creative function of difference in our lives. Difference must be . . . seen as a fund of necessary polarities between which our creativity can spark like a dialectic. Only then does the necessity for interdependency become unthreatening." To spark creativity, one among the dialectics or tensions consistent with Lorde is the relationship between religious traditionalism and various subgroup differences. For example, religious traditionalism may not embrace lesbian and gay persons. The organization can more effectively create and sustain healthy lines of communication between persons of different sexual identities if they were not shrouded in secrecy and shame and if people were allowed to speak and break those silences. Navigating those potential tensions can nurture growth beyond fear for all.

Welcoming Change Over Time

Resilience demands thorough organizational change. For resilience to be reflected in an organization's social ecology, various changes are necessary. Following from figure 3, resources, collaborations, and silences are among the most vital aspects of the "people, places, and things" 12-Step trope. Each of them will likely change. For an organization to enrich health and resilience, best practices of change include "trust, common rules, leadership . . . networks and bridging . . . within a polycentric governance structure, and a devolution of management rights and power sharing that promotes participation" (Quinlan and Gunderson 2016, 182; see also Rudzinski et al. 2017). Resources not cultivated, voice and trust impeded by silences, affiliate networks not engaged equitably, and power not shared creatively further affiliation fractures and are among the ways organizations devolve.

The figure 3 components and their related best practices are consistent with one of the primary goals of the Institute of Medicine (IOM). The IOM (2000, 6) is mentioned here because it asserts the importance in all forms of health care of being "patient-centered—providing care that is respectful of and responsive to individual patient preferences, needs, and values and ensuring that patient values guide all clinical decisions." A community organization has affiliates rather than patients. Consistent with the IOM directive, though, affiliates can be addressed with a similar level of conscientious concern. Navigating fluctuations in affiliation, collaboration, and many other dimensions of a community organization keeping its doors open is a vital means of sustaining that organization's ability to be, and contribute to, a social ecology of health and resilience.

Policy Possibilities

Despite policy not being this book's primary aim, a few policy considerations are warranted. The FACTS Ministries having an oversized sign across the front of the building, with type that would comfortably fit a building three times its size, was itself a political statement and best practice. The words referenced overcoming addiction and "sobriety," and they affirmed visibility beyond addiction's shame. Moving beyond visible, public advocacy for health services addressing stigmatized populations, the Ministries is marked by missed opportunities to further policy-related initiatives. Across the continua of initiatives, various civic engagements are possible, if not necessary, since "political empowerment is the only route to recovery, and this empowerment is braided with spirituality" (Morell 1996, 310; see also Boeri 2018; US Surgeon General 2016). A multidimensional ministries' mission of bridging best practices with public policy, includes (a) enriching health-care access to help reduce health disparities, (b) addressing housing access, (c) responding to gun violence and police brutality, and (d) doing so as part of larger economic revitalizations, as circumstances allow. Ambitious and achievable, these policy-related empowerments are briefly discussed below.

Health-Care Access

As stated by the US Surgeon General (2016, 1), "The Affordable Care Act requires the majority of United States health plans and insurers to offer prevention, screening, brief interventions, and other forms of treatment for substance use disorders." Health resources that include those for reducing substance use disorders prioritize a diverse set of "front-end" policies consistent with the Ministries' mission. Given the prevalence of illicit drug consumption in the US, policies that support harm reduction (e.g., safe using sites) *and* long-term sobriety grounded in abstinence are essential. The evidence-based summary in the Surgeon General's report details comprehensive and hopeful demonstrations of a critical category that, at its best, the Ministries aptly fulfills: community coalition models. Policy that promotes increased access to well-structured collaborative engagements is consistent with such evidence-based practices. Yet in the 2016 US Surgeon General's report, these community coalitions exclusively focused on prevention.

The FACTS Ministries' mission is consistent with the Mental Health Parity and Addiction Equity Act (2008) and the Affordable Care Act (2010). The former "requires that the financial requirements and treatment limitations imposed by health plans and insurers for substance use disorders be no more restrictive than [those] they impose for medical and surgical conditions. . . . It is difficult to overstate the importance of these two Acts for creating a public health-oriented approach to reducing substance misuse and related disorders" (US Surgeon General 2016, 1–20).

Research from Medicaid expansion states shows that "the ACA was associated with reductions in treatment disparity between Black and White clients . . . [and that] Black clients with Medicaid in expansion states had the greatest reduction in disparities" (Johnson, Choi, and Herrera 2021, 1). Community-based health services can help strengthen these improvements with their informal contributions to improvements in access to care.

In addition, section 1115 of the Social Security Act supports New Service Delivery Alternatives through Medicaid and the US Department of Health and Human Services. Such services can improve the funding base for building aftercare and addiction recovery support services, including recovery coaching, with which the FACTS Ministries' flourishing period was consistent. In the continuum of the care process, the Ministries could be a beneficial resource in relation to adult drug courts and medically assisted treatment (MAT). Drug courts and MAT are policy initiatives that contribute to harm reduction. All contributions to replacing the criminal justice response to substance misuse—i.e., mass incarceration (Drucker 2011)—with a public health response to it are beneficial policy advances.

In addition, consistent with the Ministries' health services and mission, there is strong evidence-based program support for the value of combining "standalone day treatment with [abstinence] contingency management. This intervention was originally developed to treat homeless drug users. . . . [It] consists of primarily group activities including counseling, recreational activities, skills building, [and] occurred five days per week during the first two months and two times per week for four months" (Washington State Institute for Public Policy 2019, 1; see also Boeri 2018; De Crescenzo et al. 2018). This time-intensive initiative is consistent with the Ministries' five domains of health resources (see chapter 3) and has been shown to be highly cost-effective. Public policy funding for a range of intensity structures is important for policy progress.

While contributing to the improvement of health services access and broader public health, such policy initiatives help reduce health disparities (Johnson, Choi, and Herrera 2021). The local city paper recently published multiple articles by a variety of professionals on North Lawson and the presence of health disparities in the neighborhood: infant mortality, life expectancy, obesity, drugs, and more. Health-focused outreach to one or more of these concern-specific elements, as well as to the county health department in its potential faith-based participations is possible; from hosting a neighborhood forum to well-child health practices and health screenings could take place on site. For example, the Ministries could collaborate to invite the local city council member or high-level staff member to hold an open forum. Or Ministries leadership could co-author an open letter to the state legislator to advocate on behalf of faith-based funding to contribute to reductions in health disparities (Sager 2012). While they cannot lobby as a faith-based nonprofit, they can advocate. It could initiate outreach to one or more outside experts or to issue-specific participants, or restart Friday Youth Nights during the summer and use them as a platform to address youth-centered health disparities. Consistent with the young man who gave testimony and was silenced during a church service (see chapter 5), a young fatherhood and faith initiative could align with the Youth Nights program to enrich a social ecology of resilience as both organization and neighborhood reciprocity. These are among the many ways the FACTS Ministries could further health access consistent with its mission.

Housing Access

As a 501(c)3 nonprofit, a faith-based organization like the FACTS Ministries must remain consistent with both legal and ethical standards of organizational best practices regarding political participations of all kinds (Sager 2012). Policy that improves housing alternatives is an essential part of any initiative focused on establishing and enhancing interdependent recovery capital among those most vulnerable to the destructive repetitions of active addiction. Research has shown that hiring recruiters and using loan funding helped to establish more residential aftercare centers, and taking out such loans enhanced the likelihood of long-term recovery (e.g., Jason et al. 2005). Policies toward improving access to sober homes is vital—both as a bridge step from homeless shelter settings and as a means of addressing housing insecurity and foreclosure. Real estate initiatives could offer opportunities for home ownership in North Lawson to former sober homes residents working their way to healthy living. Nearby abandoned houses have the potential for nonprofit, capital-generating resource options (e.g., sober homes, leasable properties for community development corporation property management). Ministries leadership would be able to engage longtime affiliates who live in low-income housing with property management, interpersonal, and legal skills for navigating the "slumlord" process that too often exploits them (see Cusack et al. 2019). There are many abandoned or otherwise rundown homes available in North Lawson that could be purchased at a reasonable price and renovated (see chapter 2). Such initiatives could be strengthened by pilot testing the risk versus utility of a rent-to-own "step up" properties plan of sober growth toward housing ownership for former sober homes residents, along with funding for employability and job stability (e.g., Western 2008). Options to address housing insecurities in a just manner are all the more vital given the COVID pandemic.

In other urban areas, city officials have inserted additional criteria to block another slumlord from taking over. They proposed reinvestment plans for such buildings, maintaining mixed-income—including a large number of lower-income—renters to ensure the neighborhood's support (Imbroscio 2011). Whether housing focused or not, social businesses "operate [both within, and] outside the profit-seeking economy and have been used to provide employment opportunities" (McKay 2017, 754) for returning citizens, those recovering from addiction, and people with a history of mental illness. Policy initiatives for this kind of homegrown economic revitalization could be a best practice through an innovative trust moving toward mutually beneficial owner partnerships for affiliate sober progress and an organization's programming maturation. Such housing alternatives could directly enrich a sober homes initiative, property acquisition, and broader economic participation beyond rent-to-own access in the North Lawson housing market.

Gun Violence and Police Brutality

A social ecology of resilience informed by a continuum-of-care model is also relevant to the Ministries in relation to gun violence. In June 2015, four people, including two small children, were shot in a horrific gangland-style shooting in a nearby neighborhood. The shooting was an opportunity to mobilize and to address gun violence in relation to the often violently maintained illicit-substance-using markets in the neighborhood. A health ministry contributing to individual, familial, and neighborhood public safety as a faith-health priority has a valued history in neighborhoods similar to North Lawson. In Boston and other cities, "focused deterrence strategies are designed to prevent serious youth violence by reaching out directly to [youth]. Churches and other community groups offer health services and other kinds of help" (Welsh, Braga, and Sullivan 2014, 514; see also Duck 2015) to improve faith, health, and resilience.

Recently, yet another African American young man was shot in North Lawson by police multiple times. In the aftermath of the event, there was a small, well-intentioned rally on the steps of the county courthouse. Addressing factors related to this or any other shooting is far from the responsibility of any one organization. Unfortunately, no sustained organizational mobilizing occurred. A post-rally flyer was posted at the Ministries on one of the four refrigerators in the community room. The flyer was an invitation to a neighborhood rally. No consideration of structural inequality or other related dynamics informing this violence was ever presented then, nor when a similar incident occurred again a few months later. Questions were not raised at the Ministries about collective means to challenge the interdependent oppressions that shape the criminalization of Black bodies in a predominantly African American neighborhood. No collaborations or willingness to work with others in proactive ways toward a sustainable, multiorganizational, local area resilience occurred. Given that he was a faith leader who publicly presented himself as "a minister beyond the sinister," Pastor Marshall's silence on this issue was noted by affiliates. Gun violence is a public health issue beyond the scope of this current project and contribution. Still, as one evidence-based example, the cure violence model (Butts et al. 2015; Welsh, Braga, and Sullivan 2014) and other similar initiatives are among the valuable next steps to which faith-based health organizations can contribute. Such options could be useful in moving from "focused deterrence strategies" to faith-health collaborations to further criminal justice accountability in relation to individual, organizational, and communal health and resilience.

Economic Revitalization(s)

In March 2017, the Greater Lawson Development Group (GLDG) closed its doors for the final time. Its stated mission was to collaborate with community leaders, organizations, and government entities to improve quality of life in the area through housing and economic development and community revitalization initiatives. The closing of the GLDG reduced the potential for grassroots-anchored revitalization in the neighborhood. Just one year earlier, a "Smart City" application stated:

> [This] is a richly diverse city where people of every type have succeeded in achieving the American Dream, though we recognize that our city, like many others, has pockets of isolation that handicap the success of some of our residents—particularly racial or ethnic minorities and those with lower incomes. The [North Lawson] neighborhood faces many of these challenges,

> which is the primary reason for proposing [it] for a mobility-access related project. An unemployment rate of over 15%, more than three times the rest of the city . . . a poverty level almost three times that of the city, and a median household income of less than half of the rest of the city, compels [a] focus on access to jobs and connecting citizens to community services. (Smart Cities application)

The city was awarded the grant. While hopeful, the practices that followed from it are consistent with the "colonization in the name of empowerment" caution (Evans et al. 2012, 183), where exploitive relationships remain, or get worse, after "redevelopment" or "revitalization" initiatives take place. Prioritizing indigenous process leadership and resource decision-making in the revitalization, in true collaboration with empathic outsiders, remains uncertain and formative. There were two day-care centers within a two-mile radius southward, between a homeless shelter and the Ministries. That area included a religiously grounded arts center (that closed in early 2015), eight of the fourteen corridor churches, a library a few blocks north, and the Thirteenth Street and Akron Avenue intersection of two health-care outlets, a food shop, a retail store, and the GLDG office.

In a congregational corridor, a multidimensional ministry informed by the collective leadership of its affiliates has the potential to contribute to economic stability. In 2014, a longtime FACTS Ministries affiliate was a national award winner from a well-respected entrepreneurial magazine. Consistent with this affiliate's success, organizationally monetizing his innovation into related small business models continues to have great revitalizing potential. There is potential for the Ministries to engage in a collective economic and neighborhood development vision if affiliates were invited to share ideas, participate in decision-making, and contribute their short- and long-term visions. A community development corporation 501(c)8 partial-profit model could engage with other churches, along with the Good Samaritan homeless shelter a couple miles south, in a "corridor of community among us."

A Challenging Past and Possible Future

This qualitative case study looked at how a faith-based health services organization prioritized recovery from addiction during the rising opioid crisis in an era of neoliberal decline. It follows from Tagai et al. (2018) and their aggregate, comparative, and quantitative capacity inventory of faith-based organizations that address health. To place the Tagai et al. inventory in a societal context, Jason Hackworth (2010) suggests the following: (a) the state has declined; (b) faith-based services are replacing it; (c) denying structural influences and, instead, emphasizing individual action is central to a faith-based focus; and (d) individual responsibility (and blame) focus is consistent with the neoliberal turn. Consistent with Tagai et al., and as Hackworth cautions and this book shows, organizational and other forms of collaboration, in responding to the individual and structural factors informing health disparities, can occur simultaneously and successfully.

As noted in the introduction, this research demonstrates why "resilience researchers must become more ecological in their approach . . . to tell the rest of the story on resilience and better equip individuals and whole communities for success" (Shaw et al. 2016, 39). The social ecology of health and resilience as summarized in figure 3, and explored throughout these chapters, is a framework of beliefs, communication, and organizational programs and "processes that foster healing and growth out of crisis [which] can reduce stress and vulnerability in high-risk situations, and empower to overcome prolonged adversity" (Walsh 2003, 67). These are the means by which the FACTS Ministries in North Lawson, and other likeminded organizations in similar urban neighborhoods, can engender and sustain a beneficial *collective* environment of support that works together toward individual, organizational, and social change. While many challenges remain, this new model of a social ecology of resilience, informed by the best practices and policy recommendations above, can be helpful in navigating the collision of interdependent epidemics that mark our present and future.

Faith-based organizations with supportive leadership that dedicate time to implementation and sustainability are more successful when they implement an activity that promotes health (Austin and Claiborne 2011; James and Jordan 2018; Johnson, Choi, and Herrera 2021). Such a health-promoting mission must shift in ways that are beneficial for furthering other shifts toward a possible future. A shift in philosophy could enrich a dialogue between offering MAT strategies to reduce harm and engaging others in 12-Step fellowship protocol and practices. Faith-based community organizations focused on recovery could play an important role in such a shift by prioritizing complete abstinence, as they also affirm the value of harm reduction. Doing so would value both as part of a long-term continuum-of-care model to nurture affiliates' long-term health outcomes. The foundation of the 12-Step model extends from having reached a "bottom" that leads to Step 1: "We admitted we were powerless over cocaine and all other mind-altering substances and that our lives had become unmanageable" (Cocaine Anonymous 2018, 5). However contrary to harm reduction and MAT that Step 1 may appear to be, Alcoholics Anonymous was cofounded by "Dr. Bob," a medical doctor (Alcoholics Anonymous 2001). Among the first pages assigned as homework in the step-work process using the Big Book is a section of the book's front matter titled "The Doctor's Opinion." In it is the recognition that there are health challenges of many kinds that can affect one's recovery and may require seeking outside help from medical or other health professionals. Those using MAT or other harm-reduction practices and those who are abstinent on a daily basis need not be at odds, since saving lives and promoting health and resilient well-being are goals they share. How these approaches can benefit one another to the benefit of each is a dialogue that is growing in the substance use treatment industry (Boeri 2018; US Surgeon General 2016). Both historically and today, medical innovation has a role to play to help enrich faith-based community health organizations.

Consistent with a great deal of prior research (Boeri 2018; Hackworth 2010; Johnson, Choi, and Herrera 2021; McKay 2017; Showalter 2018; Tagai et al. 2018; US Surgeon General 2016; Welsh, Braga, and Sullivan 2014), this analysis of the FACTS Ministries suggests that a shift toward a public health approach to combating addiction in government policy seems warranted and overdue. The US government has long been complicit in magnifying negative outcomes of substance-related behaviors (James and Jordan 2018). For example, despite scientific evidence that equipping users with sterile needles is a strategy that saves users from contracting AIDS-related infections, the government "prohibited federal funding for syringe-exchange programs for people who inject[ed] drugs nearly continuously from 1988 to 2015" (Showalter 2018, 95). Sadly, withdrawing this funding has prevented a lifesaving strategy. The uneven US history with regard to drug use risks and addiction recovery appears to have taken a beneficial turn with the election of the Biden administration. Though reasons for caution remain,

> President Biden has made clear that addressing the overdose and addiction epidemic is an urgent priority for his administration. In March [2021], the President signed into law the American Rescue Plan, which appropriated nearly $4 billion to enable

> the Substance Abuse and Mental Health Services Administration and the Health Resources and Services Administration to expand access to vital behavioral health services. President Biden has also said that people should not be incarcerated for drug use but should be offered treatment instead. The President has also emphasized the need to eradicate racial, gender, and economic inequities that currently exist in the criminal justice system. These drug policy priorities . . . take a bold approach to reducing overdoses and saving lives. (Executive Office of the President, Office of National Drug Control Policy 2021, 1)

However preliminary and aspirational this memo may seem, it provides reason for hope. As former surgeon general Dr. Joycelyn Elders noted a generation ago, "Much of U.S. drug policy is racist in its consequences, particularly in terms of the number of African-Americans in prison for drug offenses" (cited by Marlatt 1996, 782). What is needed is foregrounding these contradictions and the racial and class-based rationales for their continued presence. The utility of a Presidential ONDCP memo is unclear. Post-prison "secondary sanctions" and related inequalities of policy and practices are at the intersection of the prison/reentry, health/substance use, and related structural inequalities. What is not in dispute is the general decline of state participation in social welfare funding and related supports for low- and moderate-income persons (Hackworth 2010). This same population is subject to the limitations of reduced access to substance-related and other health resources for sustaining behavior change and potentially improving quality of life.

There seems to be a necessary shift in recognizing the danger of social inequity in the US regarding substance use disorder. Conservative former Federal Reserve chair Alan Greenspan, progressive professor Noam Chomsky, and many in between recognize that growing inequalities are a threat to our democracy. Likewise, the National Institutes of Health suggest that addressing the opioid crisis requires first confronting socioeconomic disparities. Informed in part by contexts of despair (Boeri 2018; D'Angelo and Her 2019), "the opioid crisis has particularly affected some of the poorest regions of the country, such as Appalachia, and . . . people living in poverty are especially at risk for addiction and its consequences like overdose or spreads of HIV" (NIDA 2017, 1). As a nation, while all markets are contingent on both, we have a demand-side problem, not a supply-side problem. Well beyond the analysis of a single faith-based organization, this book helps to disentangle this country's intersections and their many health consequences, as greater understanding can inform better organizational functioning, policy, and improved life chances.

Be it the opioid crisis, other forms of substance misuse, or so many other aspects of society, "the marginalization of Black people is highly consistent with a pattern of framing addiction affecting people of color as a pathological shortcoming to be answered by militarized policing and involvement of the criminal justice system, in lieu of treatment" (James and Jordan 2018, 404). There are reasons to have hope that the Biden administration memo cited above will help initiate a structural turnaround in these long-standing patterns, with federal mandates and state-specific adherence to these sustainable policy transformations. Especially in this era of the retreat of the neoliberal state, our current health challenges require a new, more nuanced conversation to which this book contributes. The conversation must revise interdiction and racialized criminalization priorities and instead enrich a public health approach. ACA expansion with local area matched funding and collaborations with different community-based options will improve the likelihood for better long-term recovery and health-care access. How communities that have experienced sustained downturn and neglect engage with community organizational development and the means to create new and uncharted collaborations can then have a better opportunity to succeed.

The United States has seen significant growth in grassroots recovery organizations that bridge mutual aid and social policy advocacy (Evans et al. 2012; Laudet et al. 2014; US Surgeon General 2016). Other visible, within-neighborhood activities are a part of enhancing the public-policy and best-practices potential of this declaration. More recently, some organizations have suggested that to enhance the potential for best practices across the faith-based to secular continuum, policy makers need to enhance therapies and promote social engagement strategies that initiate and sustain recovery-supportive lifestyles in community (Bliuc et al. 2017; Boeri 2018). Visible faith-health participations, petition-signing and letter-writing campaigns, supporting reform lobbying initiatives, and other related appeals to local and legislative officials are among beneficial activities consistent with the FACTS Ministries' mission.

Who is at the table having this new conversation of policy innovations and outcomes? Consistent with the "parachuting in" caution of Imani Woods (cited in Marlatt 1996), as Reuter and Caulkins (1995, 1059–60) noted, "Based on experience since 1985, the rhetorical and policy-oriented emphasis on making drug use less acceptable and drugs less available, as well as the focus on drug prevalence as the dominant indicator of program success, has probably outlived its usefulness." The last twenty years have only further reinforced the importance of calling this rhetorical and policy-oriented emphasis into further question. Faith-based and other health organizations could sponsor a needle exchange directly in front of the organization, so that people in active addiction could be protected from a health problem related to drug misuse, while not solely expecting immediate and sustained abstinence. Outreach and inclusion of volunteers in active addiction can play a role in program development toward nurturing an environment of resilience that acknowledges a substance-using continuum. Also potentially consistent with beneficial tensions, direct interaction of some kind could be made to and with nearby trap houses, as quality communication could occur with the (generally) young men navigating the drug marketplace (see Duck 2015). This could demonstrate how their decisions matter and strategize how their management, marketing, and leadership skills can be used differently. Beyond anonymity, selective visibilities can be a foundation to further a 12-Step consensus regarding harm reduction to improve the potential for saving lives.

These many process and policy uncertainties are now being influenced by the most serious of period effects: the COVID-19 pandemic occurring simultaneously with intersecting challenges of an ongoing opioid crisis, while all other substance use circumstances never went away. The social distancing requirements and increased isolations are especially challenging for those with substance use difficulties, and "although the pandemic threatens everyone, it is a particularly grave risk to the millions of Americans with opioid use disorder, who—already vulnerable and marginalized—are heavily dependent on face-to-face health care delivery. Rapid and coordinated action on the part of clinicians and policymakers is required if these threats are to be mitigated" (Alexander et al. 2020, 57). This is true for many others, and the effects are being experienced by all those with substance use challenges of any kind. Videoconferencing, conference call phone trees, and other social media alternatives consistent with maintaining social distancing have been developed (e.g., Liese and Monley 2021).

Judging from informal communication with individuals in recovery, compared to pre-pandemic participation levels, during the pandemic overall affiliation has declined. Some are suggesting that these online and alternative resources are being used unevenly, though no systematic analysis of how they have changed and what the particular consequences of these changes are has been completed. Preliminary evidence from the city of this project suggests that within Cocaine Anonymous and other mutual aid fellowships, fewer meetings are being sustained, fewer people in recovery are attending them, fewer newcomers to recovery are finding their way to them, refusals to participate in any recovery fellowship activities is increasing among once active members, and complaints about what is lost in the translation from face-to-face to videoconference settings appear to be widespread. The willingness to have confidence in "back to normal" practices like a return to face-to-face meetings is being complicated by the COVID-19 delta variant and the prospect of other variants, given the plateaued levels of COVID vaccinations as this book is being completed. All of these uncertainties regarding the availability of, and engagement with, community-based substance use recovery are occurring at a time when alcohol use and opioid overdoses are increasing, as are increases in refusing to access emergency care when needed due to fear of possible COVID infection (e.g., Boyer 2021; Wainwright et al. 2020). Be they faith-based or otherwise, organizations like the FACTS Ministries could have leveraged their organizational relationships to help fill these voids. This project ended before the pandemic began, but, given its problematic organizational relationships during normal times, the viability of the Ministries serving in that collaborative role during the pandemic was unlikely.

Like many other faith-based and health-related organizations, too often Ministries leadership denied or otherwise silenced consideration of structural and ecological factors that informed the lives of its affiliates and instead advocated an individualized narrative. Though focusing on the individual process, the 12-Step spiritual program is also centered on shared fellowship. It affirms organizational ties; values meetings, sponsorship, and peer-mentoring forms of collective service; and supports multiple levels of sober organizing as important resources for sustaining recovery. Despite the flawed decisions of leadership at the FACTS Ministries, the process and practices of faith-based community health organizations in the neoliberal era *can* (and must?) make beneficial contributions for a healthier, broader justice. For the present and probable future, community organizations are likely to matter more than they probably should. Grounded in W. E. B. Du Bois's suggested focus on the social atmosphere surrounding all citizens, may the conceptual model of ecological resilience (see figure 3) and best practices extending from it help strengthen local health-care access more broadly, and the role of community organizations in that broader access.

As this project has demonstrated, thoughtful, participatory, collaborative approaches toward a healthier, more sober future can help address today's many local challenges. The presence and absence of beneficial affiliates and resources like those analyzed here are contemporary expressions of the ethnogenic thread. When nurtured, they are the hope beyond hurt of a collective ethos and program of action in community health organizations, especially in neighborhoods like North Lawson. May this book, and valuing the best practices and related policy progress of such initiatives, encourage these organizations' ability to flourish and nurture a healthier, more resilient present and future.

Epilogue

At the FACTS Ministries, any discussion of carceral logics, or the retreat of the welfare state, or the intentional underdevelopment of neighborhoods like North Lawson (see chapter 2) never occurred. In the day-to-day, this was largely understandable. The organization had faith works to engage, outreach to complete, donations to secure, and services to provide toward the healing of challenging lives to shepherd affiliates from one sober day to the next. "Highbrow" conversations about the retreat of the welfare state and the spiritual dissonance associated with faith-based funding of social and health services were generally perceived as outside of their charge and mission. The merging of those two things—navigating the everyday oppressions of a high-poverty neighborhood and placing those realities in a broader dialogue of health and resilience, place and power—can occur if opportunities to do so are created and valued. Forms of participatory leadership within an organization are vital if the merging of them and the dialogues they demand are to exist. Sustaining organizational affiliations (with Cocaine Anonymous, for example) to enrich that combination can be an important aspect of servant-leadership possibilities. Several FACTS Ministries affiliates were interested in volunteering their time to bring these merged health and resilience dialogues into being.

Closer to home, pathways to engage in discussions about the challenges of White religious patronage, African American megachurch envy, or uncertainties of sustaining secular/faith-based affiliations for community health and resilience were never welcomed. Any efforts toward initiating that level of critical awareness and consideration of organizational mission were quickly silenced. Instead of intentionally embracing W. E. B. Du Bois's call to act against the "peculiar indifference" toward African American health disparities with innovative community health initiatives, the

FACTS Ministries repeatedly chose to renew "the veil" of White religious patronage and its downstream consequences.

Du Bois used "the veil" as a metaphor for psychosocial race differences between African Americans and Whites and its role in the creation of the "double consciousness" of a divided identity within African American individuals and the communities they reside in and to which they contribute (Du Bois [1899] 1967). These divisions can express themselves in various ways, including through tense and fractured affiliations among organizations addressing community health. These fractured affiliations soil the best expressions of "the ethnogenic thread," compromising the potential for realizing and sustaining a flourishing social ecology of health and resilience. Then when that White religious patronage trope was finally resisted in 2012, the choice to do so was shared with Ministries affiliates in a piecemeal fashion, which compromised the potential for initiating forms of collective investment among those who remained. No participatory leadership process was initiated to take the place of prior patronage. Instead, a religious autocracy was intensified, and various fractures remained unhealed.

On Saturday, February 18, 2017, Ricky, a former resident of the FACTS Ministries sober homes, returned to the Either-Or CA meeting. He was hoping to begin his post-relapse sobriety again. No one in attendance, who all went to recovery fellowship meetings regularly in the city, could recall having seen him for two years or so. This return to the Ministries happened quite rarely. Typically, when an individual ended his sober homes residence via relapse, he did not return to the Ministries for any reason. Not for CA meetings. Not for community lunch meals on Tuesdays or Thursdays. Not for anything. Ricky was greeted warmly. His return spoke favorably about the environment the Ministries was for him and for many others, as a space of individual and collective resilience. Rather than speaking on the two topics, Ricky said:

> I don't know all what the topics are. And it don't much matter, for real. I'm just glad to have made it back. 'Cause I was back out there. And it ain't nothin' nice. Not even. Not even. Naw. It ain't got no better. It's got much worse. Now I see why Marvin died way he did. I see it. It took me two years to get back here. Two years. I ain't. I ain't . . . [his voice trails; a long pause, his eyes welling with tears]. I had to get back up on my feet, you know. Had to get things goin' 'gain. 'Cause I couldn't come back up in here, tore up from the floor up, lookin' all

> raggedy, and shit. Just couldn't do it, you know. But I'm back up in here. Good to see so many of the same faces, and all. That's it. I pass.

The poignancy and urgency of Ricky's testimony resonated powerfully with all those in attendance, whether they had experienced a prior relapse or not. A caring pause of shared silence and prayer followed. What struck many was Ricky's choice to stay away from the Ministries for two full years while living in an "abandominium" just a stone's throw from the Ministries' front door, and to return only when he was "back on his feet." In conversations in the weeks that followed, questions were raised by several longtime affiliates regarding just how welcoming the Ministries now was and at what point in one's recovery can a return to its social ecology of resilience begin (again). That "should" occur at any time in one's efforts to sustain long-term sobriety. Ricky's experience required two long Midwestern winters in an abandoned house "with no running water, and bootleg electricity every now and again," he said. Everyone's addiction is their own, but his choices were surprising to many for an individual as "vested" in the Ministries, the Either-Or meetings, and their mission(s) as Ricky had been. It was a point of pride to all that the Ministries was still here and that the Either-Or meeting still had a place in it.

Since Pastor Ellwyn Marshall had ended the Ministries' hosting of the Thursday night CA meeting two years earlier, the role and value of the Ministries had been in decline in the eyes of the immediate neighborhood, the local chapter of the CA fellowship, and the recovery community. What was one to make of a Ministries where uncertain leadership decisions now seemed to be the norm, where services and access of any kind were in decline, and where tensions between the Ministries and its health mission seemed to be growing every day? For these and other reasons, questions of its social ecology of resilience that had been simmering for years seemed to boil over. Uncertainties often mark the beginning of a decline. As the National Academies of Sciences, Engineering, and Medicine (2018, 1, 4, 6–7) stated, summarizing a workshop on "Faith-Health Collaboration to Improve Population Health,"

> Faith-based groups can play an important role at the intersection of substance use disorder, homelessness, and mental health . . . to identify specific health needs [and] to build relationships across systems, communities, and particularly across race lines. . . . The faith community needs to be included in

> decision-making circles [as] partners with health-sector organizations[to] co-create, share risks and benefits [and] advance community caregiving. (See also National Academies of Sciences, Engineering, and Medicine 2021; Price-Spratlen 2015; US Surgeon General 2016.)

The FACTS Ministries had largely been true to this Academies of Sciences call to action, yet the corrosive effects of long-term choices had been initiated several years earlier. Its role at the intersection of multiple challenges to advance community caregiving had been changing (see chapter 6). In its early years its summertime tent revival and alleyway barbecue had been more a means of visibility and food-centered outreach to its North Lawson neighbors than it was a fundraiser. Even as growth was nurtured and its apex sustained, fractures and silences grew also. In slight contrast to the Ministries' relationship with the neighborhood, for the local chapter of CA, trust in the Ministries had been damaged differently (see chapter 4). An affiliation and shared mission between the fellowship and the Ministries had been initiated years earlier when Pastor Marshall had participated in CA district meetings. While each meeting is autonomous, at district meetings, representatives from individual CA meetings throughout the city meet to make leadership decisions "on behalf of CA as a whole" (Cocaine Anonymous 2019, 8). But Pastor Marshall's participation in these district meetings had ended more than ten years ago.

Ministries representation of any kind at the district meetings had not been an Either-Or priority for several years. The people most willing to serve in the role of group service representative had been alienated by various actions of indifference by Ministries leadership. Those that remained were unable to make the monthly district meetings a priority. In August 2014, when the city's CA district was planning its thirtieth anniversary celebration, the Ministries had been presented with the opportunity to participate as an organizational collaborator in a way that was consistent with CA Traditions. However, Ministries leadership balked at each of the respectfully offered ceremony alternatives of shared mission. In the end, the Ministries did not participate in the district-wide anniversary celebration in any way. This furthered the erosions of its ecology of resilience. Within the recovery community of the city, what to make of the Ministries was an increasingly open question. Answers to it and other collaboration questions within the formal treatment, recovery, and health services community vis-à-vis the Ministries were uncertain at best. With the exception of CA and the community correctional facility (CCF), organizational affiliations seldom lasted for any length of time.

A short while after Ricky's post-relapse return to Either-Or, on Saturday, April 8, 2017, the Either-Or meeting began with what had become the norm. Like Ricky's last visit before his relapse, no one knew then that this meeting would soon be homeless. The two most frequent, and now longest-term, affiliates, Kevin (see introduction) and Jerry (chapter 4), were there. Then Devonte (chapter 4), the one sober homes resident who came most regularly, soon joined them. A couple minutes later, one more sober homes resident and two other CA affiliates joined them. Finally, four men from CCF arrived late. At 10:10, with coffee prepared, five willing readers, and the chairs set up in a semicircle, the meeting began. After the meeting, Kevin spoke with Johnny, one of the newer sober homes residents. Johnny spoke about recent Ministries Bible study recordings he felt Kevin might like to hear. "You might also be interested in some old sermons, given your interest in the Word. Here are a few to take with you," Johnny said. These were from among the forty to fifty tapes that had been displayed on a chapel wall as a tape library available for Ministries affiliates to check out, listen to, and copy at their leisure. After generating a DVD copy with a couple Bible study downloads on the chapel computer, Johnny gave the DVD and the four sermon cassette tapes to Kevin. "Thanks," Kevin responded. "I'll give 'em a listen, and bring them back next week."

A half hour after Kevin got home from the meeting, his phone rang. It was Pastor Marshall, calling with a raised voice and an angry tone. Pastor Marshall called Kevin a thief and demanded that the sermon tapes be returned. "You took some things that weren't yours!" Pastor Marshall said. "Did you take some sermon tapes out of the chapel? Did you? Why did you take those tapes?! They are not yours to take! Do you like stealing other people's things?! It would be the same as me going into your work office, and taking out some things of yours! That's what it would be like! Do you think that would be okay?!" Not interested in being called a thief for borrowing something that had been available on the chapel wall display for years, Kevin asked Pastor Marshall, given his anger and urgency, if he wanted the tapes back immediately. If so, he or someone else could come by Kevin's house to pick them up. After a brief pause, Pastor Marshall said, "Just bring them with you next Saturday." All that anger, shouting, and urgent accusation, yet the tapes could be brought back seven days later. Kevin did so.

The following Saturday, while talking with Jerry, Kevin learned that earlier that week, Pastor Marshall had come to Jerry's workplace with a sober homes resident by his side. Again, with urgency and anger, they had walked past the secretary to enter Jerry's office unannounced. The two men demanded that Jerry give them the key to the Ministries. Jerry was the last Ministries affiliate not directly beholden to Pastor Marshall who had a key to the building. "You would not have believed it, Kevin. You would have thought I had stolen something from them that they wanted to strong-arm me for to insure it was returned," Jerry said. With that demand, Pastor Marshall's final words to him and whoever else cared to listen were, "That CA meeting at the Ministries is over! *Never* again for you guys!"

After Kevin recounted his phone conversation with Pastor Marshall from the prior Saturday, Devonte, the most principled sober homes resident, joined them to tell them that the Either-Or meeting had been "canceled." Not being clear about the difference between hosting a meeting and "owning" and thus being able to end a meeting, Pastor Marshall had shared with Devonte his wish to cancel the meeting, which Devonte now repeated. That meeting proceeded with the few people in attendance. Shock, anger, and uncertainty followed. These were the responses to the sudden eviction of the final Either-Or CA meeting from the FACTS Ministries. With that decision, the once fully functioning Ministries that had had one or more events on every day but Monday, with two or more activities three days a week, now had only the Wednesday night Bible study and the community lunches on Tuesday and Thursdays. What can the social ecology of resilience-as-health-ministry possibly mean when it had only these activities? Whatever the answers, the Either-Or CA meeting was now homeless.

Perhaps still more surprising, eight months later as 2018 began, the Either-Or meeting was still homeless. The home group members' desire to keep the meeting in that congregational corridor of Akron Avenue where it had been since it began was still not fulfilled. The library to the north of the Ministries (see chapter 2) had two public meeting rooms. Both of those had standing reservations from two other community organizations during those Saturday morning hours. Four of the adjacent churches said they could not host the meeting. Among those that gave a reason, one said that they had a "space constraint," which was hard to believe, since that three-story church building was nearly ten thousand square feet. Two other churches said they would have to charge a minimum of $45 and

$90 per week, respectively, to rent a basement room on Saturday mornings. That price was an impossibility under virtually any circumstance among recovery fellowships. But this was especially so when Seventh Tradition donations from those in attendance had been averaging less than $10 per week for several years. A nearby youth recreation center asked a minimum $50 per week rental fee, which was untenable for the same reasons. A conscious community restaurant nearby was willing to make space available for $10 per week—but only its outside patio, and only during the summer months. Six other churches along the corridor provided no response of any kind.

In the meantime, the drug market and related active addiction chaos right across the street from the Ministries continues. Sober homes residents living in the Ministries' duplex next door to the building could clearly see the gas station exchanges just a few feet away. People would regularly stand near the gas pumps, begging to pump gas for customers for change so they could generate slender funds to get another few shavings of dope. Dope dealers hung out on the counter inside the gas station mini-mart. Or during the summer they sat under the shady bush just to the north of the gas station. Other dealings, sexual and otherwise, took place behind the building. These were among the rituals and repetitions that remained most visible in that portion of the North Lawson neighborhood. Where would the Rickys of the Ministries' present and possible future go now when they wanted to return to a place of sober familiarity? A social ecology of resilience has its limits, even as hope remains among the home group members of an evicted CA group in search of a Saturday morning meeting place. As this book is being completed, the Either-Or meeting of Cocaine Anonymous remains homeless. The local CA district ended its efforts to house the meeting in the neighborhood. Now, three years later, that meeting has still not found a new home. Neither the library nor any of the churches—two of which already hosted recovery meetings of one or more fellowships—had any obligation to this, or any other, form of faith-based health-care access. Still, what location in the area could include "a room at the inn" that is affordable? In whatever form, the FACTS Ministries remains, and a CA group's search for a new home continues.

References

Achara-Abrahams, Ijeoma, Arthur C. Evans, Jose Ortiz, Diana Lopez Villegas, Joseph O'Dell, OmiSade Ali, and Dietra Hawkins. 2012. "Recovery Management and African Americans: A Report from the Field." *Alcoholism Treatment Quarterly* 30:263–92.

Alcoholics Anonymous. 1952. *Twelve Steps and Twelve Traditions*. New York: Alcoholics Anonymous World Services.

———. 1981. *Twelve Steps and Twelve Traditions*. New York: Alcoholics Anonymous World Services.

———. 2001. *Alcoholics Anonymous* (4th ed.). New York: Alcoholics Anonymous World Services.

Alexander, G. Caleb, Kenneth B. Stoller, Rebecca L. Haffajee, and Brendan Saloner. 2020. "An Epidemic in the Midst of a Pandemic: Opioid Use Disorder and COVID-19." *Annals of Internal Medicine* 173:57–59.

Alex-Assensoh, Yvette M. 2004. "Taking the Sanctuary to the Streets: Religion, Race, and Community Development in Columbus, Ohio." *Annals of the American Academy of Political and Social Science* 594:79–91.

Alexander, Jack. 1941. "Alcoholics Anonymous: Freed Slaves of Drink, Now They Free Others." *Saturday Evening Post* 213:9–11, 89–92.

Allen, Julie Ober, Katherine Alaimo, Doris Elam, and Elizabeth Perry. 2008. *Journal of Hunger and Environmental Nutrition* 3:418–39.

Andermann, Anne. 2016. "Taking Action on the Social Determinants of Health in Clinical Practice: A Framework for Health Professionals." *Canadian Medical Association Journal* 188: E474–E483.

Andrews, Dale P. 2002. *Practical Theology for Black Churches: Bridging Black Theology and African American Folk Religion*. Louisville, KY: Westminster Press.

Annamma, Subini Ancy, Yolanda Anyon, Nicole M. Joseph, Jordan Farrar, Eldridge Greer, Barbara Downing, and John Simmons. 2016. "Black Girls and School Discipline: The Complexities of Being Overrepresented and Understudied." *Urban Education* 54:1–32.

Ard, Kerry. 2016. "By All Measures: An Examination of the Relationship Between Segregation and Health Risk from Air Pollution." *Population and the Environment* 38:1–20.

Austin, Sandra A., and Nancy Claiborne. 2011. "Faith Wellness Collaboration: A Community-Based Approach to Address Type II Diabetes Disparities in an African-American Community." *Social Work in Health Care* 50:360–75.

Bagheri, Ghodratollah, Reihaneh Zarei, and Mojtaba Nik Aeen. 2012. "Organizational Silence (Basic Concepts and Its Development Factors)." *Ideal Type of Management* 1:47–58.

Bakken, Nicholas W., Whitney DeCamp, and Christy A. Visher. 2014. "Spirituality and Desistance from Substance Use Among Reentering Offenders." *International Journal of Offender Therapy and Comparative Criminology* 48:1321–39.

Barber, Kendra H. 2015. "Whither Shall We Go? The Past and Present of Black Churches and the Public Sphere." *Religions* 6:245–65.

Barnes, Sandra L. 2005. "Black Church Culture and Community Action." *Social Forces* 84:967–94.

Bassuk, Ellen L., Justine Hanson, R. Neil Greene, Molly Richard, and Alexandre Laudet. 2016. "Peer-Delivered Recovery Support Services for Addictions in the United States: A Systematic Review." *Journal of Substance Abuse Treatment* 63:1–9.

Bayor, Ronald H. 1988. "Roads to Racial Segregation: Atlanta in the Twentieth Century." *Journal of Urban History* 15:3–21.

Beckhard, Richard. 1969. *Organization Development: Strategies and Models*. London: Addison-Wesley.

Beheshtifar, Malikeh, Hossein Borhani, and Mahmood Nekoie-Moghadam. 2012. "Destructive Role of Employee Silence in Organizational Success." *International Journal of Academic Research in Business and Social Sciences* 2:275–82.

Bellamy, Chyrell D., Michael Rowe, Patricia Benedict, and Larry Davidson. 2014. "Giving Back and Getting Something Back: The Role of Mutual-Aid Groups for Individuals in Recovery from Incarceration, Addiction, and Mental Illness." In *Broadening the Base of Addiction Mutual Support Groups*, edited by Jeffrey D. Roth, William L. White, and John F. Kelly, 151–64. London: Routledge.

Bennett, Kate Mary, and Gillian Windle. 2015. "The Importance of Not Only Individual, but Also Community and Society Factors in Resilience in Later Life." *Behavioral and Brain Sciences* 38:22–23, E94. https://doi.org/10.1017/S0140525X14001459.

Berg, Bruce L. 2007. *Qualitative Research Methods for the Social Sciences* (6th ed.). Boston: Pearson-Allyn Bacon.

Berger, Peter L. 1969. *The Sacred Canopy*. New York: Anchor.

Best, David, Melinda Beckwith, Catherine Haslam, S. Alexander Haslam, Jolanda Jetten, Emily Mawson, and Dan I. Lubman. 2015. "Overcoming Alcohol and Other Drug Addiction as a Process of Social Identity Transition: The

Social Identity Model of Recovery (SIMOR)." *Addiction Research and Theory* 24:111–23.

Best, David, and Stephanie de Alwis. 2017. "Community Recovery as a Public Health Intervention: The Contagion of Hope." *Alcoholism Treatment Quarterly* 35:187–99.

Betancourt, Theresa S., Sarah E. Meyers-Ohki, Alexandra Charrow, and Nathan Hansen. 2013. "Annual Research Review: Mental Health and Resilience in HIV/AIDS-Affected Children—A Review of the Literature and Recommendations for Future Research." *Journal of Child Psychology and Psychiatry* 54:423–44.

Bliuc, Ana-Maria, David Best, Muhammad Iqbal, and Katie Upton. 2017. "Building Addiction Recovery Capital Through Online Participation in a Recovery Community." *Social Science & Medicine* 193:110–17.

Boeri, Miriam. 2018. *Hurt: Chronicles of the Drug War Generation*. Oakland: University of California Press.

Bogart, Cathy J., and Carol E. Pearce. 2003. "'13th-Stepping': Why Alcoholics Anonymous Is Not Always a Safe Place for Women." *Journal of Addictions Nursing* 14:43–47.

Bogosian, Robert. 2012. "Engaging Organizational Voice: A Phenomenological Study of Employees' Lived Experiences of Silence in Work Group Settings." PhD diss., George Washington University.

Borer, Michael Ian, and Tyler S. Schafer. 2011. "Culture War Confessionals: Conflicting Accounts of Christianity, Violence, and Mixed Martial Arts." *Journal of Media and Religion* 10:165–84.

Bourgois, Philippe. 1996. *In Search of Respect: Selling Crack in El Barrio*. Cambridge: Cambridge University Press.

Bourgois, Philippe, and Jeff Schonberg. 2009. *Righteous Dopefiend*. Berkeley: University of California Press.

Boyd, Josh, and Melissa Stahley. 2008. "Communitas/Corporatas Tensions in Organizational Rhetoric: Finding a Balance in Sports Public Relations." *Journal of Public Relations Research* 20:251–70.

Boyer, Corinne. 2021. "Addiction in the Pandemic: Overdose Deaths Surge As Coronavirus Adds to Opioid Crisis." Ohio Valley ReSource, Coronavirus Health, January 29, 2021. https://ohiovalleyresource.org/2021/01/29/addiction-in-the-pandemic-overdose-deaths-surge-as-coronavirus-adds-to-opioid-crisis/.

Brantingham, P. L., and P. J. Brantingham. 1993. "Environment, Routine, and Situation: Toward a Pattern Theory of Crime." In *Routine Activity and Rational Choice: Advances in Criminological Theory*, vol. 5., edited by R. V. Clarke and M. Felson, 259–94. New Brunswick, NJ: Transaction.

Bricker, Diane. 1995. "The Challenge of Inclusion." *Journal of Early Intervention* 9:179–94.

Briggs, Daniel. 2012. *Crack Cocaine Users: High Society and Low Life in South London*. London: Routledge.

Brinsfield, Chad T., Marissa S. Edwards, and Jerald Greenberg. 2009. "Voice and Silence in Organizations: Historical Review and Current Conceptualizations." In *Voice and Silence in Organizations*, edited by Jerald Greenberg and Marissa S. Edwards, 3–33. Bingley, UK: Emerald.

Brown, Emma J. 2006. "The Integral Place of Religion in the Lives of Rural African-American Women Who Use Cocaine." *Journal of Religion and Health* 45:19–39.

Brown, Howard P., and John H. Peterson Jr. 1991. "Assessing Spirituality in Addiction Treatment and Follow-Up: Development of the Brown-Peterson Recovery Progress Inventory (B-PRPI)." *Alcoholism Treatment Quarterly* 8:21–50.

Brown, Teresa L. Fry. 1997. "Avoiding Asphyxiation: A Womanist Perspective on Intrapersonal and Interpersonal Transformation." In *Embracing the Spirit: Womanist Perspectives on Hope, Salvation & Transformation*, edited by Emilie M. Townes, 72–96. Maryknoll, NY: Orbis Books.

Buckingham, Sarah A., Daniel Frings, and Ian P. Albery. 2013. "Group Membership and Social Identity in Addiction Recovery." *Psychology of Addictive Behaviors* 27:1132–40.

Butler, Michelle, and Shadd Maruna. 2016. "Rethinking Prison Disciplinary Processes: A Potential Future for Restorative Justice." *Victims and Offenders* 11:126–48.

Butts, Jeffrey A., Caterina Gouvis Roman, Lindsay Bostwick, and Jeremy R. Porter. 2015. "Cure Violence: A Public Health Model to Reduce Gun Violence." *Annual Review of Public Health* 36:39–53.

Cacioppo, John T., Amy B. Adler, Paul B. Lester, Dennis McGurk, Jeffrey L. Thomas, His-Yuan Chen, and Stephanie Cacioppo. 2015. "Building Social Resilience in Soldiers: A Double Dissociative Randomized Controlled Study." *Journal of Personality and Social Psychology* 109:90–105.

Canetti, Elias. 1984. *Crowds and Power*. New York: Farrar, Straus, and Giroux.

Castells, Manuel. 1970. *The Urban Question: A Marxist Approach*. Cambridge, MA: MIT Press.

CelebrateOne. 2016. *2016 Annual Report: Our Community, Our Babies, Our Future*. Columbus, OH: CelebrateOne Info.

Chappel, John N. 1995. "Teaching and Learning Recovery." *Substance Abuse* 16:141–53.

Cheney, Ann M., Brenda M. Booth, Tyrone F. Borders, and Geoffrey M. Curran. 2016. "The Role of Social Capital in African Americans' Attempts to Reduce and Quit Cocaine Use." *Substance Use & Misuse* 51:777–87.

Cheney, Ann M., Geoffrey M. Curran, Brenda M. Booth, Steve Sullivan, Katharine Stewart, and Tyrone F. Borders. 2014. "The Religious and Spiritual Dimensions of Cutting Down and Stopping Cocaine Use: A Qualitative Exploration Among African Americans in the South." *Journal of Drug Issues* 44:94–113.

Chilton, Mariana, and Sue Booth. 2007. "Hunger of the Body and Hunger of the Mind: African American Women's Perceptions of Food Insecurity, Health and Violence." *Journal of Nutrition Education and Behavior* 39:116–25.

Chitwood, Dale D., Michael L. Weiss, and Carl G. Leukefeld. 2008. "A Systematic Review of Recent Literature on Religiosity and Substance Use." *Journal of Drug Issues* 38:653–88.

Christle, Christine A., Kristine Jolivette, and C. Michael Nelson. 2005. "Breaking the School to Prison Pipeline: Identifying School Risk and Protective Factors for Youth Delinquency." *Exceptionality: A Special Education Journal* 13:69–88.

Chu, Doris C., and Hung-En Sung. 2009. "Racial Differences in Desistance from Substance Abuse: The Impact of Religious Involvement on Recovery." *International Journal of Offender Therapy and Comparative Criminology* 53:696–716.

Cinar, Orhan, Fatih Karcioglu, and Zisan Duygu Aliogullari. 2013. "The Relationship Between Organizational Silence and Organizational Citizenship Behavior: A Survey Study in the Province of Erzurum, Turkey." *Procedia—Social and Behavioral Sciences* 99:314–21.

City-Data. 2010. https://www.city-data.com/neighborhood/.

Clear, Todd. 2007. *Imprisoning Communities: How Mass Incarceration Makes Disadvantaged Neighborhoods Worse.* New York: Oxford.

Clebsch, William A., and Charles R. Jaekle. 1975. *Pastoral Care in Historical Perspective.* New York: Jason Aronson.

Cleveland, H. Harrington, Kitty S. Harris, Amanda K. Baker, Richard Herbert, and Lukas R. Dean. 2007. "Characteristics of a Collegiate Recovery Community: Maintaining Recovery in an Abstinence-Hostile Environment." *Journal of Substance Abuse Treatment* 33:13–23.

Cocaine Anonymous. 2018. *Cocaine Anonymous World Services Manual.* Long Beach, CA: CAWSO.

———. 2019. *Cocaine Anonymous World Services Manual.* Long Beach, CA: CAWSO.

Cockburn, Alexander, and Jeffrey St. Clair. 1999. *Whiteout: The CIA, Drugs and the Press.* London: Verso.

Cole, Luke W., and Sheila R. Foster. 2001. *From the Ground Up: Environmental Racism and the Rise of the Environmental Justice Movement.* New York: New York University Press.

Collard, Carol S., Terri Lewinson, and Karen Watkins. 2014. "Supportive Housing: An Evidence-Based Intervention for Reducing Relapse Among Low Income Adults in Addiction Recovery." *Journal of Evidence-Based Social Work* 11:468–79.

Conger, J. A. 1999. "Charismatic and Transformational Leadership in Organizations: An Insider's Perspective on These Developing Streams of Research." *Leadership Quarterly* 10:145–80.

Connerly, Charles E. 2002. "From Racial Zoning to Community Empowerment: The Interstate Highway System and the African American Community in Birmingham, Alabama." *Journal of Planning Education and Research* 22:99–114.

Coombs, Robert Holman. 2001. *Addiction Recovery Tools*. Thousand Oaks, CA: SAGE.

Cummings, Lorine L. 1995. "A Womanist Response to the Afrocentric Idea: Jarena Lee, Womanist Preacher." In *Living the Intersection: Womanism and Afrocentrism in Theology*, edited by Cheryl J. Sanders, 57–66. Minneapolis, MN: Fortress Press.

Cummins, Steven, Sarah Curtis, Ana V. Diez-Roux, and Sally Macintyre. 2007. "Understanding and Representing 'Place' in Health Research: A Relational Approach." *Social Science & Medicine* 65:1825–38.

Cusack, Meagan, Ann Elizabeth Montgomery, Anneliese E. Sorrentino, Melissa E. Dichter, Manik Chhabra, and Gala True. 2019. "Journey to Home: Development of a Conceptual Model to Describe Veterans' Experiences with Resolving Housing Instability." *Housing Studies* 34:1–23.

Dackis, Charles A., and Charles P. O'Brien. 2001. "Cocaine Dependence: A Disease of the Brain's Reward Centers." *Journal of Substance Abuse Treatment* 21:111–17.

D'Amato, Alessia, and Nigel Roome. 2009. "Toward an Integrated Model of Leadership for Corporate Responsibility and Sustainable Development: A Process Model of Corporate Responsibility Beyond Management Innovation." *Corporate Governance* 9:421–34.

D'Angelo, Karen A., and Wonbin Her. 2019. "'The Drug Issue Really Isn't the Main Problem': A Photovoice Study on Community Perceptions of Place, Health, and Substance Abuse." *Health & Place* 57:257–64.

Darrah, Mary C. 2001. *Sister Ignatia: Angel of Alcoholics Anonymous*. Center City, MN: Hazelden.

De Crescenzo, Franco, Marco Ciabattini, Gian Loreto D'Alò, Riccardo De Giorgi, Cinzia Del Giovane, Carolina Cassar, Luigi Janiri, Nicolas Clark, Michael Joshua Ostacher, and Andrea Cipriani. 2018. "Comparative Efficacy and Acceptability of Psychosocial Interventions for Individuals with Cocaine and Amphetamine Addiction: A Systematic Review and Network Meta-Analysis." *PLoS Medicine* 15: e1002715. https://doi.org/10.1371/journal.pmed.1002715.

De Leon, George. 2000. *The Therapeutic Community: Theory, Model, and Method*. New York: Springer.

Denhardt, Janet, and Robert Denhardt. 2010. "Building Organizational Resilience and Adaptive Management." In *Handbook of Adult Resilience*, edited by John W. Reich, Alex J. Zautra, and John Stuart Hall, 333–49. New York: Guilford.

DeVerteuil, Geoffrey, and Robert Wilton. 2009. "Spaces of Abeyance, Care and Survival: The Addiction Treatment System as a Site of 'Regulatory Richness.'" *Political Geography* 28:463–72.

Doehring, Carrie. 1992. "Developing Models of Feminist Pastoral Counseling." *Journal of Pastoral Care* 46:23–31.

Dorrien, Gary. 2016. "Breaking White Supremacy: The Black Social Gospel as New Abolitionism." *American Journal of Theology and Philosophy* 37:197–216.

Dossett, Wendy. 2017. "A Daily Reprieve Contingent on the Maintenance of Our Spiritual Condition." *Addiction* 112:942–43.

Douglass, Frederick. 1855. *My Bondage and My Freedom*. New York: Miller, Orton, and Mulligan.

Draus, Paul, and Robert G. Carlson. 2009. "Down on Main Street: Drugs and the Small-Town Vortex." *Health & Place* 15:247–54.

Drucker, Ernest. 2011. *A Plague of Prisons: The Epidemiology of Mass Incarceration in America*. New York: New Press.

Du Bois, W. E. B. (1899) 1967. *The Philadelphia Negro*. New York: Schocken Books.

———, ed. 1903. *The Negro Church*. Atlanta, GA: Atlanta University Press.

———. (1903) 1969. *The Souls of Black Folk*. New York: Signet Classic.

———. 1904. "The Development of a People." *International Journal of Ethics* 14:292–311.

———, ed. 1906. *The Health and Physique of the Negro American: Report of a Social Study Made Under the Direction of Atlanta University*. Together with the Proceedings of the Eleventh Conference for the Study of the Negro Problems, Atlanta University, on May 29, 1906. Atlanta, GA: Atlanta University Press.

Duck, Waverly. 2015. *No Way Out: Precarious Living in the Shadow of Poverty and Drug Dealing*. Chicago: University of Chicago Press.

Duff, Cameron. 2011. "Networks, Resources and Agencies: On the Character and Production of Enabling Places." *Health & Place* 17:149–56.

Dunlap, Eloise, Andrew Golub, and Bruce D. Johnson. 2006. "The Severely-Distressed African American Family in the Crack Era: Empowerment Is Not Enough." *Journal of Sociology and Social Welfare* 33:115–39.

Esbensen, Finn-Aage, and David Huizinga. 1990. "Community Structure and Drug Use: From a Social Disorganization Perspective." *Justice Quarterly* 7:691–709.

Evans, Arthur C., Jr., Ijeoma Achara-Abrahams, Roland Lamb, and William L. White. 2012. "Ethnic-Specific Support Systems as a Method for Sustaining Long-Term Addiction Recovery." *Journal of Groups in Addiction and Recovery* 7:171–88.

———. 2014. "Ethnic-Specific Support Systems as a Method for Sustaining Long-Term Addiction Recovery." In *Broadening the Base of Addiction Mutual Support Groups*, edited by Jeffrey D. Roth, William L. White, and John F. Kelly, 99–116. London: Routledge.

Evans, Arthur C., Jr., and Beverly J. Haberle. 2009. "Foreword." In *Peer-Based Addiction Recovery Support: History, Theory, Practice and Scientific Evaluation*, edited by William L. White, 3–5. Philadelphia, PA: Great Lakes Addiction Technology Transfer Center, Philadelphia Department of Behavioral Health and Mental Retardation Services.

Evans, Joshua, Dyanne Semogas, Joshua G. Smalley, and Lynne Lohfeld. 2015. "'This Place Has Given Me a Reason to Care': Understanding 'Managed Alcohol Programs' as Enabling Places in Canada." *Health & Place* 33:118–24.

Executive Office of the President, Office of National Drug Control Policy (ONDCP). 2021. "The Biden-Harris Administration's Statement of Drug Policy Priorities for Year One." Executive Office of the President, Office of National Drug Control Policy: Washington, DC 20503. https://www.whitehouse.gov/wp-content/uploads/2021/03/BidenHarris-Statement-of-Drug-Policy-Priorities-April-1.pdf.

Faces and Voices of Recovery. 2012. *Recovery Community Organization Toolkit*. Washington, DC: Face and Voices of Recovery.

Ferme, Mariane C. 2002. *The Underneath of Things*. Berkeley: University of California Press.

Fields, Errol Lamont, Laura M. Bogart, Katherine C. Smith, David J. Malebranche, Jonathan Ellen, and Mark A. Schuster. 2015. "'I Always Felt I Had to Prove My Manhood': Homosexuality, Masculinity, Gender Role Strain, and HIV Risk Among Young Black Men Who Have Sex with Men." *American Journal of Public Health* 105:122–31. https://doi.org/10.2105/AJPH.2013.301866.

Flores, Edward Orozco. 2013. *God's Gangs: Barrio Ministry, Masculinity, and Gang Recovery*. New York: New York University Press.

Flynn, Patrick M., George W. Joe, Kirk M. Broome, D. Dwayne Simpson, and Barry S. Brown. 2003. "Looking Back on Cocaine Dependence: Reasons for Recovery." *American Journal on Addictions* 12:398–411.

Foreman, James, Jr. 2017. *Locking Up Our Own: Crime and Punishment in Black America*. New York: Farrar, Straus, and Giroux.

Forrest-Bank, Shandra S., Nicole Nicotera, Elizabeth K. Anthony, and Jeffrey M. Jenson. 2015. "Finding Their Way: Perceptions of Risk, Resilience, and Positive Youth Development Among Adolescents and Young Adults from Public Housing Neighborhoods." *Children and Youth Services Review* 55:147–58.

Fox-Wolfgramm, Susan J. 1997. "Towards Developing a Methodology for Doing Qualitative Research: The Dynamic-Comparative Case Study Method." *Scandinavian Journal of Management* 13:439–55.

Frazier, E. Franklin. 1930. "Occupational Classes Among Negros in Cities." *American Journal of Sociology* 35:718–38.

Freeman, Edith M. 2001. *Substance Abuse Intervention, Prevention, Rehabilitation, and Systems Change Strategies*. New York: Columbia University Press.

Galanter, Marc, Helen Dermatis, Stephen Post, and Courtney Santucci. 2013. "Abstinence from Drugs of Abuse in Community-Based Members of Narcotics Anonymous." *Journal of Studies on Alcohol and Drugs* 74:349–52.

Gecas, Viktor. 2000. "Value Identities, Self-Motives, and Social Movements." In *Self, Identity, and Social Movements*, edited by Sheldon Stryker, Timothy Joseph Owens, and Robert W. White, 93–109. Minneapolis: University of Minnesota Press.

Gems, Gerald R. 2004. "The Politics of Boxing: Resistance, Religion, and Working Class Assimilation." *International Sports Journal* 8:89–103.

Giffin, William W. 2005. *African Americans and the Color Line in Ohio, 1915–1930*. Columbus: Ohio State University Press.

Gilkes, Cheryl Townsend. 1980. "The Black Church as a Therapeutic Community: Suggested Areas for Research into the Black Religious Experience." *Journal of the Interdenominational Theological Center* 8:29–44.

———. 1998. "Plenty Good Room: Adaptation in a Changing Black Church." *Annals of the American Academy of Political and Social Science* 55:101–21.

Goffman, Erving. (1963) 1986. *Stigma: Notes on the Management of Spoiled Identity*. New York: Touchstone.

Gray, Barbara. 1985. "Conditions Facilitating Interorganizational Collaboration." *Human Relations* 38:911–36.

Greenfield, Shelly F., Audrey J. Brooks, Susan M. Gordon, Carla A. Green, Frankie Kropp, R. Kathryn McHugh, Melissa Lincoln, Denise Hien, and Gloria M. Miele. 2007. "Substance Abuse Treatment Entry, Retention, and Outcome in Women: A Review of the Literature." *Drug and Alcohol Dependence* 86:1–21.

Greenleaf, Robert K. 2002. *Servant Leadership: A Journey into the Nature of Legitimate Power and Greatness*. Mahwah, NJ: Paulist Press.

Grim, Brian J., and Melissa E. Grim. 2019. "Belief, Behavior, and Belonging: How Faith Is Indispensable in Preventing and Recovering from Substance Abuse." *Journal of Religion and Health* 58:1713–50.

Gubrium, Aline C. 2008. "Writing Against the Image of the Monstrous Crack Mother." *Journal of Contemporary Ethnography* 37:11–27.

Hackworth, Jason. 2010. "Faith, Welfare, and the City: The Mobilization of Religious Organizations for Neoliberal Ends." *Urban Geography* 31:750–73.

———. 2019. *Manufacturing Decline: How Racism and the Conservative Movement Crush the American Rust Belt*. New York: Columbia University Press.

Hall, Stuart. 1997. *Culture, Media and Identities Representation: Cultural Representations and Signifying Practices*. Newbury Park, CA: SAGE/Open University Press.

Harmon, Brook E., Sei-Hill Kim, Christine E. Blake, and James R. Hebert. 2014. "Health Care Information in African-American Churches." *Journal of Health Care for the Poor and the Underserved* 25:242–56.

Harris, Christine R., and Peter Salovey. 2008. "Reflections on Envy." In *Envy: Theory and Research*, edited by Richard H. Smith, 335–56. New York: Oxford University Press.

Haslam, S. Alexander, Jolanda Jetten, Tom Postmes, and Catherine Haslam. 2009. "Social Identity, Health and Well-Being: An Emerging Agenda for Applied Psychology." *Applied Psychology* 58:1–23.

Health Affairs Blog. 2020. "COVID-19 and Health Disparities: Insights from Key Informant Interviews." October 27, 2020. https://doi.org/10.1377/hblog20201023.55778.

Health Map. 2016. [Source details withheld for confidentiality.]

Hein, David. 2005. "The Reverend Mr. Shegog's Easter Sermon: Preaching as Communion in Faulkner's 'The Sound and the Fury.' " *Mississippi Quarterly* 58:559–80.

Helgeson, Vicki S., and Lindsey Lopez. 2010. "Basic Dimension of Resilience: Social Support and Growth Following Adversity." In *Handbook of Adult Resilience*, edited by John W. Reich, Alex J. Zautra, and John Stuart Hall, 309–30. New York: Guilford.

Hemphill, Essex. 1991. *Ceremonies: Prose and Poetry*. New York: Plume.

Hennessy, Emily A. 2017. "Recovery Capital: A Systematic Review of the Literature." *Addiction Research and Theory* 25:349–60.

Herd, Denise. 1991. "The Paradox of Intemperance: Blacks and the Alcohol Question in Nineteenth-Century America." In *Drinking: Behavior and Belief in Modern History*, edited by Susanna Barrows and Robin Room, 354–75. Berkeley: University of California Press.

Heslin, Kevin C., Trudy Singzon, Otaren Aimiuwu, Dave Sheridan, and Alison Hamilton. 2012. "From Personal Tragedy to Personal Challenge: Responses to Stigma Among Sober Living Home Residents and Operators." *Sociology of Health and Illness* 34:379–95.

Heyer, Jeremy, Zachary Schmitt, Lynn Dombrowski, and Svetlana (Lana) Yarosh. 2020. "Opportunities for Enhancing Access and Efficacy of Peer Sponsorship in Substance Use Disorder Recovery." In *CHI '20: Proceedings of the 2020 CHI Conference on Human Factors in Computing* Systems, 1–14. https://doi.org/10.1145/3313831.3376241.

Hinton, Elizabeth, MaryBeth Musumeci, Robin Rudowitz, Larisa Antonisse, and Cornelia Hall. 2019. *Section 1115 Medicaid Demonstration Waivers: The Current Landscape of Approved and Pending Waivers*. Issue Brief. San Francisco: Kaiser Family Foundation.

Hirsch, Arnold. 1998. *Making of the Second Ghetto* (2nd ed.). Chicago: University of Chicago Press.

Hodge, Lauren M., and Karen M. T. Turner. 2016. "Sustained Implementation of Evidence-Based Programs in Disadvantaged Communities: A Conceptual Framework of Supporting Factors." *American Journal of Community Psychology* 58:192–210.

Hodges, John Q., and Eric R. Hardiman. 2006. "Promoting Healthy Organizational Partnerships and Collaboration Between Consumer-Run and Community Mental Health Agencies." *Administration and Policy in Mental Health and Mental Health Services Research* 33:267–78.

Holden, Kisha B., Brian S. McGregor, Starla H. Blanks, and Carlos Mahaffey. 2012. "Psychosocial, Socio-Cultural, and Environmental Influences on Mental Health Help-Seeking Among African-American Men." *Journal of Men's Health* 9:63–69.

Holmes, Jeremy. 2017. "Roots and Routes to Resilience and Its Role in Psychotherapy: A Selective, Attachment-Informed Review." *Attachment & Human Development* 19:364–81.

Hood, Daniel E. 2012. *Redemption and Recovery: Further Parallels of Religion and Science in Addiction Treatment*. New Brunswick, NJ: Transaction.

Humphreys, Keith. 2004. *Circles of Recovery: Self-Help Organizations for Addictions*. New York: Cambridge University Press.

Humphreys, Keith, and Anna Lembke. 2014. "Recovery-Oriented Policy and Care Systems in the UK and USA." *Drug and Alcohol Review* 33:13–18.

Hunter, Marcus Anthony. 2013. "A Bridge Over Troubled Urban Waters: W. E. B. Du Bois's *The Philadelphia Negro* and the Ecological Conundrum." *Du Bois Review* 10:7–27. https://doi.org/10.1017/S1742058X13000015.

Imbroscio, David. 2011. "Beyond Mobility: The Limits of Liberal Urban Policy." *Journal of Urban Affairs* 34:1–20.

Institute of Medicine [IOM] (Committee on Quality of Health Care in America). 2000. *Crossing the Quality Chasm: A New Health System for the 21st Century*. Washington, DC: National Academy Press.

Jacobs, Gregory S. 1998. *Getting Around Brown: Desegregation, Development, and the Columbus Public Schools*. Columbus: Ohio State University Press.

James, Keturah, and Ayana Jordan. 2018. "The Opioid Crisis in Black Communities." *Journal of Law, Medicine & Ethics* 46:404–21.

Jason, Leonard A., Jordan Braciszewski, Bradley D. Olson, and Joseph R. Ferrari. 2005. "Increasing the Number of Mutual Help Recovery Homes for Substance Abusers: Effects of Government Policy and Funding Assistance." *Behavior and Social Issues* 14:71–79.

Jason, Leonard A., Bradley D. Olson, Joseph R. Ferrari, and Anthony T. Lo Sasso. 2006. "Communal Housing Settings Enhance Substance Abuse Recovery." *American Journal of Public Health* 96:1727–29.

Jarrett, Robin L. 1997. "Resilience Among Low-Income African American Youth: An Ethnographic Perspective." *Journal of the Society for Psychological Anthropology* 25:218–29.

Johnson, E. Patrick. 1998. "Feeling the Spirit in the Dark: Expanding Notions of the Sacred in the African-American Gay Community." *Callaloo* 21:399–416.

Johnson, Natrina L., Sugy Choi, and Carolina-Nicole Herrera. 2021. "Black Clients in Expansion States Who Used Opioids Were More Likely to Access Medication for Opioid Use Disorder After ACA Implementation." *Journal of Substance Abuse Treatment*. Epub ahead of print. https://doi.or10.1016/j.jsat.2021.108533. PMID: 34218991.

Johnson, Rucker C. 2010. "The Place of Race in Health Disparities: How Family Background and Neighborhood Conditions in Childhood Impact Later-Life Health." In *Neighborhood and Life Chances: How Place Matters in Modern*

America, edited by Harriet B. Newburger, Eugenie L. Birch, and Susan M. Wachter, 18–36. Philadelphia: University of Pennsylvania Press.

———. 2018. "Addressing Racial Health Disparities: Looking Back to Point the Way Forward." *Annals of the American Academy of Political and Social Sciences* 680:132–71.

Jones-Eversley, Sharon D., and Lorraine T. Dean. 2018. "After 121 Years, It's Time to Recognize W. E. B. Du Bois as a Founding Father of Social Epidemiology." *Journal of Negro Education* 87:230–45.

Kanter, Rosabeth Moss. 1968. "Commitment and Social Organization: A Study of Commitment Mechanisms in Utopian Communities." *American Sociological Review* 33:499–517.

Kaskutas, Lee Ann, Thomasina J. Borkman, Alexandre Laudet, Lois A. Ritter, Jane Witbrodt, Meenakshi Sabina Subbaraman, Aina Stunz, and Jason Bond. 2014. "Elements That Define Recovery: The Experiential Perspective." *Journal for Studies of Alcohol and Drugs* 75:999–1010.

Kawachi, Ichiro, and Lisa Berkman. 2000. "Social Cohesion, Social Capital, and Health." In *Social Epidemiology*, edited by Lisa F. Berkman and Ichiro Kawachi, 174–90. Oxford: Oxford University Press.

Kelly, J. F., and J. Yeterian. 2008. "Mutual-Help Groups." In *Evidence-Based Adjunctive Treatments*, edited by W. O'Donohue and J. R. Cunningham, 61–106. New York: Elsevier.

Kirwan Institute. 2012. *Neighborhoods & Community Development in Franklin County: Understanding Our Past & Preparing for Our Future*. Columbus, OH: Community Development Collaborative.

Knight, Kelly Ray. 2015. *Addicted.Pregnant.Poor.* Durham, NC: Duke University Press.

Krentzman, Amy R. 2013. "Review of the Application of Positive Psychology to Substance Use, Addiction, and Recovery Research." *Psychology of Addictive Behaviors* 27:151–65.

Krohn, Elise. 2013. "Recovering Health Through Cultural Traditions." *Fourth World Journal* 12:93–98.

Kübler-Ross, Elisabeth. (1969) 1997. *On Death and Dying*. New York: MacMillan.

Kubrin, Charis E., and Ronald Weitzer. 2003. "New Directions in Social Disorganization Theory." *Journal of Research in Crime and Delinquency* 40:374–402.

Kumpfer, Karol L. 1999. "Factors and Processes Contributing to Resilience: The Resilience Framework." In *Resilience and Development: Positive Life Adaptations*, edited by M. D. Glantz and J. L. Johnson, 179–224. New York: Kluwer/Plenum.

Kumpfer, Karol L., and Julia Franklin Summerhays. 2006. "Prevention Approaches to Enhance Resilience Among High-Risk Youth: Comments on the Papers of Dishion and Connell and Greenberg." *Annual New York Academy of Sciences* 1094:151–63.

Kumpfer, Karol L., and Charles W. Turner. 1990. "The Social Ecology Model of Adolescent Substance Abuse: Implications for Prevention." *International Journal of the Addictions* 25:435–63.

Landers, Bernard. 1954. *Towards an Understanding of Juvenile Delinquency*. New York: Columbia University Press.

Landmarks Foundation. 2014. *African-American Settlements and Communities in Columbus, Ohio: A Report*. Columbus, OH: Columbus Landmarks Foundation Press.

Lanier, Jacqueline, Julie Schumacher, and Kerri Calvert. 2015. "Cultivating Community Collaboration and Community Health Through Community Gardens." *Journal of Community Practice* 23:492–507.

Laudet, Alexandre B. 2008. "The Impact of Alcoholics Anonymous on Other Substance Abuse-Related Twelve-Step Programs." In *Recent Developments in Alcoholism*, vol. 18, edited by Marc Galanter and Lee Ann Kaskutas, 71–89. New York: Springer.

Laudet, Alexandre B., Kitty Harris, Thomas Kimball, Ken C. Winters, and D. Paul Moberg. 2014. "Collegiate Recovery Communities Programs: What Do We Know and What Do We Need to Know?" *Journal of Social Work Practice in the Addictions* 14:84–100.

Lavack, Anne. 2007. "Using Social Marketing to De-Stigmatize Addictions: A Review." *Addiction Research & Theory* 15:479–92.

Lee, Shayne. 2007. "Prosperity Theology: T. D. Jakes and the Gospel of the Almighty Dollar." *CrossCurrents* 57:227–36.

Lejuez, C. W., Marina A. Bornovalova, Elizabeth K. Reynolds, Stacey B. Daughters, and John J. Curtin. 2007. "Risk Factors in the Relationship Between Gender and Crack/Cocaine." *Experimental and Clinical Psychopharmacology* 15:165–75.

Leverentz, Andrea. 2010. "People, Places, and Things: How Female Ex-Prisoners Negotiate Their Neighborhood Context." *Journal of Contemporary Ethnography* 39:646–81.

Levin, Jeff. 2014a. "Faith-Based Initiatives in Health Promotion: History, Challenges, and Current Partnerships." *American Journal of Health Promotion* 28:139–41.

———. 2014b. "Faith-Based Partnerships for Population Health: Challenges, Initiatives, and Prospects." *Public Health Reports* 129:127–31.

Liese, Bruce S., and Corey M. Monley. 2021. "Providing Addiction Services During a Pandemic: Lessons Learned from COVID-19." *Journal of Substance Abuse Treatment* 120:1–4.

Lincoln, C. Eric, and Lawrence H. Mamiya. 1990. *The Black Church in the African American Experience*. Durham, NC: Duke University Press.

Lindberg, Annika, and Tobias Georg Eule. 2020. "Organisational Ethnography as a Project of Unease." *Journal of Organisational Ethnography* 9:237–47. https://doi.org/10.1108/JOE-12-2019-0043.

Lindeman, Eduard C. 1921. *The Community: An Introduction to the Study of Community Leadership and Organization*. New York: Association Press.

Lipari, R. N., E. Park-Lee, and S. Van Horn. 2016. *America's Need for and Receipt of Substance Use Treatment in 2015: The CBHSQ Report*. September 29, 2016. Rockville, MD: Center for Behavioral Health Statistics and Quality, Substance Abuse and Mental Health Services Administration.

Lissack, Michael R., and Hugo Letiche. 2002. "Complexity, Emergence, Resilience, and Coherence: Gaining Perspective on Organizations and their Study." *Emergence* 4:72–94.

Lorde, Audre. 1984. *Sister Outsider: Essays and Speeches*. Trumansburg, NY: Crossing Press.

Luthar, Suniya S., Dante Cicchetti, and Bronwyn Becker. 2000. "The Construct of Resilience: A Critical Evaluation and Guidelines for Future Work." *Child Development* 71:543–62.

Madras, Bertha K. 2018. "The President's Commission on Combating Drug Addiction and the Opioid Crisis: Origins and Recommendations." *Clinical Pharmacology & Therapeutics* 103:943–45.

Mallett, Christopher A. 2017. "The School-to-Prison Pipeline: Disproportionate Impact on Vulnerable Children and Adolescents." *Education and Urban Society* 49:563–92. https://dx.doi.org/10.1177/0013124516644053.

Marlatt, G. Alan. 1996. "Harm Reduction: Come as You Are." *Addictive Behaviors* 21:779–88.

Maruna, Shadd, and Kevin Roy. 2007. "Amputation or Reconstruction? Notes on the Concept of 'Knifing Off' and Desistance from Crime." *Journal of Contemporary Criminal Justice* 23:104–24.

Massey, Douglas S., and Nancy A. Denton. 1993. *American Apartheid: Segregation and the Making of the Underclass*. Cambridge, MA: Harvard University Press.

Matto, Holly C. 2004. "Applying an Ecological Framework to Understanding Drug Addiction and Recovery." *Journal of Social Work Practice in the Addictions* 4:5–22.

Mayo, Anna T., and Anita Williams Woolley. 2016. "Teamwork in Health Care: Maximizing Collective Intelligence via Inclusive Collaboration and Open Communication." *American Journal of Ethics* 18:933–40.

McGuire, Keon M., Jesus Cisneros, and T. Donté McGuire. 2017. "Intersections at a (Heteronormative) Crossroad: Gender and Sexuality Among Black Students' Spiritual-and-Religious Narratives." *Journal of College Student Development* 58:175–97.

McKay, James R. 2017. "Making the Hard Work of Recovery More Attractive for Those with Substance Abuse Disorders." *Addiction* 112:751–57.

McNamara, Madeleine W., Katrina Miller-Stevens, and John C. Morris. 2020. "Exploring the Determinants of Collaboration Failure." *International Journal of Public Administration* 43:49–59. https://doi.org/10.1080/01900692.2019.1627552.

McRoberts, Omar M. 2003. *Streets of Glory: Church and Community in a Black Urban Neighborhood.* Chicago: University of Chicago Press.

Mericle, Amy A., Douglas L. Polcin, Jordana Hemberg, and Jennifer Miles. 2017. "Recovery Housing: Evolving Models to Address Resident Needs." *Journal of Psychoactive Drugs* 49:352–61.

Michener Lloyd, Sergio Aguilar-Gaxiola, Philip M. Alberti, Manuel J. Castaneda, Brian C. Castrucci, Lisa Macon Harrison, Lauren S. Hughes, Al Richmond, and Nina Wallerstein. 2020. "Engaging with Communities—Lessons (Re) Learned from COVID-19." *Preventing Chronic Disease* 17:1–8. https://doi.org/10.5888/pcd17.200250.

Mizelle, Richard M., Jr. 2014. *Backwater Blues: The Mississippi Flood of 1927 in the African American Imagination.* Minneapolis: University of Minnesota Press.

Molina-Markham, Elizabeth. 2014. "Finding the 'Sense of the Meeting': Decision Making Through Silence Among Quakers." *Western Journal of Communication* 78:155–74.

Monroe, Irene. 2004. "When and Where I Enter, Then the Whole Race Enters with Me: Que(e)rying Exodus." In *Loving the Body: Black Religious Studies and the Erotic*, edited by Anthony B. Pinn and Dwight N. Hopkins, 121–32. New York: Palgrave Macmillan.

Mooney, Alyssa C., Eric Giannella, M. Maria Glymour, Torsten B. Neilands, Meghan D. Morris, Jacqueline Tulsky, and May Sudhinaraset. 2018. "Racial/Ethnic Disparities in Arrests for Drug Possession after California Proposition 47, 2011–2016." *American Journal of Public Health* 108:987–93.

Moore, Dawn, Lisa Freeman, and Marian Krawczyk. 2011. "Spatio-Therapeutics: Drug Treatment Courts and Urban Space." *Social & Legal Studies* 20:157–72.

Morell, Carolyn. 1996. "Radicalizing Recovery: Addiction, Spirituality, and Politics." *Social Work* 41:306–12.

Morgan, Oliver J. 2009. "Thoughts on the Interaction of Trauma, Addiction, and Spirituality." *Journal of Addictions & Offender Counseling* 30:5–15.

Morjaria, Asesha, and Jim Orford. 2002. "The Role of Religion and Spirituality in Recovery from Drink Problems: A Qualitative Study of Alcoholics Anonymous Members and South Asian Men." *Addiction Research & Theory* 10:225–56.

Morton, Sarah, Laura O'Reilly, and Karl O'Brien. 2016. "Boxing Clever: Utilizing Education and Fitness to Build Recovery Capital in a Substances Use Rehabilitation Program." *Journal of Substance Use* 5:521–26.

Muhammad, Khalil Gibran. 2010. *The Condemnation of Blackness: Race, Crime, and the Making of Modern Urban America.* Cambridge, MA: Harvard University Press.

Mukku, Venkata K., Timothy G. Benson, Farzana Alam, William D. Richie, and Rahn K. Bailey. 2012. "Overview of Substance Use Disorders and Incarceration of African American Males." *Frontiers in Psychiatry* 3:1–5.

Myrdal, Gunnar. (1944) 1964. *An American Dilemma: The Negro Problem and Modern Democracy*. New York: Harper and Brothers.

Naifeh, Sam. 1995. "Archetypal Foundations of Addiction and Recovery." *Journal of Analytical Psychology* 40:133–59.

National Academies of Sciences, Engineering, and Medicine. 2018. Faith-Health Collaboration to Improve Population Health: Proceedings of a Workshop—in Brief. Washington, DC: National Academies Press.

———. 2021. Faith-Health Collaboration to Improve Community and Population Health: Proceedings of a Workshop. Washington, DC: National Academies Press.

National Institute on Drug Abuse (NIDA). 2003. *Preventing Drug Use Among Children and Adolescents: A Research-Based Guide for Parents, Educators, and Community Leaders* (2nd ed.). Bethesda, MD: National Institute of Drug Abuse.

———. 2017. "Addressing the Opioid Crisis Means Confronting Socioeconomic Disparities." *National Institutes of Health (NIH) Advancing Addiction Science*, October 25, 2017. https://www.drugabuse.gov/about-nida/noras-blog/2017/10/addressing-opioid-crisis-means-confronting-socioeconomic-disparities.

Neff, James Alan, Clayton T. Shorkey, and Liliane Cambraia Windsor. 2006. "Contrasting Faith-Based and Traditional Substance Abuse Treatment Programs." *Journal of Substance Abuse Treatment* 30:49–61.

Netherland, Julie, and Helena B. Hansen. 2016. "The War on Drugs That Wasn't: Wasted Whiteness, 'Dirty Doctors,' and Race in Media Coverage of Prescription Opioid Misuse." *Cultural Medicine and Psychiatry* 40:664–86.

Norris, Fran H., Susan P. Stevens, Betty Pfefferbaum, Karen F. Wyche, and Rose L. Pfefferbaum. 2008. "Community Resilience as a Metaphor, Theory, Set of Capacities, and Strategy for Disaster Readiness." *American Journal of Community Psychology* 41:127–50.

Oglesby, William B. 1973. "Pastoral Care and Counseling in Biblical Perspective." *Interpretation* 27:307–26.

Ohmer, Mary L., Pamela Meadowcroft, Kate Freed, and Ericka Lewis. 2009. "Community Gardening and Community Development: Individual, Social and Community Benefits of a Community Conservation Program." *Journal of Community Practice* 17:377–99.

Okvat, Heather A., and Alex J. Zautra. 2011. "Community Gardening: A Parsimonious Path to Individual, Community, and Environmental Resilience." *American Journal of Community Psychology* 47:374–87.

Ostrom, Elinor, and Marco Janssen. 2004. "Multi-Level Governance and Resilience of Social-Ecological Systems." In *Globalisation, Poverty and Conflict*, edited by Max Spoor, 239–59. Dordrecht, Netherlands: Kluwer Academic.

Padfield, Stefan J., and Maria E. Pagano. 2018. "The Helper Therapy Principle: Using the Power of Service to Save Addicts." *University of Memphis Law Review* 48:1165–91.

Pagano, Maria E., Karen B. Friend, J. Scott Tonigan, and Robert L. Stout. 2004. "Helping Other Alcoholics in Alcoholics Anonymous and Drinking Outcomes: Findings from Project MATCH." *Journal of Studies on Alcohol and Drugs* 65:766–73.

Pagano, Maria E., Stephen G. Post, and Shannon M. Johnson. 2011. "Alcoholics Anonymous-Related Helping and the Helper Therapy Principle." *Alcoholism Treatment Quarterly* 29:23–34.

Parson, Sean. 2014. "Breaking Bread, Sharing Soup, and Smashing the State: Food Not Bombs and Anarchist Critiques of the Neoliberal Charity State." *Theory in Action* 7:33–51.

Passetti, Lora L., Susan H. Godley, and Mark D. Godley. 2014. "Youth Participation in Mutual Support Groups: History, Current Knowledge, and Areas for Future Research." In *Broadening the Base of Addiction Mutual Support Groups*, edited by Jeffrey D. Roth, William L. White, and John F. Kelly, 183–208. London: Routledge.

Pattillo-McCoy, Mary E. 1998. "Church Culture as a Strategy of Action in the Black Community." *American Sociological Review* 63:767–84.

Pawlak, Roman, and Sarah Colby. 2009. "Benefits, Barriers, Self-Efficacy and Knowledge Regarding Healthy Foods: Perception of African Americans Living in Eastern North Carolina." *Nutrition Research and Practice* 3:56–63.

Pecora, Vincent P. 2002. "The Culture of Surveillance." *Qualitative Sociology* 25:345–58.

Perkins, Rachel, and Catheryn Khoo-Lattimore. 2020. "Friend or Foe: Challenges to Collaboration Success at Different Lifecycle Stages for Regional Small Tourism Firms in Australia." *Tourism and Hospitality Research* 20:184–97. https://doi.org/10.1177/1467358419836719.

Perry, James L., Annie Hondeghem, and Lois Recascino Wise. 2010. "Revisiting the Motivational Bases of Public Service: Twenty Years of Research and an Agenda for the Future." *Public Administration Review* 70:681–90.

Peterson, Jane, Jan R. Atwood, and Bernice Yates. 2002. "Key Elements for Church-Based Health Promotion Programs: Outcome-Based Literature Review." *Public Health Nursing* 19:401–11.

Pidd, Ken, Ann Roche, and Jane Fischer. 2015. "A Recipe for Good Mental Health: A Pilot Randomised Controlled Trail of a Psychological Wellbeing and Substance Use Intervention Targeting Young Chefs." *Drugs: Education, Prevention and Policy* 22:352–61.

Pinn, Anthony B. 2004. "Introduction." In *Loving the Body: Black Religious Studies and the Erotic*, edited by Anthony B. Pinn and Dwight N. Hopkins, 1–10. New York: Palgrave Macmillan.

Pollard, Alton B. 2004. "Teaching the Body: Sexuality and the Black Church." In *Loving the Body: Black Religious Studies and the Erotic*, edited by Anthony B. Pinn and Dwight N. Hopkins, 315–46. New York: Palgrave MacMillan.

Polson, Edward C. 2008. "The Inter-Organizational Ties That Bind: Exploring the Contributions of Agency-Congregation Relationships." *Sociology of Religion* 69:45–65.

Price-Spratlen, Townsand. 1999. "Livin' for the City: African American Community Development and Depression Era Migration." *Demography* 36:553–68.

———. 2003. "The Urban Context of Historical Activism: NAACP Depression Era Insurgency and Organization-Building." *Sociological Quarterly* 44:303–28.

———. 2008. "Urban Destination Selection Among African Americans During the 1950s Great Migration." *Social Science History* 32:437–69.

———. 2015. *Nurturing Sanctuary: Community Capacity Building in African American Churches*. New York: Peter Lang.

Price-Spratlen, Townsand, and William Goldsby. 2012. *Reconstructing Rage: Transformative Reentry in the Era of Mass Incarceration*. New York: Peter Lang.

Putnam, Robert D., and Lewis M. Feldstein. 2003. *Better Together: Restoring the American Community*. New York: Simon and Schuster.

Quinlan, Allyson, and Lance Gunderson. 2016. "Ecological & Social-Ecological Resilience: Assessing and Managing Change in Complex Systems." In *IRGC Resource Guide on Resilience*, edited by Marie-Valentine Florin and Igor Linkov, 180–83. Lausanne, Switzerland: EPFL International Risk Governance Center.

Quinn, Sandra Crouse, and Stephen B. Thomas. 2001. "The National Negro Health Week, 1915 to 1951: A Descriptive Account." *Minority Health Today* 2:44–49.

Rayburn, Rachel, and James D. Wright. 2009. "Homeless Men in Alcoholics Anonymous: Barriers to Achieving and Maintaining Sobriety." *Journal of Applied Social Science* 3:55–70.

Reich, Michael S., Mary S. Dietrich, A. J. Reid Finlayson, Edward F. Fischer, and Peter R. Martin. 2008. "Coffee and Cigarette Consumption and Perceived Effects in Recovering Alcoholics Participating in Alcoholics Anonymous in Nashville, TN." *Alcohol Clinical Experience Research* 32:1799–1806.

Reid, Graeme, and Liz Walker. 2003. "Secrecy, Stigma and HIV/AIDS: An Introduction." *African Journal of AIDS Research* 2:85–88.

Reissman, Frank. 1965. "The 'Helper' Therapy Principle." *Social Work* 10:27–32.

Reuter, Peter, and Jonathan P. Caulkins. 1995. "Public Health Policy Forum—Redefining the Goals of National Drug Policy: Recommendations from a Working Group." *American Journal of Public Health* 85:1059–63.

Roth, Jeffrey D. 2010. "Addiction as a Family Disease." *Journal of Groups in Addiction & Recovery* 5:1–3.

Roth, Jeffrey D., William L. White, and John F. Kelly, eds. 2014. *Broadening the Base of Addiction Mutual Support Groups: Bringing Theory and Science to Contemporary Trends*. New York: Routledge.

Rothstein, Richard. 2017. *The Color of Law: A Forgotten History of How Our Government Segregated America*. New York: Liveright Publishing.

Rudzinski, Katherine, Peggy McDonough, Rosemary Gartner, and Carol Strike. 2017. "Is There Room for Resilience? A Scoping Review and Critique of Substance Use Literature and Its Utilization of the Concept of Resilience." *Substance Abuse Treatment, Prevention, and Policy* 12:41–75. https://doi.org/10.1186/s13011-017-0125-2.

Sager, Rebecca. 2007. "The Cultural Construction of State Sponsored Religion: Race, Politics, and State Implementation of the Faith-Based Initiative." *Church and State* 49:467–85.

———. 2011. "Faith-Based Social Services: Saving the Body or the Soul? A Research Note." *Journal for the Scientific Study of Religion* 50:201–10.

———. 2012. *Faith, Politics, and Power: The Politics of Faith-Based Initiatives*. Oxford: Oxford University Press.

Sanders, Edwin C., II. 1997. "New Insights and Interventions: Churches Uniting to Reach the African American Community with Health Information." *Journal of Health Care for the Poor and Underserved* 8:373–75.

Sandoz, Charles J., and Christie Dupuis. 1998. "The AA 'Home Group' Effect: There's No Place Like Home." *Journal of Ministry in Addiction & Recovery* 5:57–63.

Scheirer, Mary Ann, Sherie Lou Z. Santos, Erin K. Tagai, Janice Bowie, Jimmie Slade, Roxanne Carter, and Cheryl L. Holt. 2017. "Dimensions of Sustainability for a Health Communication Intervention in African Americans Churches: A Multi-Methods Study." *Implementation Science* 12:1–12.

Schilt, Kristen, and Laurel Westbrook. 2009. "Doing Gender, Doing Heteronormativity: 'Gender Normals,' Transgender People, and the Social Maintenance of Heteronormativity." *Gender & Society* 23:440–64.

Sharpe, Tanya Telfair. 2005. *Behind the Eight Ball: Sex for Crack Cocaine Exchange and Poor Black Women*. New York: Haworth.

Shaw, Clifford R., and Henry D. McKay. 1942. *Juvenile Delinquency and Urban Areas*. Chicago: University of Chicago Press.

Shaw, Jessica, Kate C. McLean, Bruce Taylor, Kevin Swartout, and Katie Querna. 2016. "Beyond Resilience: Why We Need to Look at Systems Too." *Psychology of Violence* 6:34–41. https://doi.org/10.1037/vio0000020.

Shaw, Todd C., and Eric L. McDaniel. 2007. " 'Whosoever Will': Black Theology, Homosexuality, and the Black Political Church." In *The Expanding Boundaries of Black Politics*, edited by Georgia A. Persons, 137–55. New Brunswick, NJ: Transaction.

Showalter, David. 2018. "Federal Funding for Syringe Exchange in the U.S.: Explaining a Long-Term Policy Failure." *International Journal of Drug Policy* 55:95–104.

Siddiqi, Arjumand, Ichiro Kawachi, Daniel P. Keeting, and Clyde Hertzman. 2013. "A Comparative Study of Population Health in the United States and Canada During the Neoliberal Era, 1980–2008." *International Journal of Health Services* 43:193–216.

Simon, Barbara Levy. 1994. *The Empowerment Tradition in American Social Work: A History*. New York: Columbia University Press.

Sittig, Dean F., Joan S. Ash, and Hardeep Singh. 2014. "The SAFER Guides: Empowering Organizations to Improve the Safety and Effectiveness of Electronic Health Records." *American Journal of Managed Care* 20:418–23.

Snow, David A., and Doug McAdam. 2000. "Identity Work Processes in the Context of Social Movements: Clarifying the Identity/Movement Nexus." In *Self, Identity, and Social Movements*, edited by Sheldon Stryker, Timothy J. Owens, and Robert W. White, 41–67. Minneapolis: University of Minnesota Press.

Spitzer, Dean R. 1996. "Power Rewards: Rewards That Really Motivate." *Management Review* 85:45–50.

Stajduhar, Kelli I., Laura Funk, Audrey L. Shaw, Joan L. Bottorff, and Joy Johnson. 2009. "Resilience from the Perspective of the Illicit Injection Drug User: An Exploratory Descriptive Study." *International Journal of Drug Policy* 20:309–16.

Stansbury, Kim L., Gillian L. Marshall, Jodi Hall, Gaynell M. Simpson, and Karen Bullock. 2012. "Community Engagement with African American Clergy: Faith-Based Model for Culturally Competent Practice." *Aging & Mental Health* 22:1510–15.

Strike, Carol, Katherine Rudzinski, Jessica Patterson, and Margaret Millson. 2012. "Frequent Food Insecurity Among Injection Drug Users: Correlates and Concerns." *BMC Public Health* 12:1–9.

Substance Abuse and Mental Health Services Administration (SAMHSA). 2014. *The Next Step . . . Toward a Better Life*. Rockville, MD: US Department of Health and Human Services.

———. 2015. *Behavioral Health Trends in the United States: Results from the 2014 National Survey on Drug Use and Health*. Rockville, MD: US Department of Health and Human Services.

———. 2020. "Double Jeopardy: COVID-19 and Behavioral Health Disparities for Black and Latino Communities in the U.S. (Submitted by OBHE)." https://www.samhsa.gov/sites/default/files/covid19-behavioral-health-disparities-black-latino-communities.pdf.

Sumners, Ann D. 1988. "Humor: Coping in Recovery from Addiction." *Issues in Mental Health Nursing* 9:169–79.

Tagai, Erin Kelly, Mary Ann Scheirer, Sherie Lou Z. Santos, Muhiuddin Haider, Janice Bowie, Jimmie Slade, Tony L. Whitehead, Min Qi Wang, and Cheryl L. Holt. 2018. "Assessing Capacity of Faith-Based Organizations for Health Promotion Activities." *Health Promotion Practice* 19:714–23.

Tangenberg, Kathleen M. 2005a. "Faith-Based Human Services Initiatives: Considerations for Social Work Practice and Theory." *Social Work* 50:197–206.

———. 2005b. "Twelve-Step Programs and Faith-Based Recovery: Research Controversies, Provider Perspectives, and Practice Implications." *Journal of Evidence-Based Social Work* 2:19–40.

Taylor, Jill McLean, Carol Gilligan, and Amy Sullivan. 1995. *Between Voice and Silence: Women and Girls, Race and Relationships*. London: Harvard University Press.

Taylor, Robert Joseph, Linda M. Chatters, and Jeff Levin. 2004. *Religion in the Lives of African Americans: Social, Psychological, and Health Perspectives*. Thousand Oaks, CA: SAGE.

Taylor, Ronald C. 1979. "Black Ethnicity and the Persistence of Ethnogenesis." *American Journal of Sociology* 84:1401–23.

Teo, Winnie L., Mary Lee, and Wee-Shiong Lim. 2017. "The Relational Activation of Resilience Model: How Leadership Activates Resilience in an Organizational Crisis." *Journal of Contingency and Crisis Management* 25:136–47. https://doi.org/10.1111/1468-5973.12179.

Timmons, Shirley M. 2012. "A Christian Faith-Based Recovery Theory: Understanding God as Sponsor." *Journal of Religion and Health* 51:1152–64.

Travis, Trysh. 2009. "'Handles to Hang On to Our Society': Commonplace Books and Surrendered Masculinity in Alcoholics Anonymous." *Men and Masculinities* 12:175–200.

Tribble, Jeffery L., Sr. 2005. *Transformative Pastoral Leadership in the Black Church*. New York: Palgrave Macmillan.

Turner, Victor. 1974. *Dramas, Fields, and Metaphors: Symbolic Action in Human Society*. Ithaca, NY: Cornell University Press.

Ungar, Michael. 2011. "The Social Ecology of Resilience: Addressing Contextual and Cultural Ambiguity of a Nascent Construct." *American Journal of Orthopsychiatry* 81:1–17.

———. 2012. "Introduction to the Volume." In *The Social Ecology of Resilience: A Handbook of Theory and Practice*, edited by Michael Ungar, 1–9. New York: Springer.

Ungar, Michael, Mehdi Ghazinour, and Jorg Richter. 2013. "Annual Research Review: What Is Resilience Within the Social Ecology of Human Development?" *Journal of Child Psychology and Psychiatry* 54:348–66.

US Surgeon General. 2016. *Facing Addiction in America: The Surgeon General's Report on Alcohol, Drugs, and Health*. Washington, DC: US Department of Health and Human Services.

Vaillant, George E. 2002. "Singleness of Purpose." *About AA: A Newsletter for Professionals* 31:F12–F13.

Vangen, Siv, and Chris Huxham. 2003. "Nurturing Collaborative Relations: Building Trust in Interorganizational Collaboration." *Journal of Applied Behavioral Science* 39:5–31.

Vivolo-Kantor, Alana Marie, Brooke Hoots, Felicia David, and Matthew Gladden. 2019. "Suspected Heroin Overdoses in U.S. Emergency Departments, 2017–2018." *American Journal of Public Health* 109:1022–24.

Wacquant, Loïc. 2010. "Crafting the Neoliberal State: Workfare, Prisonfare, and Social Insecurity." *Sociological Forum* 25:197–220.

Wainwright, Jacob J., Meriam Mikre, Penn Whitley, Eric Dawson, Angela Huskey, Andrew Lukowiak, and Brett P. Giroir. 2020. "Analysis of Drug Test Results Before and After the US Declaration of a National Emergency Concerning the COVID-19 Outbreak." *Journal of the American Medical Association* 324:1674–77.

Walker, Rennee E., Christopher R. Keane, and Jessica G. Burke. 2010. "Disparities and Access to Healthy Food in the United States: A Review of the Literature." *Health & Place* 16:876–84.

Wallace, R., and D. Wallace. 1997. "Resilience and Persistence of the Synergism of Plagues: Stochastic Resonance and the Ecology of Disease, Disorder and Disinvestment in U.S. Urban Neighborhoods." *Environment and Planning A* 29:789–804.

Walsh, Froma. 2003. "Crisis, Trauma, and Challenge: A Relational Resilience Approach for Healing, Transformation, and Growth." *Smith College Studies in Social Work* 74:49–71.

Walter, Tony. 2014. "Organizations and Death—A View from Death Studies." *Culture & Organization* 20:68–76.

Walton-Moss, Benita, Ellen M. Ray, and Kathleen Woodruff. 2013. "Relationship of Spirituality or Religion to Recovery from Substance Abuse: A Systematic Review." *Journal of Addictions Nursing* 4:217–26.

Wandersman, Abraham. 2014. "Getting to Outcomes: An Evaluation Capacity Building Example of Rationale, Science, and Practice." *American Journal of Evaluation* 35:100–106.

Warner, R. Stephen. 1993. "Work in Progress Toward a New Paradigm for the Sociological Study of Religion in the United States." *American Journal of Sociology* 98:1044–93.

Washington State Institute for Public Policy. 2019. "Day Treatment with Abstinence Contingencies and Vouchers." *Benefit-Cost Results*. Olympia: Washington State Institute for Public Policy. http://wsippweb-prod.us-west-2.elasticbeanstalk.com/BenefitCost/Program/299.

Washington, Olivia G. M., and David P. Moxley. 2003. "Group Interventions with Low-Income African American Women Recovering from Chemical Dependency." *Health & Social Work* 28:146–56.

Waters, Richard D., and Denise Sevick Bortree. 2012. " 'Can We Talk About the Direction of This Church?': The Impact of Responsiveness and Conflict on Millennials' Relationship with Religious Institutions." *Journal of Media and Religion* 11:200–15.

Waters, Sonia. 2015. "Identity in the Empathic Community: Alcoholics Anonymous as a Model Community for Storytelling and Chance." *Pastoral Psychology* 64:769–82.

Wechsberg, Wendee M., S. Gail Craddock, and Robert L. Hubbard. 1998. "How Are Women Who Enter Substance Abuse Treatment Different Than Men? A Gender Comparison from the Drug Abuse Treatment Outcome Study (DATOS)." *Drugs & Society* 12:97–115.

Weissmann, Peter, William T. Branch, Catherine F. Gracey, Paul Haidet, and Richard M. Frankel. 2006. "Role Modeling Humanistic Behavior: Learning Bedside Manner from the Experts." *Academic Medicine* 81:661–67.

Welsh, Brandon C., Anthony A. Braga, and Christopher J. Sullivan. 2014. "Serious Youth Violence and Innovative Prevention: On the Emerging Link Between Public Health and Criminology." *Justice Quarterly* 31:500–23.

Werner, Emmy E., and Ruth S. Smith. 1982. *Vulnerable but Invincible: A Longitudinal Study of Resilient Children and Youth*. New York: McGraw Hill.

Western, Bruce. 2008. "Reentry: Reversing Mass Imprisonment." *Boston Review* 33:7–11.

———. 2018. *Homeward: Life in the Year After Prison*. New York: Russell Sage Foundation.

Western, Bruce, and Becky Pettit. 2010. "Incarceration & Social Inequality." *Daedalus* 139:8–19.

White, Kellee. 2011. "The Sustaining Relevance of W. E. B. Du Bois to Health Disparities Research." *Du Bois Review* 8:285–93.

White, Ronald C., and C. Howard Hopkins. 1975. *The Social Gospel: Religion and Reform in Changing America*. Philadelphia: Temple University Press.

White, William L. 1996. *Pathways from the Culture of Addiction to the Culture of Recovery*. Center City, MN: Hazelden.

White, William. 2007. "Addiction Recovery: Its Definition and Conceptual Boundaries." *Journal of Substance Abuse Treatment* 33:229–241.

———, ed. 2009. *Peer-Based Addiction Recovery Support: History, Theory, Practice and Scientific Evaluation*. Philadelphia, PA: Great Lakes Addiction Technology Transfer Center, Philadelphia Department of Behavioral Health and Mental Retardation Services.

White, William L., John F. Kelly, and Jeffrey D. Roth. 2012. "New Addiction Recovery Support Institutions: Mobilizing Support Beyond Professional Addiction Treatment and Recovery Mutual Aid." *Journal of Groups in Addiction & Recovery* 7:2–4, 297–317.

———. 2014. "New Addiction-Recovery Support Institutions: Mobilizing Support Beyond Professional Addiction Treatment and Recovery Mutual Aid." In *Broadening the Base of Addiction Mutual Support Groups*, edited by Jeffrey D. Roth, William L. White, and John F. Kelly, 227–47. London: Routledge.

Williams, David R., and Michelle Sternthal. 2010. "Understanding Racial-Ethnic Disparities in Health: Sociological Contributions." *Journal of Health and Social Behavior* 51:S15–S27.

Williams, Joseph M., and Julia Bryan. 2013. "Overcoming Adversity: High-Achieving African American Youth's Perspectives on Educational Resilience." *Journal of Counseling and Development* 91:291–300.

Wilson, Bill. 1984. *Pass It On*. New York: Alcoholics Anonymous World Services.

Windle, Gill, and Kate M. Bennett. 2012. "Caring Relationships: How to Promote Resilience in Challenging Times." In *The Social Ecology of Resilience: A Handbook of Theory and Practice*, edited by Michael Ungar, 219–31. https://doi.org/10.1007/978-1-4614-0586-3_18.

Windsor, Liliane Cambraia, and Vithya Murugan. 2012. "From the Individual to the Community: Perspectives About Substance Abuse Services." *Journal of Social Work Practices in Addiction* 12:412–33.

Witbrodt, Jane, Lee Ann Kaskutas, Jason Bond, and Kevin Delucchi. 2012. "Does Sponsorship Improve Outcomes Above Alcoholics Anonymous Attendance? A Latent Class Growth Curve Analysis." *Addiction* 107:301–11. https://doi.org/10.1111/j.1360-0443.2011.03570.x.

Woods, LaKeesha N., A. Stephen Lanza, William Dyson, and Derrick M. Gordon. 2013. "The Role of Prevention in Promoting Continuity of Health Care in Prisoner Reentry Initiatives." *American Journal of Public Health* 103:830–38.

Wulff, Katharine, Darrin Donato, and Nicole Lurie. 2015. "What Is Health Resilience and How Can We Build It?" *Annual Review of Public Health* 36:361–74.

Zautra, Alex J., John Stuart Hall, and Kate E. Murray. 2010. "Resilience: A New Definition of Health for People and Communities." In *Handbook of Adult Resilience*, edited by John W. Reich, Alex J. Zautra, and John Stuart Hall, 3–29. New York: Guilford.

Index

Addiction, active, xv, xvi, 3, 6, 7, 13, 14, 17, 20, 49, 53, 79, 91, 100, 105, 120, 135, 139, 172, 212; carceral consequences of, 48; as a family disease, 31; heroin, 11, 13, 52, 128

Addiction Equity Act, 210

Affordable Care Act (ACA), 91, 183, 204, 207, 210

African American/Black, affiliates, 21, 30, 164; agency, 6; Black Baptist, 163; Black Social Gospel, 150, 152, 184; body, war on, 2; Bug's Borough, 54–55; church(es), 12–13, 93, 119, 133, 138, 141, 148–150, 161, 170, 181–182, 205, 223, 224; church tradition, 93, 133; communities/neighborhood(s), 58, 190, 196, 203, 214; crackhead identity, 98; double consciousness, 224; families post-Civil War, 54; Great Migration, 57; health/well-being, 1–3, 7–8, 99–100; heroin addiction, 11; liberation, 141; lynching, 8; marginalization, 58, 219; mass incarceration/imprisonment, 8, 10, 140, 218; media, 9–10; men, 82, 91; negro(es), 8, 53; neighborhood/community, 66, 70; racialization/demonization, 8–9; war on, 2, 3; women, 88–89, 137

Akron Avenue. *See* Places [of the FACTS Ministries]: Akron Avenue

Alcoholics Anonymous, 48, 84, 101–102; and food, 112; How It Works, 120

Alexander, Jack, 112

American apartheid, 55, 57, 62, 65

Anchor churches, 82, 116, 162, 164, 181; evangelical, 154, 170, 171, 174

Andermann, Anne, 71

Barnes, Sandra, 93, 150, 176

Bassuk, Ellen L., 117

Beckhard, Richard, 106, 117

Beheshtifar, Malikeh, 106, 132, 154

Bellamy, Chyrell D., 69, 70

Bellringer, 14

Bennett, Kate Mary, 4, 117, 173, 183, 192

Best, David, 128, 134

Best practices, 199–209

Biden administration, 217

Big Book, xiv, 42, 48, 102–104, 105, 108, 141, 217

Black(s). *See* African American(s)

Bluic, Ana-Maria, 202, 204

Boeri, Miriam, 2, 3, 50

Bottom, xiv; xvi, 14, 45, 49, 77, 100, 217
Bourgois, Phillipe, 2, 6, 13, 109
Boxing club. *See* FACTS Ministries: Fists of Faith
Boyer, Corinne, 207, 221
Bug's Borough. *See* African American(s): Bug's Borough

Call to the Altar, 146
Call-and-response, 103, 113, 164, 170, 182
Castells, Manuel, 54, 66
Cedar Tree Church, 18
Charity, 149, 153, 160; apolitical, 85; corporate, 165; evangelical, 48, 101, 174, 175, 185; 12-Step meetings and, 101
Cheney, Ann M., 12, 99, 161, 172, 178, 199
Christ Faith Church, 166
Christian service, 48
Christle, Christine A., 57, 59
Cocaine Anonymous (CA), xi, xv, xvi, 16, 23, 29, 36, 38, 39, 41, 42, 43, 48, 71, 74, 94, 97–129, 134, 157–159, 178, 182, 183, 189, 195, 221, 223, 226, 229; GSR in, 98, 102, 106, 107, 126. *See also* FACTS Ministries: Either-Or
Collaborations among organizations, 205–207
Colored Temperance Society, 10–11
Community, -based interventions, 12, coalitions, 210; organization(s), 5, 6, 12, 69, 93. *See* FACTS Ministries: Community lunches
Community Correctional Facility (CCF), 110–111, 126, 142, 149, 152, 155, 182–183, 227
Connecticut Community for Addiction Recovery, 12
COVID-19 pandemic, 1, 11, 59, 63, 204, 213, 220, 221
Crack cocaine, xv, 11, 12, 13, 15, 39, 43, 98–99; and sex, 109
Criminal justice, 2. *See also* Mass incarceration/imprisonment

D'Angelo, Karen A., 2, 6, 13, 218
Darwinian individualism. *See* Social Darwinism
De Leon, George, 42, 74
Deed restrictions, 55
Disparities, 1–2, 7, 10–13, 20, 47, 50, 58, 67, 73, 92, 140, 149, 151, 189
Domains. *See* FACTS Ministries: Domains of
Dope. *See* Drug(s)
Dorrien, Gary, 150
Dossett, Wendy, 102, 132, 199
Douglass, Frederick, 11
Drucker, Ernest, 7, 19, 191, 211
Drug(s), 11–13, 60; court(s), 183, 211; culture, 20, 37, 74; dealers, 229; druggists, 8; policy, 190, 217–220; -related offences; sales, 98, 159; sexual control, 109; testing, 172; use, 66, 220; use risks, 217; traffic, 10; War on, 2, 11, 20, 74, 193. *See also* Substance misuse
Drug-Abuse Treatment Outcomes Studies (DATOS), 135
Drug treatment, 1, 6, 28, 32, 84, 93, 127, 190, 195, 210, 218, 219; aftercare, 41, 212; center, 18, 48, 69, 82, 128, 144; industry, 20, 217; Intensive Outpatient (IOP), xiv, xv; medically assisted treatment (MAT), 211, 217; services, 12; shortage, 10; policy, 211; staff, 40, 74
Du Bois, W. E. B., 1, 2, 3, 7, 8, 52–53, 79, 89, 93, 99, 150, 189, 191, 192, 205, 206, 221, 222, 224

Duck, Waverly, 202, 213, 220
Duff, Cameron, 47, 50, 65
Dunlap, Eloise, 28, 61, 71

Ecological framework, 52
Ecology of resilience. *See* Social ecology of resilience
Either-Or. *See* FACTS Ministries: Either-Or
1115 Substance Use Disorder (SUD) Waiver, 2, 211
Ethnogenesis. *See* Ethnogenic thread
Ethnogenic thread, 6, 10, 65–66, 92, 127, 129, 202, 224
Evans, Arthur C., 12, 173, 215, 219

FACTS Ministries, xv, xvi, 3, 5, 7, 13–21, 27–28, 40; anniversary, 158–160; barbeque, 119, 160, 226; benefactor charity, 153; beneficial attributes, 106; Black faith, 102; celebrations, 113; church and Bible study domain, 30–34; decline of, 129, 173–183; community lunches, 82–83, 119–120; domains of, 29–30, 50, 93–94, 176; Either-Or, 16, 36, 38–43, 48, 71, 74, 97–129, 178, 182; faith-health ministry, 150; Fists of Faith, 85–87; flourishing and decline of, 157–185; Friday Youth Nights, 45, 87, 135, 148, 177–178, 212; health referrals, 91; health resources of, 70–94; health screenings, 83–84, 88, 91; heteronormativity, 141–144; Men's Prayer Breakfasts, 46, 84, 149, 172, 176, 180, 182; men's workout group, 88, 90; mission of, 43, 178; nonprofit, 163–169, 175, 212; partnerships, 97; Partnership Dinner, 163–164, 181; participatory leadership, 117; pastoral care/counseling domain, 77–81; peer monitoring, 171; Praise and Worship Team (PWT) 35, 102, 110, 137, 142, 162; public-health approach, 217; race-class silences, 138–140; safe space, 83; as sanctuary, 97–129; self-assessment, 198; substance abuse recovery domain, 71–77, 98; Sunday service, 142; supportive space of, 38; nutritional/meal-based support domain, 82–85; Thanksgiving Day meal, 84, 165, 179; youth, 145–155, 176, 178; youth, developmental/preventive domain, 85–88; vision, 167–168. *See also* People [of the FACTS Ministries]; Places [of the FACTS Ministries]; Things [of the FACTS Ministries]
Faith-based organization(s), 6, 12, 18, 206, 217, 225–226; Faith-Based and Community Initiatives, 153–154
Faith-Health mission/reciprocity, 14, 34, 70, 99, 150, 191, 205, 214, 219, 225
Flores, Edward Orozco, 76, 102, 145, 155, 176
Food, attraction of, 181; -centered, 226; desert, 61, 64, 82; insecurity, 47, 82; resource, 111–112
Frazier, E. Franklin, 56
Freeman, Edith M., 28, 161
From Punishment to Public Health, 12

Gap in the literature, 54
Geographic cure, 79
Gilkes, Cheryl Townsend, 93, 138
Goffman, Erving, 99, 142
Gray, Barbara, 116, 117, 127, 128
Group Conscience, 106, 124–125
GSR (Group Service Representative). *See* Cocaine Anonymous: GSR

Gun violence, 213–214

Hackworth, Jason, 153, 191, 192, 207, 216–218
Hayworth Street. *See* Places [of the FACTS Ministries]: Hayworth Street
Health care, 192; access, 91, 210,–212; disparities in, 1, 2, 13, 70, 210–212; equity-oriented, 71; racialized, 10
Health ministry/organization(s), 6, 7, 13, 15, 18, 49, 100, 171
Helgeson, Vicki S., 28
Helper therapy principle (HTP), 84
Hemphill, Essex, 134
Herd, Denise, 10, 11
Heroin addiction: *See* Addiction: Heroin
Heyer, Jeremy, 76
Higher power, 37–38
Hodge, Lauren M., 97, 99
Hodges, John Q., 127, 128
Holden, Kisha B., 91
Housing, access, 212–213; color line, 55; insecurity, 212. *See also* Places [of the FACTS Ministries]: Sober homes
Howston Street. *See* Places [of the FACTS Ministries]: Howston Street
Humphreys, Keith, 12, 48, 99, 113

Identity amplification, 134
Imprisonment. *See* Mass incarceration/imprisonment
Incarceration. *See* Mass incarceration/imprisonment
Institute of Medicine, 209
Intensive outpatient (IOP) treatment, xiv

Jackleg preacher, 15, 65, 81
James, Keturah, 6, 10, 12, 203, 206, 207, 216, 217, 219
Johnson, Natrina, 211, 216, 217
Johnson, Rucker, 7, 58
Jones-Eversley, Sharon D., 53

King, Rev. Dr. Martin Luther, Jr., 114
Kubler-Ross, Elizabeth, 115
Kumpfer, Karol L., 74–75, 117

Laudet, Alexandre B., 12, 101, 102, 112, 202, 219
Lawson-Lee High. *See* North Lawson: High school
Leadership, 193–194, 199.
Leadership, 36, 49, 73, 84, 93, 97, 126, 190, 193–194, 223; church/faith, 3, 81, 85, 102, 123, 150, 172, 177, 189, 198–199, 212, 215–216; pastor-centered, 199; 12–Step, 101, 116, 163, 226; youth, 145–149. *See also* People [of the FACTS Ministries]: Charismatic/participatory leadership and service of; People [of the FACTS Ministries]: Women's leadership
Leverentz, Andrea, 28, 44, 66
Levin, Jeff, 92, 189, 190, 199
Liese, Bruce, S., 220
Lincoln, C. Eric, 89, 102, 148, 149, 150, 184
Lindeman, Eduard, 204
Living testimony, 32, 34
Lorde, Audre, 37, 109, 131–133, 152, 208
Lunch program, at school, 57, 59, 169
Luthar, Suniya S., 183

Malcom X, 102
Male-centered caring, 84
Marijuana maintenance plan, 20
Marlatt, G. Alan, 190, 218, 219
Marshall, Cheryl. *See* People [of the FACTS Ministries]: Cheryl Marshall

Marshall, Pastor Ellwyn, 7, 13–20, 32, 38, 49, 77, 79, 85–86, 89, 98, 116, 214; agency of, 185; authoritarian, 197; interview with, 166–168; dismissive, 197; lack of compassion, 145–148, 150, 151, 173; pastoral training, 80; style of ministry, 138–139; toward poverty/the poor, 139–140, 150; traditional role models, 136; and 12 steps, 117, 171
Maruna, Shadd, 79
Mass incarceration/imprisonment, 6, 10, 12, 20, 161, 184, 218; blaming the victim, 151; cradle-to-prison pipeline, 59, 62; school-to-prison pipeline, 59
Massey, Douglas S., 57
Matto, Holly C., 52, 93
McGandry Street. *See* Places [of the FACTS Ministries]: McGandry Street
McRoberts, Omar M., 56, 66, 202
Medically assisted treatment (MAT). *See* Drug treatment: Medically assisted treatment
Mental Health Parity Act, 210
Mericle, Amy A., 53, 54
Methods, 20–22; neighborhood ethnography, 51–67; organizational ethnography, 5, 22, 23; participant observation, 5, 22, 29, 195
Millwood Fellowship Church, 13, 17, 18, 19, 46, 121, 166, 174, 176–177
Ministries. *See* FACTS Ministries
Morell, Carolyn, 12, 102, 129, 134, 155, 196, 198, 210
Morgan, Oliver J., 135
Mutual aid societies, 99, 127
Mutual help culture, 74

Narcotics Anonymous, 39, 102
National Academies of Sciences, 225, 226
National Institutes of Drug Abuse (NIDA), 88, 206, 218
National Institutes of Health, 52, 88
National Negro Health Week, 100, 129
National Prescription Drug Abuse and Heroin Summit, 11
Negro. *See* African American
New York Times, on racialization of drugs, 8, 9, 13
Normative ideal, 142
Norris, Fran H., 202
North Lawson, 13, 14, 19, 29–31, 43, 48, 51–67, 120, 124, 148, 175, 183, 212–214, 229; abstinence-hostile, 202–203; community garden, 51, 53–54, 64–65; crime, 61; Crooked Walkway, 120; disinvestment/divestment in, 58, 61; Greater Lawson Development Group, 21; high school, 57–58, 60; highway construction in, 56; history of, 54–58; homicide, 150; infant mortality, 59, 89; library, 62–65; mortality rate, 88–89; outreach to, 119; racial segregation in, 55–57; resilient ecology of, 61–65, 93; returning GIs, 55; sex industry work, 120; today, 58–61; toddler health, 91; white flight, 57; women's faith-health group, 136; women's clinic, 91–92; World War I era, 54; World War II, 55

Obama, President [Barack], 11, 113, 184
Office of National Drug Control Policy, 218
Opioid crisis/epidemic, 6, 10, 13, 206, 218–219; health challenge, 10, 18, 20

Organizations, healthy, 106; impact of funding, 155

Pagano, Maria E., 36, 84
Pandemic. *See* COVID-19 pandemic
Parker United Methodist Church, 33
Pastoral therapy, 80
Pattillo, Mary, 150, 164
People [of the FACTS Ministries], 27–50; Albert, 35–36, 76–77, 110, 113–114, 121, 158, 160, 162, 179–180; Andrew, 46; Arnold, 111, 162; Brother Darryl Hasten, 31–32, 47, 48, 199; Brother Warren Pomely, 31–34, 46, 47; Calvin Sandorn, 168, 171, 174–175, 177; Carol, 45; Carla, 38–41, 91, 98, 99; Chance, 44; charismatic/participatory leadership and service of, 107–111, 117–119, 120, 123, 128, 135, 177; Cheryl Marshall, 14, 17, 88, 136, 178; Claretta, 141–142, 144; Conrad, 41–43, 50; Copter, 44–45; Dawn, 141–142, 144; Devonte, 125, 227–228; Darnell, 90; Donald, 90; Dorren, 142, 144; Douglass, 35–37, 49, 75; Edward, 179; families of, 112–113; Isaac H., 171, 179–180; Jack, 112–113; Jaleel, 145–146; Jerry, 109–110, 120–121, 162, 227–228; Jess, 91, 144–145; Joe, 112; Johnny, 227; Jonathan, 39, 108, 112; Larry, 43–44, 48; Kevin, 227–228; Lawrence, 46; LGBTQ+, 140–145; Major, 114–115; Marla, 141–142; Martell, 142–144; Mason, 144–145; millennials, 145; Raymond Daughtry, 13, 15, 17; Richard, 178–179; Ricky, 224–225; Roman and Cindy, 79–80; Sarah, 107–108; silencing/alienation of, 45, 121–128, 131–155, 198; silencing of women, 135–137; Sonja, 112; Troy-Allen, 108–110; sponsor churches, 168–169; Tyler, 145; valuing people, 199–201; volunteer(s), 87, 148, 170, 199, 201, 204; women, 40, 87, 89; women's leadership [absence of], 136–137; Women of Faith and Wellness, 88, 136
People Advocating Recovery in Kentucky, 12
People, places, and things, 27, 28, 66, 25–94, 199–200. *See also* People [of the FACTS Ministries]; Places [of the FACTS Ministries]; Things [of the FACTS Ministries]
Peterson, Jane, 71, 203
Pinn, Anthony B., 133
Places [of the FACTS Ministries], 51–67; Akron Avenue, 17, 32, 38, 51, 56, 60, 66, 70, 89, 125, 170, 172, 173; Hayworth Street, 59–60; Howston Street, 56; McGandry Street, 60; nurturing paces, 201–203; sober homes, 19, 35–38, 48–49, 74–76, 98, 122–123, 126–127, 171, 180, 212; triggers, 170; North Lawson. *See* North Lawson
Pollard, Alton B., 141, 142
Price-Spratlen, Townsand, 6, 7, 31, 57, 107, 116, 145, 184, 199, 226
Prosperity ministry/narrative, 138–140, 149, 169, 181

Qualitative methods. See Methods
Quinn, Sandra Crouse, 1, 2, 100, 205

Racial segregation. *See* North Lawson: Racial segregation in
Reciprocity, x, 13, 34, 36, 40, 41, 48, 129, 153, 212
Reconstruction, 16
Recovery [from drug addiction], 1, 11, 12, 14, 16, 27, 28, 48, 52, 53,

77, 82, 93, 100, 202; active, 98; best practices, 128–129; Christian Recovery, 195–196; defined as, 109; Faces & Voices of, 12, 201, 204, 208; and God's plan, 47; and mourning/grief, 114–116; organization(s), 12, 216; person in, 79; program of, 107; Rally for Recovery, 195; religiously grounded, 34; and sexuality, 109. *See also* FACTS Ministries: Substance abuse recovery domain; Resilience; 12-Steps [Recovery Program]

Reid, Graeme, 132, 135, 155

Relapse, 6, 34–35, 126; and death, 111, 114–116, 162; and eviction, 171; prevention, 23, 76, 136; risk, 19, 27, 38, 74, 75, 109–110, 115

Resilience, 4, 5, 6, 16, 50, 52, 64–65, 70, 80, 83, 93, 125, 128, 182, 191; centered, 93; communal, 164; compromised, 154, 198; dialogues of, 97–185; mission, 133; and organizational change, 209; reciprocity of, 40; research, 216. *See also*: Social ecology of resilience; Social resilience; Recovery

Resilient ecology. *See* Social ecology of resilience

Returning citizens, 3, 19, 20, 28, 44, 67, 123, 142, 152, 213

Reuter, Peter, 219, 220

Roth, Jeffrey D., 3, 31, 69, 78, 81

Sacred Calling Fellowship, 18

Sacred space, 48

Safe space, 79, 100, 101. *See also* FACTS Ministries: Safe space

Sager, Rebecca, 1, 23, 93, 94, 149, 153, 154, 177, 193, 198, 204, 212

Screenings. *See* Health screenings

Second Tradition. *See* Twelve Traditions: Second

Seventh Tradition. *See* Twelve Traditions: Seventh

Shaw, Clifford, 52

Shaw, Jessica, 3, 4, 53, 216

Shell game, 56

Silence, beneficial role of, 133; shared, 105; toxic, 131; transformation of. 133; tyrann(ies) of, 131–132, 152

Silencing/alienation of members. *See* People [of the FACTS Ministries]: Silencing/alienation of members

Sixth Tradition: *See* Twelve Traditions: Sixth

Snow, John, 53

Sober housing. *See* Places [of the FACTS Ministries]: Sober homes

Sober living homes/Sober homes. *See* Places [of the FACTS Ministries]: Sober homes

Sober, anniversaries/celebrations, 113, 117; healing, 34; hours, xiv; xvi; service, 49; shame, 98. *See also* Sobriety

Sobriety, 15, 16, 34, 38, 40, 44, 82, 93; continuous/long-term/sustained, 19–20, 113, 114, 126, 210; faith-driven, 102; fragility of, 115; length of, 105; renewal, 126. *See also* Sober

Social, Darwinism, 140, 150; disorganization model, 52; epidemiology, 52; reconstruction, 3, 5, 16. *See also* Social ecology of resilience

Social ecology of resilience, xvi, 3, 4, 5, 14, 13, 16, 20, 28, 29, 50, 51, 53, 60, 61–67, 69, 70–94, 97, 100, 203, 212; at the Ministries, 102, 120, 132, 134, 145, 226, 229

Social Gospel, Black, 150, 152, 184

Social justice silences, 149–152

Southern Pentecostal church, 80

Spiritual dissonance, 42

Sponsor, 40–41
St. Priscilla Evangelical Church, 173–174
Stajduhar, Kelli, I., 50, 53, 62
Stem, 15, 60
Stevie Wonder format, birthday song, 114
Stigma, 3, 47, 70, 74, 132, 134, 142–143, 153, 155, 159, 192; neighborhood, 66, 92; racialized, 7, 10, 98–99; reduction of, 206, 208, 210
Substance abuse. *See* Substance misuse, substance use disorder
Substance Abuse and Mental Health Services Administration (SAMHSA), 1, 3, 27, 191, 204, 250
Substance, misuse, 7–14; 190, 211; use disorder, 2, 11, 18, 218. Use treatment. *See* Drug treatment

Task Force Report on Black and Minority Health, 2
Taylor, Jill McLean, 133, 134, 145
Taylor, Robert Joseph, 31, 89
Taylor, Ronald C., 6
Teo, Winnie L., 4, 124, 192, 207
Therapeutic community, 74
Things [of the FACTS Ministries], 69–94; capacity-building assets, 203
Timmons, Shirley M., 47
Travis, Trysh, 75, 109, 110
Turner, Victor, 132
12-Step(s) [Recovery Program], xiv, xv, xvi, 15, 20, 36, 38, 41, 47, 48, 71, 76, 116, 117, 124, 128–129, 189, 208, 220–221; meetings, 101–106, 111; Step Nine, 79, 104; Step One, 16, 101, 217; Step Zero, 16; trope, 209; *Twelve Steps and Twelve Traditions*, 102. *See also* Recovery; Twelve Traditions
Twelve Traditions, 71, 102, 104, 117, 122–123, 178, 226; first, 102, 104; second, 36; seventh, xvi, 106, 229; sixth, 158

U.S. Surgeon General, 11, 12, 14, 128, 191, 204, 207, 210, 217–219, 226
Ungar, Michael, 4, 28, 32, 47, 50, 53, 65, 93, 102, 183, 192

Vamped, 15

Wacquant, Loic, 153
Wallace, R., 191
Walsh, Froma, 3, 4, 28, 31, 48, 53, 85, 128, 216
War on Drugs. *See* Drug(s): War on
Washington State Institute for Public Policy, 211
Welfare state, 193
Western, Bruce, 44, 176, 213
White, William L., 2, 4, 6, 10, 12, 19, 37, 78, 99, 112, 124, 128, 129, 134, 191, 202
Women of Faith and Wellness: *See* People [of the FACTS Ministries]: Women of Faith and Wellness
Women. *See* People [of the FACTS Ministries]: Women; Women of Faith and Wellness; silencing of women
Women's clinic. *See* North Lawson: Women's clinic
Women's leadership. *See* People [of the FACTS Ministries]: Women's leadership
Wulff, Katharine, 69, 70, 93, 158

Youth. *See* FACTS Ministries: Friday Youth Nights; youth; youth, developmental/preventive domain

Zautra, Alex J., 4

www.ingramcontent.com/pod-product-compliance
Lightning Source LLC
LaVergne TN
LVHW050150080826
844660LV00002B/144

* 9 7 8 1 4 3 8 4 8 7 3 7 3 *